All the Families of the Earth

All the Families of the Earth

Recovering Scripture's Vision Beyond Nationalism

STEVEN D. KURTZ

Foreword by Brian Kaylor

WIPF & STOCK · Eugene, Oregon

All the Families of the Earth
Recovering Scripture's Vision Beyond Nationalism

Wipf & Stock
An Imprint of Wipf and Stock Publishers
199 W. 8th Ave., Suite 3
Eugene, OR 97401

www.wipfandstock.com

PAPERBACK ISBN: 979-8-3852-6895-5
HARDCOVER ISBN: 979-8-3852-6896-2
EBOOK ISBN: 979-8-3852-6897-9

VERSION NUMBER 021826

Cover photo by Maria Orlova.

To Jennifer

The will to give ourselves to others and "welcome" them, to readjust our identities to make space for them, is prior to any judgment about others, except that of identifying them in their humanity.

—Miroslav Volf, *Exclusion and Embrace*

Contents

Foreword

In the fall of 2025, the US Department of Defense (also calling itself the Department of War) created several promotional videos adding Bible verses to its arsenal. The videos featured the text of a verse overlaid on clips of the US military in action, like fighter jets flying, tanks rolling along, missiles firing, and soldiers shooting. One video used Ps 18:37: "I pursued my enemies and overtook them; I did not turn back till they were destroyed." Another took a verse from the classic Twenty-Third Psalm, not to create a peaceful vibe at a funeral but to cheerlead for war: "Though I walk through the valley of the shadow of death I will fear no evil; for YOU are with me." Yet another video employed a verse—Josh 1:9—from a passage that's been historically used to justify genocide: "Be strong and of good courage. Do not be afraid, nor dismayed. For the Lord your God is with you wherever you go." Another video even used the Lord's Prayer, creating a particularly wild disconnect between the words and the images:

> Hallowed be thy name [missiles shooting into the sky]. Thy kingdom come [fleet of naval vessels], thy will be done [close up of a fighter jet in the air] on earth [tank rolling by] as it is in heaven [paratroopers launching from plane]. . . . For thine is the kingdom [close up of a soldier aiming a gun] and the power [aerial shot of fighter jets and helicopters on a runway] and the glory [a waving American flag] forever and ever [Donald Trump, J. D. Vance, and Pete Hegseth saluting], amen [Department of War logo and name].

On social media, the videos quickly spread, sparking a divided reaction. Many celebrated the mash-up of Scripture and the American military, adding Christian nationalistic remarks like "God bless America" and this proves the US is "one nation under God." Others criticized the videos as going against the US's constitutional principle of church-state separation and for heretically co-opting the sacred texts. It quickly became a sort of hermeneutical Rorschach test exposing one's theology and political philosophy.

As one who found the videos civically and theologically problematic, I think a lot about how to reach those who embrace Christian nationalism while calling themselves Christians and say they take the Bible seriously (perhaps even claiming they take it literally, though no one actually does). Somewhere along the way, those of us who are ministers, Bible teachers, and church leaders have failed a large swath of people. Too many have been converted into Christian nationalism with no understanding of how such an ideology twists essential Christian doctrines. As Christian nationalist ideas—and often related racist, anti-immigrant, and patriarchal beliefs—find an audience in various countries, we need people who carefully and persuasively point to a better way. And that's why this book from Steven Kurtz is so important.

How we read the Bible matters. As we see with the US military's videos, Christian nationalism often picks a verse or two out of its historical and literary context, making the sacred text malleable enough to support just about any preconceived political proposal. Too few people who sit in the pews of our churches or claim to cherish the Bible actually read verses within a larger context. Kurtz brilliantly walks us through the Bible, guiding us to see an overarching narrative. Like putting on glasses, this allows us to see the whole story and the individual narratives with fresh clarity.

Whether you're a pastor seeking a resource to help you prepare your sermons, a small group wanting to dig deeper with your next book study, or an individual Christian hoping to read the Bible better, turn the page because you've picked up the right book.

Rev. Dr. Brian Kaylor
President of Word&Way and author of
The Bible According to Christian Nationalists

Acknowledgments

I AM INDEBTED TO a huge number of scholars who have been my professors and the authors of commentaries, monographs, and articles over the years. These scholars are the giants on whose shoulders I am fortunate to stand. They have raised the curtain to allow me glimpses of the ancient, often inscrutable stages that the Bible's many texts played on.

I am also deeply grateful for the colleagues and friends without whose encouragement and support this book would not have been possible. I profoundly appreciate my brother Mark, whose meticulous editing and helpful suggestions were a godsend. I want to thank Roger Berry and David Scherer, who have been my dialogue partners and challenge network over many years, and Professor Emeritus Paul Borgmann for his interest and engagement. I am endlessly thankful to my wife, Jennifer, for believing in me and encouraging me throughout the long writing process that occupied me during our travels from Fairbanks to Quito.

Abbreviations

Ag. Ap. — Josephus. *Against Apion*. In *The Life; Against Apion*, translated by H. St. J. Thackeray, 162–412. Loeb Classical Library 186. Cambridge: Harvard University Press, 1926

Apol. — Tertullian. *The Apology of Tertullian*. Translated by Jeremy Collier. London: Griffith Farran Okeden & Welsh, 1889

BDAG — Danker, Frederick W., Walter Bauer, William F. Arndt, and F. Wilbur Gingrich. *Greek-English Lexicon of the New Testament and Other Early Christian Literature*. 3rd ed. Chicago: University of Chicago Press, 2000. Accordance Bible Software

BDB — Brown, Francis, S. R. Driver, and Charles A. Briggs. *A Hebrew and English Lexicon of the Old Testament*. Oxford: Clarendon Press, 1907. Accordance Bible Software

Hist. — Tacitus. *The Complete Works of Tacitus*. Edited by Sara Bryant, translated by Alfred John Church and William Jackson Brodribb. 1873. Repr., New York: Random House, 1942

KJV — King James Version

LXX — Septuagint (the Greek Old Testament)

NASB — New American Standard Bible

NRSV — New Revised Standard Version

Phaed. — Plato. *Phaedo*. In *Euthyphro; Apology; Crito; Phaedo; Phaedrus*, translated by Harold N. Fowler, 195 406. Loeb Classical Library 36. Cambridge: Harvard University Press, 1914

Rom. Hist. — Cassius Dio. *Dio's Roman History*. Translated by Earnest Cary. Vol. 8. London: Heinemann, 1925

Introduction

Who Are the Chosen?

The ancient Romans thought Christians were atheists. They did not believe in Jupiter, Venus, Mars, or any of the other Roman gods, so they were unbelievers. Christians did not see it that way; they would say they believed in the one true God, the God of Abraham, Isaac, and Jacob, the God of Moses and the prophets—the God revealed in Jesus, the Christ. One person's atheist is another person's true believer. Which identity is correct?

Why does the Bible spend so much time circling around the question of identity: who is *in* and who is *out*? Who is a true child of Abraham and who is not? Who can lay claim to being part of the chosen people? How should Jews and Gentiles coexist? If God created the world and all its people, how is he the God of Israel in a particular way? (In the Hebrew Bible, God is mostly but not always described as male—that was then.) If those seem like odd questions settled long ago, consider how much time is spent today circling around similar questions of identity. Are we a Christian nation? Should we be? How should we coexist with others?

My question is, Can we learn something about that by examining the biblical narratives? I hope so. In this book, we will be entering into the world of the Bible, acknowledging that it is not our world, separated as we are now by so much time. The people of the ancient world, wherever we meet them—in the Hebrew Bible or in the poetry of the *Iliad* and the *Odyssey*—saw things differently. Some have remarked, for example, that we can no longer look at the stars and imagine that they are *up there*. Situated on a globe in space, the stars can only be *out there*. But they were *up there* in the sky to people in former times. Until Galileo, we conceived of a three-story universe. We believed that we inhabit middle-earth, between the heavens above and the realms of the dead below. The three-story universe is gone from our minds but was assumed in the ancient world.

Even to say "the world of the Bible" is saying too much, as if there were one single world to enter. The narratives of the Hebrew patriarchs—Abraham, Isaac, and Jacob—and their wives are set hundreds of years before Moses, before there was a state called Israel, and long before there was a Roman Empire. The world of Jesus was Judea, a province of Rome, where people spoke Aramaic. Paul's world was mostly Syria, also a Roman province, where everyone spoke and wrote in Greek.

We will enter these narratives with the awareness that we are like tourists who have gone abroad. We use our Google Translate app with the taxi driver and hope the app gets it right. We look at the walls of ancient churches and notice that there are uneven stones at the base, bricks a bit higher, and cut stones above; civilizations have come and gone, building on each other, the oldest ones buried in the past. We are like foreign tourists as we visit Genesis or Deuteronomy. We rely on guides who know the language and can tell the sacred stories.

Of course, we know that people will disagree about the details of the texts and their meanings. There are many questions to ask. What really happened in history? How many people repeated the stories before one of them wrote them down for the first time? What has been lost in translation? Questions abound. But our focus will be broader. We will take the narratives as we have them now and try our best to be good tourists in their worlds: good listeners, careful readers. We know that we will miss things, but we will understand enough to catch the big ideas. Big ideas are what we are after. We will enter these texts remembering that we come with twenty-first century eyes and Western perspectives—what some have called pre-understandings. When Abraham looks *up* at the stars, we will try to look up with him and suspend our knowledge that we are looking *out* from one place on our planet. When Ruth is called a foreigner, we will try to feel the emotional distance the narrator felt about Moabites, whom we have never encountered. When Jonah gets depressed at Nineveh's repentance, we will try to "feel his pain" as God suspends judgment on his repentant archenemy. We will try to be open to letting these sacred stories that have been treasured by so many for so long teach us their lessons. There is hope that we can learn from them. There is even the possibility that they will surprise us, showing us new ideas that may help us even today with our questions of identity. Where should we begin?

We begin by setting out the problem that will come up in all the texts we will consider: a tension about identity runs through all of them. The tension is created by the narratives themselves. Let's have a quick bird's-eye review. The Bible begins "In the beginning" with one God, the Creator of everything and everyone. All is well in the beginning; the first man and woman live in a perfect garden world where all their needs are met by nature itself without "the sweat of your face" (Gen 3:19) needed to produce food, euphemistically called bread, and where no thorns need to be weeded away.

All that changes after they fall to the temptation offered by the serpent to eat the forbidden fruit from the tree of the knowledge of good and evil (Gen 2:15). Their "eyes are opened" when they eat it, and they "become like God, knowing good and evil," just as the serpent told them (Gen 3:5). They also become aware of their nakedness; for the first time, they feel shame. They are then cast out of the garden of Eden into a world that knows plenty of good and evil but is not at all like God intended. They are fruitful and they do multiply (Gen 1:28), bearing sons Cain and Abel, who became the first murderer and the first victim of violence. When God confronts Cain, he replies with a question that will haunt almost every story in the rest of the Bible: "Am I my brother's keeper?" (Gen 4:9). It is perhaps the saddest question imaginable: how can you not know that most basic fact? And yet Cain's question is the most common dodge to avoid that fact.

Without explaining how, civilization develops. Technology develops with it; people learn to herd animals, to play instruments like the lyre and pipe, and to make a variety of bronze and iron tools (Gen 4:21). But violence also increases. A character called Lamech appears who boasts to his wives, "I have killed a man for wounding me" (Gen 4:23), as if that is something to be proud of. The narrator is showing us how we got to where we are in the story world. Who would want to live without domesticated animals, metal tools, and musical instruments? But on the other hand, who can live in such a world of violence? Does one necessarily have to entail the other? Whether by necessity or not, that is the world that is, the one we inhabit, the one we love and the one that appalls us.

The pace of the story quickens. Events are compressed into summary statements that encompass generations: "People began to multiply on the face of the ground" (Gen 6:1). This may appear to be a good thing, a fulfillment of the first command God ever gave, the call to "be fruitful and multiply." And yet, that blessing becomes a curse because the people who are so fruitful are fallen people. The narrator sums them up, painting them all with one brush, saying, "The wickedness of humankind was great in the earth and that every inclination of the thoughts of their hearts was only evil continually" (Gen 6:5). The reader is stunned: *Every inclination*? *Only evil? Continually*? The garden world has descended into depravity. Giving us the first glimpse of the emotions of the God who made everything and everyone good "in the beginning" but now watches it descend into violent chaos, we read, "The LORD was sorry that he had made humankind on the earth, and it grieved him to his heart" (Gen 6:6). The God of the garden has become the God of regret.

If plan A was to start the world with a perfect yet naïve couple who do not yet know good and evil, now we see what a failure it was. Perhaps plan B would be to start over with imperfect people whose eyes are wide open; people who refuse to participate in the violent status quo and who listen to the voice of divine guidance about how to escape it. Noah and his family are such people to begin the do-over. "Noah was a righteous man, blameless in his generation; Noah walked with God" (Gen 6:9). He sounds like Adam 2.0. Just as the waters covered the earth in the beginning, so waters will again cover the earth. The ancient understanding of the inhabitable earth is on display. It is a bubble of firmament protecting it from "the windows of the heavens" and earth, holding back "fountains of the deep" (Gen 7:11, 8:2). Both of them break open as grieving God sends a flood because, as we hear him say, "I have determined to make an end of all flesh, for the earth is filled with violence because of them" (Gen 6:13). In other words, it is time for plan B.

God commands and Noah obeys; that is how it should go. God commands an ark to be built, big enough to restart the earth with animals of every kind. Noah does so. He and his family and their floating zoo alone survive the flood. When it is safe for them to exit, God repeats and renews the original blessing given to Adam and Eve, saying again that they should be fruitful and multiply, and even fill the earth (Gen 1:28). Plan B now begins. The God who regretted creating the people who turned out to be "only evil continually" now seems also to regret their destruction. He promises that he will "never again curse the ground because of humankind, for the inclination of the human heart is evil from youth; nor will I ever again destroy every living creature as I have done" (Gen 8:21). He puts away his weapons. He sets his battle bow in the sky (Gen 9:13), now pointing away from the earth, its arrows of rain never again to threaten its destruction. The rainbow is the sign of the first covenant that God makes with humankind. It is, God says, an "everlasting covenant between God and every living creature of all flesh that is on the earth" (Gen 9:16).

We all know too well how plan B turns out. The descendants of Noah, we will soon learn, fare no better morally than those of Adam and Eve. The first three sons of Noah are Shem, Ham, and Japheth. Shem, we are told, is the father, meaning ancestor, of Eber (Gen 12:21). That does not sound meaningful to us, but Eber is the root of Hebrew. Shem then is the father of the Hebrews, the Semites; a foreshadowing of narratives to come.

The three brothers all have families of their own whose descendants eventually become nations, each with their own territories. Nevertheless, they all speak the same language. What follows is an enigmatic story about how they all decide to build a tower so high that its top reaches the heavens (Gen 11:4). That sounds benign enough to us, but ancient Hebrews read foreboding in those words. It sounds like the description of the tower built as a temple to Marduk, chief god of the Babylonians, the people who are destined to conquer the Hebrew people and carry them off into exile many years hence. It sounds like the motivation, or temptation, that Adam and Eve succumbed to: the quest to *be like God*.

There is implicit hubris in the temple-tower building plan; we are told that by it they intend to make a name for themselves (Gen 11:4). God appears almost threatened by their effort, saying, "Look, they are one people, and they have all one language; and this is only the beginning of what they will do; nothing that they propose to do will now be impossible for them" (Gen 11:6). His response, using the royal we/us, is "Come, let us go down, and confuse their language there, so that they will not understand one another's speech" (Gen 11:7). They called the tower Babel, meaning confuse or mix up and also a second oblique reference to Babylon. (In Babylonian [Akkadian], *Babel* means "the gate of God.")[1]

Generations follow in quick succession. Eventually, one of Shem's descendants—and thus one of Eber's—produces a man called Abram who marries a woman named Sarai. We will know them better as the people renamed Abraham and Sarah. They migrated from Ur in Mesopotamia (modern Iraq), intending to go to Canaan, we are told, but settling in Haran (in modern Turkey).

In a dramatic change of focus, the narrator takes us from the global view of the earth and its inhabitants to one specific family. We have by now been thoroughly accustomed to imagining the God of the Bible as the God of the whole earth. God created it and can affect it with blessings and curses that have worldwide consequences. He can send floods on a global scale. God, we have learned, also has a moral agenda: he hates violence. He hates it when people treat one another as means rather than as ends. And he frustrates the arrogance of people who seem to want to displace him with a tower-temple, as if some alternative moral order would be an improvement. He can confuse languages, also on a global scale. God is universally God.

But suddenly our attention is shifted from all the families of the earth to one family. And again, without any explanation, God decides to bless this one particular family: the family of Abraham and Sarah. God says, "I will make of you a great nation, and I will bless you, and make your name great, so that you will be a blessing. I will bless those who bless you, and

1. BDB, s.v. "בָּבֶל."

the one who curses you I will curse; and in you all the families of the earth shall be blessed" (Gen 12:2–3). God's concerns seem to migrate from the universal to the particular. Abraham alone is the chosen. The perfect plan A of creation starting with one innocent couple ended in a disastrously violent world, and the plan B of restarting a new world with one particular family after the flood produced no better world, so the reader may feel a sense of angst about this turn of events. Is the problem of the divided world now going to be solved by yet another attempt to identify one particular family to bless? What are the implications of such a choice? Has God then, after choosing Abraham and Sarah, lost interest or concern for the rest of the families of the earth? Or do they still matter? There is a tension between the particularity of the chosen family of Abraham and the God of the universe and all its people. That tension runs throughout all the narratives of the Bible, sometimes in the background and at other times foregrounded.

Perhaps we are meant to hear a hint at the universal nature of God's concern for humanity when God's choice to bless Abraham in particular is said to have consequences for all the families of the earth. That hint is present, but the primary focus is on this one person.

Thus begins the essential tension that will haunt most of the rest of the Bible. God is both the universal God of the whole world whose moral concerns are global and whose eyes see everything, and he is the special God of Abraham, the God of the Hebrew people. They alone are promised a blessing that includes a great name, a great nation, and special protection. God is now on their side. God makes a covenant or binding treaty with Abraham and his descendants alone. Note that this treaty should not imply mutual agreement; God acts as God has chosen to act, and Abraham is merely the recipient.

Soon the narrator will describe this second covenant that God makes with people. The first covenant after the flood was with Noah and "every living creature of all flesh that is on the earth" (Gen 9:16). This covenant with Abraham is, however, exclusive. The narrator says, "On that day the Lord made a covenant with Abram, saying, 'To your descendants I give this land, from the river of Egypt to the great river, the river Euphrates'" (Gen 15:18). This covenant is with Abraham, as he will become known, and his "descendants"—literally his "seed." And so begins the story of the chosen people, the descendants of Abraham and Sarah. It is as complicated a family story as there ever was. There are obstacles in the way of that promised blessing coming true. It begins with multiple generations of barren wives—in that world, infertility is always a female problem—lack of marriageable women, and heel-grabbing trickery (referring to the story of Jacob and Esau, which would lead us off the point here).

The descendants of Abraham have a hard time staying in the land they have been promised. Jacob has to flee to his uncle's house for years but eventually returns. His sons' generation endures famine and migrates to Egypt for survival. They survive but are eventually enslaved for hundreds of years under Pharaoh. Most of us are familiar with the way that story goes: Moses calls down plagues on Egypt, which forces Pharaoh to relent and allow them to leave. Then after a change of heart, Pharaoh sends his army out after them only to have them drown in the sea that the Israelites have just crossed on dry land. Moses then leads his people circuitously through a wilderness on a forty-year journey. On Mount Sinai—or Horeb, it has both names—Moses receives the Ten Commandments and all of the rest of the Law, or Torah, from God and announces it to the people. Another covenant is made as the people promise to obey.

The point not to lose sight of is that this is still a story about the descendants of one particular family. These Hebrews, or Israelites, are all the descendants of Abraham and Sarah. They are the chosen people. God, the LORD, is their God, on their side. They are the ones to whom the promised land has been promised. God is present uniquely to them. At his instruction, they build a tabernacle—that is, a tent-shrine comprising concentric rooms of increasing holiness, the center being the "holy of holies" where God dwells. He told them, "I will dwell among the Israelites, and I will be their God. And they shall know that I am the LORD their God, who brought them out of the land of Egypt that I might dwell among them; I am the LORD their God" (Exod 29:45–46). Yes, "their" God in a unique, particular way.

How can God have it both ways? How can God be both the creator of all the world's people and at the same time be the particular God of one people? That's the God side of the problem. The human side of the problem is this: how should the Hebrew people exist among non-chosen people? Are they automatically enemies? Are they potential enemies? Should their gods be despised as idols and the priests of their shrines eliminated? Is it okay with Israel's God that his people use violence against them? The answer we will see is both yes and no. It is a tension running through the whole Bible.

The question comes into sharp focus in the New Testament. Jesus is born into the family of the Hebrews as a descendant of Abraham, Isaac, and Jacob (Matt 1:1–2). For followers of Jesus, he is the long-awaited Messiah, the Christ—that is, the one anointed by God, the Savior. (*Messiah* comes from the Hebrew word for *anointed*, which is also what *Christ* means in Greek.)[2] The message he brings as he announces the arrival of the kingdom of God is considered good news, or in older English, "gospel" (Mark

2. BDB, s.v. "מָשַׁח"; BDAG, s.v. "Χριστός."

1:14–15). But the question early followers of Jesus had was who is the gospel for? Is it for the descendants of Abraham, the recipient of the original promise and covenant alone? "Yes," said the Jerusalem-based followers of Jesus. "No," said Paul. It is rather for everyone. It is not particular, it is universal in scope. It is not for Jews alone but for Gentiles as well.

Paul was a trained Jewish rabbi. He made arguments the way rabbis argued about the meaning of the Bible, or, as he called it, the law of Moses. This is one of those places in which we have to try to imagine their world, as different as it is from ours, because Paul's argument makes little sense to us. It is based on a play on words. Paul argues that when God made his promise to Abraham, he did not make it to him alone but also to his descendants. In English, *descendants* is plural—there are many descendants, which is why in the NRSV it is translated "offspring." But in Hebrew and in its Greek translation that Paul used, the word is *seed*, which is a singular noun (as in other English translations). The promise is to Abraham and his seed. We call this an "uncountable noun." Words for things too many and too small to count individually we use singular nouns for, like *sand*, *fish*, and for liquids like *water*. Curiously, there are exceptions: we do say *stars*. But anyway, Paul makes a point out of the singular word *seed*. He says, "Now the promises were made to Abraham and to his seed; it does not say, 'And to seeds,' as of many; but it says, 'And to your seed,' that is, to one person, who is Christ" (Gal 3:16). What is the effect? Paul says, "In Christ Jesus the blessing (or promises) of Abraham might come to the Gentiles, so that we might receive the promise of the Spirit through faith" (Gal 3:14). Notice that the promised blessings God gave to Abraham have become, according to Paul, not a literal nation and a land but *the Spirit*, which, to Paul, is the best blessing of all. And so the law of Moses, which came many years after that promise to Abraham, requiring circumcision, Sabbath-keeping, and kosher rules, applied to only Jews; but the promise first made to Abraham and "his seed" is for all who are "in Christ" by faith. We will look more closely at this in chapter 17.

In other words, Paul has universalized the promise to Abraham. He sums it up this way: "All of you are one in Christ Jesus. And if you belong to Christ, then you are Abraham's seed, heirs according to the promise" (Gal 3:28).

That opening up to Gentiles of the promised blessings to Abraham was too much for one branch of the early Christian community, and there was a big dispute about it according to both Paul and the book of Acts. Acts describes a conference in Jerusalem called to settle the matter. Paul's side won, the gospel was preached to Gentiles, the church spread, and here we are today.

But the question that remains is: Was that a legitimate move for Paul to make? Sure, like a good rabbi, he could wrestle a text until it cried "uncle" and submitted to his interpretation, but even if rabbis might have conceded the argument on the basis of that wordplay, should we? To put it another way, many texts in the Hebrew Bible, or the Old Testament, proclaim and defend particularism: the Jews are God's chosen people. The question is, are there also other texts that give voice to another, more universal perspective? Is the God of Abraham also a God whose moral concerns have a worldwide scope? Was Paul seeing a trajectory in the Hebrew Bible that included a global intention in God's plan, balancing the particularism of *chosen-ness*?

Yes, Paul would have found such texts in his Hebrew Bible, and this is what we will see as we walk through some of the narratives of the Bible. They will help us wrestle with questions that still present themselves to us today as we consider what it means to be a Christian in America. The claim has been made that America is God's chosen nation like Israel was. Some have argued that God has blessed America, making it the inheritor of Israel's role as "the city on the hill," the "light to the nations." America is blessed, the claim is made, because it is a Christian nation in origin and in purpose. God's continued blessing on America has been based on—and will only continue on—the condition of faithfulness to God as a Christian nation. Blessings for obedience and withdrawal of blessings, and even punishment for disobedience, was Israel's experience and has been and will be America's experience. This, we are told, is the biblical teaching.

Not wishing to grant that belief that America is chosen by God in some particular way, we must ask ourselves if this perspective is actually faithful to the Bible as we have it now, or is it only a selective reading of part of the story to the neglect of other parts? If we want to be biblical, then let us read the Bible without ignoring any of it. When we do, we will of course read texts about the particular chosen status of Abraham and his *seed* (or descendants/offspring). And we will also read texts that highlight God's continual concern for all the humans made in the image and likeness of God, indeed for all the families of the earth.

Part 1

Old Testament Narratives

Israelite Nationalism

1

The Perfect World

Most people agree that the stories of the Bible, probably like all ancient texts, were circulated by word of mouth long before anyone chiseled them in stone or put pen to parchment. We can picture people sitting around a campfire, listening to the elders recounting family histories and hero stories to their young. We imagine someone looking up at the stars and wondering out loud, "Where did we come from? How did we get here?" And then an elder would say, "Well, my father said it happened this way: 'In the beginning. . .'" It could have happened that way. It must have been something like that.

When we read the creation account in Gen 1, we are not asking, "Did it really happen that way?" Nor are we asking, "Can you believe that story and also believe in evolution?" Either way, the question remains: Why repeat the story generation after generation? Why eventually write it down? After all, writing was expensive in the ancient world. Not everyone had the luxury necessary to become literate; it required enough leisure to afford the time away from productive work. This means that only the stories they thought were important were written down, and only the best of them were copied and recopied so they could be handed down the generations. The Hebrew Bible as we have it now is a collection of the stories the Israelites considered important enough to invest in—and keep investing in—over many years.

We can go down to the local bookstore or order online a book called the Bible. We are used to thinking of the Bible as one single book. But a "book" is actually an amazing innovation. In ancient times, people wrote on scrolls. There was a limit to how long a scroll could get before it became too big and unwieldy. A person could have a collection of scrolls, but they were always considered individual texts. Genesis was a scroll. Exodus was a separate scroll. All of the "books" of the Bible began their life in written form as individual scrolls. Then someone got the idea to cut up the scroll into separate sections—let's call them "pages"—and bind them together on one end, thus creating a "book"—scholars call it a *codex*.

Soon, in ancient Rome, the codex replaced scrolls as an obvious improvement, the way email replaced fax machines. Now a new possibility was born: you could take several scrolls and, after cutting them into pages, bind them all together into one "book." Once that happens, people start thinking of that "book" as if each of those formerly separate scrolls was actually conceived as a unity with a common theme and purpose. Even though a careful reader can see all kinds of different perspectives and ideas from scrolls that were produced over many centuries and from different places, nevertheless, once they get stitched together into a "book," they start to be read as if there must be one perspective, one voice, one central idea connecting them all together, not just a binder's string and glue. After all these years, we might be used to thinking of the Bible as one thing, but that mistake must be resisted. Each voice that speaks from those different scrolls deserves to be heard as its original author(s) intended.

We will also need to be aware of how meanings of originally individual texts can be influenced by their order in an organized collection. The order matters and affects how texts are understood. As we will see, the one that comes first becomes a lens through which subsequent texts are read.

The story of creation in Gen 1 now stands as the first narrative in the Bible. Many scholars, however, believe it conveys the mature theological reflections of the Israelite community from centuries after Moses, David, Solomon, and many of the prophets. There are many unresolved questions. Did the narrative of creation have an oral period before it was written down? Most scholars believe it did. Was it edited by later hands? Most scholars believe it was. The scholarly consensus has evolved on these questions, but as some have observed, a consensus is only a consensus, not a certainty. That is true, but the study of history is never about certainty; that is no barrier to asking about what its message is (or messages are) in its current, final form.

We have mentioned that scrolls and the individual narratives that comprise them had lives of their own before they were joined together, like pearls with separate lives before being united on a necklace. But over the years, Israelite faith-leaders developed a growing collection of texts that they valued. Many centuries after the Hebrew Bible was written, by the time of Jesus, people spoke of several categories or collections of these originally separate texts. When a Pharisee asked Jesus what the greatest commandment was, according to Matthew, he identified the love of God and of neighbor as first and second, then said, "On these two commandments hang all the law and the prophets" (Matt 22:40). Jesus was identifying two categories, the Law—meaning the law of Moses—and the Prophets. Two categories may not have been exhaustive of the way Jews of Jesus's day thought of their sacred texts. Luke tells us that the risen Jesus referred to three groups of texts when he told the two disciples he met on the road to Emmaus, "everything written about me in the law of Moses, the prophets, and the psalms must be fulfilled" (Luke 24:44). Those three groups of texts—Law (of Moses), Prophets, and Psalms (or, as some refer to them, Writings)—have become the standard way the Jewish community has spoken of their sacred texts. The Jewish Bible is known by the acronym TaNaK, derived from the first letters of the Hebrew words for its three main sections: Torah (Law), Nevi'im (Prophets), and Ketuvim (Writings).

For clarity, the first section, called *Law*, has a lot more than laws in it. It includes the law of Moses and also all the Genesis and Exodus stories that preceded it. But *Torah* or "Law"—or better, "guidance" or "instruction"[1]—is the name given to the first division of the Hebrew Bible. (*Torah* will eventually stand for the Pentateuch, or first five books, Genesis to Deuteronomy.) As it stands now, the creation narrative is the first story in the *Tanak*.

The creation story originally existed independently but was eventually incorporated into a collection of narratives called the *Law* or *Torah*. Let us take a moment to reflect on what it meant to ancient people to have an account of the origin of the universe and of the origin of the first humans. Gen 1 was neither solitary nor unique.

Ancient Middle Eastern Creation Stories

Many ancient peoples had stories of their origins, explaining where their people came from and how they came to be identified with a particular place. Some of those stories trace their origins all the way back to the creation of the cosmos. Those creation stories are hence called cosmologies. The first chapter of Genesis is one such cosmology. As it stands now, it bears signs of having a relationship with other ancient cosmologies. Here are some examples:

The Sumerian people, who inhabited Mesopotamia about 4000 BCE, told a story of how the gods first separated heaven and earth. In council among themselves, the gods decided to create people to work the earth to relieve them of some of their labor, like irrigating the fields. They began by creating Enki and Ninma, an original man and woman, from clay.

1. BDB, s.v. "תּוֹרָה."

The Hittites, who were ascendant during the fourteenth and thirteenth centuries BCE, had a cosmology that included a serpent named Illuyanka, who represented chaos and fought with a storm god that represented order.

The ancient cosmology that probably shows the most extensive evidence of a relationship with the narrative of Genesis chapter 1 comes from Babylon. It was the Babylonians who captured Israel, or what was left of it, in the sixth century BCE, taking the survivors captive and making them exiles. Every year at their new year's festival, the Babylonians conducted an elaborate ritual in which the king of Babylon was ceremoniously defrocked by the priests and then reinvested with royal authority to reign in the name of their patron god, Marduk. As part of the annual festival, they would retell their cosmology, or creation myth, which told the tale of how Marduk became the chief god of Babylon by leading a victorious battle against other gods. That myth, named for its opening words "When, on high" (Enuma Elish), has a number of similar details as well as structural parallels with the Genesis narrative:

Babylonian Enuma Elish	**Genesis Chapter 1**
The divine spirit and cosmic material are already present eternally	The divine spirit creates matter and is independent of it
Chaos is the original condition	The world is without form, a watery chaos
Light is produced from the gods	God creates light
The creation of the firmament	The creation of the firmament
The creation of dry land	The creation of dry land
The creation of the luminaries	The creation of the luminaries
The creation of humankind	The creation of humankind
The gods rest and celebrate	God rests and sanctifies the seventh day

The cross-pollination of these cosmologies shows that ancient cultures shared some elements in common but also diverged in important ways. In the Babylonian story, for example, humans are created as an afterthought. After Marduk defeats the god Tiamat, humans are made from the wreckage of her corpse. This is a far different understanding of the essence of humankind according to the Genesis cosmology, as we will see. The point to remember is that these narratives had a history prior to their final form in the texts we have today. They were preserved because their meanings were important.

The creation story of Genesis is one of those stories worth the investment of retaining and recopying. Why? Because it offers answers to fundamental human questions. To ask, "Where do we come from?" is to imply a deeper question: What are we supposed to be? What is our purpose? To tell a story that begins with a perfect world, even if it did not stay perfect for very long, is to tell a story about how the world should have been. If we know how we were meant to be before things went wrong, then we know what we should want to become—our quest as humans. The desire we have to make things right again means we have an idea of what "right" should look like. A creation story told the way the Bible tells us shows us what to aim for: the world before things go wrong.

The Universal Image of God

After centuries of thinking of themselves as the chosen people who have a special, unique relationship with God, the Jewish community embraced the understanding that all people share common origins. The creation narrative now stands at the beginning of the Torah as a preface, the lens through which to read all the subsequent narratives. Here is what we find: the narrator quotes the Creator saying, "Let us make humankind [*adam*] in our image, according to our likeness" (Gen 1:26). *Adam* first meant "people" or "humankind" before it became the name of the first created human. It comes from the word for "ground" or "soil," *adamah*.[2] That wordplay is explicit in Gen 2:7, which says, "Then the Lord God formed man [*Adam*] from the dust of the ground [*adamah*]." Humans are *groundlings*. Groundlings in some respects, but also much more. They are groundlings created in the image and likeness of God.

We should not rush past this because the Genesis account is both similar to, but vastly different from, other ancient cosmologies in significant respects. In Sumer and Babylon, the gods are many; in Genesis, God is One, uncontested, and needing no consultation. In the Hittite cosmology, there is a struggle between the serpent of chaos and the god of order. In Genesis, the Spirit of God hovers over the waters of chaos and tames them by the simple words "Let there be," after which we are told "and it was" (Gen 1). In Babylon, violence is at the heart of the cosmology as rival gods battle it out for power. In Genesis, there is no violence whatsoever in the world as it was before things went wrong.

In Babylon, humans are created as an afterthought. In Genesis, humans are the pinnacle of creation. In Babylon, the purpose of the humans is drudgery; like janitors, their work is to keep the canals of Babylon clean and free-flowing so that the gods can have some rest. In Genesis, humans

2. BDB, s.v. "אדם."

are made in the *image and likeness* of God. They are not cursed to be janitors but blessed to *be fruitful and multiply* and given dominion over the rest of creation. All of this is the product of deep theological reflection over many years by the Israelite community. It stands now, at the beginning of the whole collection of texts they preserved as sacred, as the lens through which all subsequent texts must be read.

Let us slow down and focus on one specific insight from the Genesis text. The narrator asserts that humans of both genders are equally created, quoting God, "in our image, according to our likeness," as he explains, "male and female he created them" (Gen 1:27). What could it possibly mean that physical humans bear a resemblance to the invisible God? There has been speculation for centuries about the meaning of *image and likeness*, but in any case, humans are given a status that somehow differentiates them from all beings created before them. Yes, the narrator says, we are superior to the animals. This perspective may cause a bit of discomfort to modern people who do not believe such a sharp distinction between humans and nature is warranted—and is even a dangerous one—but remember, we are trying to enter the world of the text as tourists to a land not our own. Back then, whenever "back then" was, the separation of humans from animals and human superiority were assumed. The point is that this lens through which we are to read all of the following narratives about chosen-ness is one that shows the true picture: even if one family is chosen, nevertheless, they are part of a human family that includes everyone. We all descended from one original pair of groundlings. And, as we will see, the very narrative of choosing one family explicitly predicts that the blessings to Abraham and his descendants will produce blessings for "all the families of the earth" (Gen 12:3).

This perspective of the single origin of all humans creates a tension that remains unresolved in the Hebrew Bible. God is the Creator God of all people. All humans bear God's *image and likeness*. Yet one particular family is the subject of the whole story from the call of Abraham on. How do the chosen people then treat other people? It is a mixed picture. Abraham and his descendants enslave people, starting with Sarah's handmaid Hagar. Later, especially in the battles of conquest for the promised land led by Joshua, they have enemies who they slaughter and enemies that they cry out for God's help against. They expect God to be on their side, and in many of the stories, God is. After all, they are the chosen. The tension is real—and remains. In the back of their minds, however, is the knowledge that this world of violence was not the world as it was created to be. This world of *us* and *them* is part of what has gone wrong. The world as it should be is a nonviolent, peaceful world—a world of *shalom* or peace, well-being, welfare—in which every person is respected and treated with dignity befitting those made in God's image and likeness.

In fact, the goal of shalom will become the motif many of the Bible's writers will return to as they imagine the world as it should be. The blessing that Aaron pronounces includes shalom: "The Lord lift up his countenance upon you, and give you peace [shalom]" (Num 6:26). Isaiah sings, "How beautiful upon the mountains are the feet of the messenger who announces peace [shalom]" (Isa 52:7). Jeremiah, in his letter to the exiles in Babylon, envisions a future of shalom: "For surely I know the plans I have for you, says the Lord, plans for your welfare [shalom] and not for harm, to give you a future with hope" (Jer 29:11). The prophet Micah can see a future deliverer who brings shalom: "But you, O Bethlehem of Ephrathah, who are one of the little clans of Judah, from you shall come forth for me one who is to rule in Israel . . . and he shall be the one of peace [shalom]" (Mic 5:2, 5). These words have now become familiar to Christians because Matthew applies them to the baby Jesus (Matt 2:6). Isaiah speaks of an expected prince of peace (Isa 9:6). Zechariah's vision of the future includes a peaceful king, saying poetically,

> Rejoice greatly, O daughter Zion!
>   Shout aloud, O daughter Jerusalem!
> Lo, your king comes to you;
>   triumphant and victorious is he,
> humble and riding on a donkey,
>   on a colt, the foal of a donkey.
> He will cut off the chariot from Ephraim
>   and the war horse from Jerusalem;
> and the battle bow shall be cut off,
>   and he shall command peace to the nations. (Zech 9:9–10a)

Christians will recognize that each of these has been taken up by the New Testament and applied to Jesus. Luke describes the angels appearing to the shepherds announcing Jesus's birth, singing, "Glory to God in the highest heaven, and on earth peace among those whom he favors!" (Luke 2:14). Who does the Lord favor? Not one particular ethnic group of chosen people, but rather, as Luke's second volume, the book of Acts, describes, the entire Jewish and Gentile world.

According to Matthew, Jesus's Sermon on the Mount includes the beatitude: "Blessed are the peacemakers, for they will be called children of God" (Matt 5:9). The original creation hope of a nonviolent world in which a former enemy nation "shall not lift up sword against nation, neither shall they learn war any more" (Isa 2:4) receives its climax in Jesus's words, "I say to you that listen, Love your enemies, do good to those who hate you" (Luke 6:27).

Despite all the stories in the Hebrew Bible of centuries of violence as Israel evolved from a confederacy of family tribes into a monarchy—and as that monarchy finally collapsed in ruin—nevertheless, every faithful Israelite knew that the world was created to be a world at peace between all the families of the earth. That creation-vision was so compelling that, even after all those years, it was still the future that they believed one day God would create. Peace was the hope of the prophets. Peace was what the New Testament says Christ, the Messiah, would establish. Though the world has always experienced the opposite, nevertheless, the world as it was meant to be is a world without any enemies to hate and kill; it is a nonviolent world of peace between nations and people, all of whom have been created in the image and likeness of God.

Universal Sabbath

In the perfect world of the first chapter of Genesis, before things went wrong, the vision of a peaceful world is deepened by the concept of Sabbath. As the succeeding texts unfold, Sabbath will have profound implications for the way Israelites are instructed to think about their lives, their relationship with God, with labor, and with all of humanity. Remember, Gen 1 was not written first, but after many years of reflections and a long history. In its present form, as the opening of the Torah section of the *Tanak*, the story of creation is a preface. As such, it introduces themes and concepts that will be developed further in subsequent texts, such as the law of Moses and the prophets. Sabbath implications will continue into the New Testament as a source of conflict between Jesus and law-of-Moses expert scribes, and law-of-Moses policers, Pharisees.

Consider how the narrator situates the concept of Sabbath. Genesis begins with the wind—or spirit or breath—of God hovering over chaotic, formless waters. God begins to make order out of this chaos by creating spaces, separating those spaces from each other, and then populating those spaces appropriately. God creates light, separates light from darkness, and then populates the space with heavenly luminaries. Another of the ways the Genesis account differs from the Babylonian creation story appears here, although it is less apparent in English than in the original. The narrator of Genesis does not use the words *sun* or *moon*, but rather *greater light* and *lesser light*. This is because to say the word *sun* in Hebrew, *shemesh*, is to say the name of the ancient Mesopotamian sun-god, *Shamash*. The same is true of the moon, *Yarih*, which is the name of the moon god. In an ancient world that believed the stars controlled destinies, Genesis presents them as an afterthought. The text reads, "God made the two great lights—the greater light to rule the day and the lesser light to rule the night—and the stars" (Gen 1:16). Stars were described in an almost off-handed manner; that is a far lower role for stars than the controllers of human destiny, as many ancients believed. In the world before things went wrong, no one looked to the sun, the moon, or the stars for direction. The whole of the physical world is shown as a product of a Creator God who has no competition nor limits on his creative power, in complete control.

Importantly, there is nothing inherently wrong with this physical world. In fact, the opposite is the case. Repeatedly, the narrator tells us that at the end of each of the days of creation, "God saw that it was good" (Gen 1:10, 12, 18, 21, 25). The physical world is not a realm of profane matter, as if it were of a lower nature than spirit, but is pronounced good. Nor is the body to be considered the prison in which a soul is incarcerated, as Plato saw it.[3] Rather, after the creation of the groundlings in his image and likeness, we read, "God saw everything that he had made, and indeed, it was very good" (Gen 1:31). Physical life, the physical world, and our own physical bodies are very good. This is how the world should be; it is a very good place of fruitfulness and blessedness. It is a place where people are instructed, "Be fruitful and multiply, and fill the earth and subdue it; and have dominion over the fish of the sea and over the birds of the air and over every living thing that moves upon the earth" (Gen 1:28). We should not be bothered by the ancient words of *subdue* and *dominion*, as if they were license to despise and defile this very good world that God has made. It was simply a matter of fact to the ancient narrator that, unlike any other known beings, humans had obvious dominion. Humans had fished the waters, farmed the earth, and domesticated animals for food, clothing, and labor. As a gift given to humans, the very good world was under their "care, custody, and control," implying an obligation to use it well. Humans made in God's image and likeness are the culmination point of this narrative of good, good, very good, blessed creation story.

After this six-day work of creation, the narrator says, "And on the seventh day God finished the work that he had done, and he rested [*shabbat*, i.e., Sabbath] on the seventh day from all the work that he had done" (Gen 2:2).

In the Babylonian cosmology, the rest after the bloody creation process was for the gods and the gods alone, but this concept of Sabbath rest

3. Plato, *Phaed.*

introduced here will be developed in the texts that follow. Notice that God did not create the day of rest. Unlike other days, when God separates light from darkness or land from sea, there is nothing to separate, nor was there any space to populate. The Sabbath stands alone, outside the pattern of the other elements of creation. Rather, the day of rest was already present in God as a possibility or even a state of being. The Sabbath, the seventh day of rest, now becomes the ultimate paradigm for the world as it should be. *Sabbath* is a concept, like *shalom*, that will develop throughout the narratives of the Hebrew Bible to follow. After generations of Sabbath-keeping practice, this narrative of creation was placed as the preface to the stories to follow to elevate its status as high as it could possibly be. The Sabbath principle is what God intended for the perfect world, for all people, for all time, before any division of people into separate nations and before it all went wrong.

The word "rest" in Hebrew, *shabbat*, is the root of the phrase in our English Bibles for "sabbath feast" or "sabbath rest," *shabbaton*.[4] Sabbath feast, as the Hebrew Bible will tell us, is not just for the seventh day of the week. A Sabbath feast or rest is also to be observed every seventh year so that the land itself may rest. "When you enter the land that I am giving you, the land shall observe a sabbath for the LORD. Six years you shall sow your field, and six years you shall prune your vineyard, and gather in their yield; but in the seventh year there shall be a sabbath of complete rest [*shabbaton*] for the land, a sabbath for the LORD" (Lev 25:1–4). The seventh day of rest for humans is extended to a seventh year of rest for the land.

The seventh year is more than rest for the land; it is also rest from the burden of carrying debt. In the seventh year, all debts were to be forgiven. "Every seventh year you shall grant a remission of debts. . . . Every creditor shall remit the claim that is held against a neighbor, not exacting it, because the LORD's remission has been proclaimed" (Deut 15:1–2). The people who were created in the image and likeness of God were not to be degraded as debtors. In the ancient world, which was an agrarian one, debts were not created by overspending on consumer products. Debts were acquired by farming hardship, the result of bad harvests, plagues, droughts, or disease. For this reason every seven years, people with dignity needed to have a chance to start over by having their debts forgiven.

And there is more. The principle of Sabbath rest is once more intensified. After seven cycles of seven years, after the forty-ninth year, in the following fiftieth year, the concept of Sabbath rest is expanded even further. The fiftieth year, called the year of Jubilee, is also called a year of liberty. In the ultimate Sabbath of Jubilee, everyone will be able to return to their

4. BDB, s.v. "שָׁבַת."

ancestral land. Any land that had been lost to a family in the preceding forty-nine years would be restored. Whether the people had lost their land by selling it due to poverty caused by famine, drought, or the sickness or death of the land-working man of the household, in the fiftieth Sabbath year of Jubilee, the land was to be returned. "You shall count off seven weeks of years, seven times seven years, so that the period of seven weeks of years gives forty-nine years. Then . . . you shall proclaim liberty throughout the land to all its inhabitants. It shall be a jubilee for you: you shall return, every one of you, to your property and every one of you to your family" (Lev 25:8–10).

Some immediately raise the questions: "But did that ever really happen? Did they ever actually do that?" To raise that question is to misunderstand the purpose of a narrative that gave us that account. The law of Moses, whether obeyed or disobeyed, is meant to convey how the community should be. They were meant to understand themselves as more than merely an extended clan or a confederation of tribes. They were meant to understand each other as bound to one another in a covenant-community. They were to see each other as "neighbor" with special obligations to each other. Among these obligations was the mandate to prevent a permanent poverty class from ever developing. Every fifty years there would be a restart for each family as they returned to the land, their inheritance from God, to begin a new legacy. The law of Moses was not a description of how it was but a template for how it should be. The Sabbath principle was therefore included in the story of creation to convey God's will for all people and all times.

Was the Sabbath principle really for all people, or was it meant only for the Israelite community, the descendants of Abraham, the ones privileged to receive the law of Moses? The answer is clear: the Sabbath principle is for everyone. In the Ten Commandments, which set forth the requirement to keep the Sabbath, we read this: "But the seventh day is a sabbath to the Lord your God; you shall not do any work—you, your son or your daughter, your male or female slave, your livestock, or the alien resident in your towns" (Exod 20:10). The requirement of Sabbath rest extended specifically "to the alien resident in your towns." Aliens were noncitizens. In other English Bible versions, they are called strangers. Noncitizens were non-Israelites. It was taken for granted that there would be foreigners among the Israelite community. Some may have been servants, such as handmaids—remember this is an ancient world that we ourselves are strangers to—they may have been former occupant-survivors of conquest or spouses from surrounding peoples. The manner in which these non Israelites found themselves within Israel's territory was not the question. Slave or free, male or female, all of them were to have a Sabbath of rest from labor every seven days. It is therefore altogether fitting that the story of creation itself should culminate in Sabbath. God himself rested on the Sabbath, the seventh day, as the version of the Ten Commandments in Exodus says:

> But the seventh day is a sabbath to the LORD your God; you shall not do any work—you, your son or your daughter, your male or female slave, your livestock, or the alien resident in your towns. For in six days the LORD made heaven and earth, the sea, and all that is in them, but rested the seventh day; therefore the LORD blessed the sabbath day and consecrated it. (Exod 20:10–11)

The creation account was most likely originally handed on orally from generation to generation. Over the years, it was molded and shaped by evolving circumstances and developing understandings. Similarities to other cosmologies of the ancient world have long been known to scholars, showing that the text we now have has been influenced by its environment. But the places of departure from those ancient cosmologies are also noteworthy. In Israel's narrative, one Creator God makes all people in God's image and likeness, placing them in a good physical world and blessing them with fertility and abundance. They are somehow superior to all the other created beings. They alone are somehow godlike. Eventually, they will acquire the godlike knowledge of good and evil, but in doing so, things will go wrong for them and their descendants. Nevertheless, the world as it was meant to be begins with people created with dignity, from whom all humanity descends.

All the families of the earth are blessed with the paradigmatic rest of God on the seventh day, the Sabbath. The Sabbath rest in Israel's texts expands from the seventh day of rest for everyone, including noncitizens, to the seventh year rest for the land and forgiveness of indebtedness, and finally culminates in the fiftieth year of liberty, the Year of Jubilee, in which all property returns to its original owners. The Sabbath principle is universally for all the families of the earth before they are divided by language, ethnicity, or territorial boundary.

All of these elements of the creation narrative come together to form a stark counterpoint to the accounts of Israelite particularism that will follow. The creation of all people in the image and likeness of God and the nonviolent world of shalom are true of and for the sake of everyone. The vision of Sabbath rest, liberation, and ultimately restoration is for everyone. This perspective of God's care and concern for all the families of the earth will, from this narrative on, become one pole of tension always tugging against the texts of particularity of one chosen people, as we will see in our exploration of the narratives to follow.

2

The Mixed Multitude

Exodus continues the story of the family of Abraham, but the Genesis scroll has reached its maximum size. A new scroll will have to be started. If ancient authors wanted to connect a new scroll to a previous one to continue the story, they had to connect them in a literary manner. This is what the Exodus narrator does. He (we will assume he is male, writing in a time before it was customary for women to be educated—though some were, like king Ahab's wife Jezebel) linked his new scroll with the Genesis story by repeating the exact six Hebrew words from Genesis that enumerated Jacob's family: "These are the names of the sons of Israel who came to Egypt" (Gen 46:8 = Exod 1:1). Calling them, not Hebrews, but sons of Israel shows that this family story has now become the story of a nation; another foreshadowing of a future reality yet to be realized.

The theme of the story is about the promise God made to Abraham. In fact, the theme of the whole Hebrew Bible, some have observed, is the partial fulfillment of that promise. If the promise is partly fulfilled, then it is also partly unfulfilled—another tension that tugs at the story to the end. The promise to Abraham included descendants who would become a nation, divine protection, and the assurance that Abraham's descendants would be the means by which God would bless all the families of the earth.

The interplay of the promise and its fulfillment being so often in the hands of non-Israelites is another tension running throughout. Abraham and Sarah begin their part of the story in a foreign land we call Mesopotamia.

> Now the Lord said to Abram, "Go from your country and your kindred and your father's house to the land that I will show you.

> I will make of you a great nation, and I will bless you, and make your name great, so that you will be a blessing. I will bless those who bless you, and the one who curses you I will curse; and in you all the families of the earth shall be blessed. (Gen 12:1–3)

Abraham obeys the call to go and, when he gets to Canaan, the promise is expanded, as God says, "To your offspring [literally "seed"] I will give this land" (Gen 12:7).

From Joseph to Baby Moses

As Exodus opens, what has happened to the promise? Childlessness, the initial challenge to the promise, has been overcome. Now, the narrator tells us, the family numbers seventy, probably enough to ensure future survival. But they are no longer in the promised land. Famine has forced them to move to a foreign country. The cycle of Joseph-stories that starts with the "coat of many colors"—the one that makes his brothers jealous—has concluded in Egypt. Joseph has risen from houseboy, through the status of wrongfully imprisoned man, to become an official in Egypt. Joseph's uncanny experiences with dreams and dream interpretations has been the vehicle for his reversal of fortunes. Dreams are a frequent leitmotif throughout the narratives of the Hebrew Bible. The covenant that sealed the promise to Abraham itself was given to him in a deep, dark dream (Gen 15). We could say that the dream of a peaceable future of justice and righteousness, so prominent in the prophets, extends this theme further. However that may be, Joseph the dreamer-turned-public-official is able to extend an invitation to his family to escape the famine in Canaan and join him in Egypt, which they do. The promise is partly being fulfilled, but partly not. The family survives, but they are outside the promised land. Somehow, for the promise to come true, they will have to get back home. They are now strangers in a land not their own.

The memory of this time of placeless-ness will become part of their liturgically repeated self-identity. Moses will instruct the people to say, "A wandering Aramean was my ancestor; he went down into Egypt and lived there as an alien" (Deut 26:5). The word *alien* or *stranger* also means *sojourner*, a person a long way from home. As Israel reflects on the tension between being singled out as a particular nation and blessed with promise, they are regularly reminded that they wore the garments of a stranger. That identity will inform their treatment of strangers in the law of Moses to come. The tension is real.

Let us set the stage. As Exodus opens, time has passed—in fact so much time that Joseph's work, so appreciated by the empire in past times, is now long forgotten. There is a new Pharaoh in town who does not even remember him. In the meantime, the family of seventy has been so fruitful that, from the Egyptian's perspective, they filled the land (Exod 1:7). The creation mandate to the groundlings to be fruitful and the promised blessing of many descendants is coming true. By the way, when this story is retold in Acts 7:14, the number of the family is seventy-five. The author of Acts is quoting the Greek translation of the Hebrew Bible (LXX), which, for reasons not known, has that number. Ancient books were copied and recopied, passed down the generations, and translated; things happen along the way.

The blessing of increase, however, is also a curse in the eyes of the Egyptians, who now fear the growing number of them (Exod 1:1). The Pharaoh sees them as a potential threat to his power, so he announces, presumably to his court officials, "Come, let us deal shrewdly with them, or they will increase and, in the event of war, join our enemies and fight against us and escape from the land" (Exod 1:10). The word *shrewdly* is also the word *wisely*, but we will soon find out Pharaoh's plan is anything but wise. This is irony, of which the Hebrew narratives are full. You can picture the author winking as he writes *shrewdly*. The Pharaoh is a fool—a murderous fool, but a fool nonetheless.

The first part of Pharaoh's solution to the multiplying Israelites is to enslave them. "The Egyptians became ruthless in imposing tasks on the Israelites and made their lives bitter with hard service in mortar and brick and in every kind of field labor. They were ruthless in all the tasks that they imposed on them" (Exod 1:13–14). Twice, for emphasis, the narrator repeats the word *ruthless*. The people's lives are *bitter*. How this enslavement plan fixes the problem of numerousness and fertility is not clear. Did *shrewd* Pharaoh think they would just be too tired to make babies? If so, he is not as clever as he thinks

His plan has no effect, and so he comes up with plan B. He instructs the two Hebrew midwives named Shiphrah and Puah to kill the newborns if they are male. The fact that the narrator tells us the midwives' names is significant. Names were important in that world. Why? The ancient Israelites, for most of their history, had no concept of a conscious afterlife. They referred to the dead as shadows of their former selves. In death, they rest—with their families, if they are lucky—but beyond the grave, there is neither joy nor sorrow, bliss nor punishment, communication nor community. The way they lived on was through the continuation of their family line, their name. When a narrator tells a story, the reader will notice who is named and who remains namelessly lost to memory. Pharaoh is never named.

Ironically, two women are named and thus remembered forever. Shiphrah and Puah are names appropriate to northwest Semitic people from that time. Pharaoh instructs Shiphrah and Puah to kill newborn Hebrew baby boys as if eliminating the male labor pool is a great plan for a Pharaoh, and as if any surviving males could not potentially marry many women and continue to produce more babies. The two women defeat this plan, claiming that the vigorous Hebrew women give birth too fast for them to get to them in time. Two lowly women have just outfoxed a powerful man. Could this be part of the promise to Abraham coming true?

Not so fast. Shrewd Pharaoh what's-his-name comes up with plan C. He summons Shiphrah and Puah and orders them, "When you act as midwives to the Hebrew women, and see them on the birthstool, if it is a boy, kill him; but if it is a girl, she shall live" (Exod 1:16). But the narrator tells us that the midwives feared God more than Pharaoh, so they disobeyed the order and let the boys remain alive (Exod 1:17). This act of noncompliance, which we would label an act of civil disobedience, outfoxes the Pharaoh again. The fact that Shiphrah and Puah make up a lie to Pharaoh, telling him that the Hebrew women were not like the Egyptian women, Hebrew women gave birth before they could get to them (Exod 1:19), should not detain us. It did not bother the narrator, whose ethic of the preservation of life took priority over strict rules of honesty. If that feels awkward to our modern sensibilities, let it stand as another example of the historical distance between ourselves and this ancient text. Again, we aim to hear the text on its own terms. God, we are told, rewards Shiphrah and Puah with families. The word is literally *houses* but "families" are exactly what is meant. Unlike the nameless Pharaoh who has disappeared from history, these two lowly Israelite women live on into the future; their names continue through their families.

Now Pharaoh must come up with plan D, which he promptly does and which sets the stage for the hero of the story, Moses. Pharaoh commanded his people to throw every Hebrew boy into the Nile (Exod 1:22). The promise could not be in graver danger. Pharaoh's *decree*, as later rabbis will call it, combines infanticide and genocide. It puzzled rabbis throughout the years why anyone would risk having a baby under such circumstances. They developed a story, or *midrash*, to explain it. Without getting lost down that rabbit trail, suffice it to say that it was belief in the reliability of God's promise to Abraham that enabled the Hebrews to continue having babies, and one of them became God's means of deliverance. Did not the rescue of the newborns by the clever midwives prove that the promise was still in operation? So reasoned the rabbis.

The story of how Moses was born and hidden in a basket, literally an *ark*, is well known. It is full of drama and irony. Moses's own mother is enlisted as a wet nurse and paid by Pharaoh's daughter to suckle him. Though Moses's name is Egyptian in origin, appearing in names like Thutmosis, the Hebrew narrator does what others did: invented an origin for the word—an etymology—using a Hebrew pun. As if the Egyptian daughter of Pharaoh would have known Hebrew well enough to make such a pun, we are told that "She named him *Moses*, 'because,' she said, 'I *drew him out* of the water'" (Exod 2:10). *Moses* puns on the Hebrew word *masha*, "to draw."[1] After weaning, Moses is then raised in Pharaoh's house as his adopted son. The ironies multiply as the Pharaoh who ordered his murder now houses, feeds, clothes, and presumably educates this Hebrew baby boy. Once again, it is non-Israelites who intervene on behalf of the chosen people in significant ways. The ancient world apparently delighted in stories of rescued heroes. From Mesopotamia comes the story of their famous Sargon of Akkad. His mother, a high priestess, hid this baby, her illegitimate love child, in a bitumen-coated basket of reeds and set him afloat on the Euphrates River. Discovery of her baby would have endangered her position; priestesses were supposed to be childless. The basket was found and the baby was rescued and adopted by Akki, the water drawer. Later Sargon won the favor of the goddess Ishtar and eventually won the throne of Akkad. Scholars have noted the similarity of structure in stories of this sort: the hero is abandoned by his parents and raised by others before rising to prominence. Recall the stories of Oedipus, Romulus, King Arthur, and even Superman, to name a few.

Moses Comes of Age

The story of the Exodus, central to the Hebrew Bible, relies on the actions of a man whose life was spared by a foreigner who found him in a basket and raised him as her son. The narrative does not lift the curtain for us to see what it would have been like to have grown up in Pharaoh's household, dining on the best Egyptian cuisine, or receiving a first-class Egyptian education. All of that is left to the imagination. We do get to see that the values Moses absorbed in that foreign context included a sense of justice and fairness, even if they initially produced mixed results. The tension between the acknowledged positive role that foreigners play in Israel's story, on the one hand, and the particularity of their self-understanding as distinctly blessed people, on the other, is almost everywhere present. Immediately after Moses's rescue by the daughter of Pharaoh, the narrator jumps to Moses as an adult man. Somehow, despite his entire childhood in an Egyptian palace, he has managed to know himself as distinctly Hebrew, as the next scene

1. BDB, s.v. "מָשָׁה."

illustrates. "One day, after Moses had grown up, he went out to his people [literally "brothers"] and saw their forced labor. He saw an Egyptian beating a Hebrew, one of his kinsfolk [literally "brothers"]. He looked this way and that, and seeing no one he killed the Egyptian and hid him in the sand" (Exod 2:11–12). Repeatedly in the Hebrew Bible, events are narrated without any moralizing comment. A reader is supposed to know right from wrong and make moral judgments accordingly. The narrator does not approve of Moses's violence and attempted cover-up any more than the other Hebrew people do, as the next lines make clear: "When he went out the next day, he saw two Hebrews fighting; and he said to the one who was in the wrong, 'Why do you strike your fellow Hebrew?' He answered, 'Who made you a ruler and judge over us? Do you mean to kill me as you killed the Egyptian?'" (Exod 2:13–14). Did the narrator intend to be ironic by depicting the man who would famously proclaim the law of "an eye for an eye and a tooth for a tooth" (Exod 21:24) being so disproportionate? Even though the author of Acts 7:23–29 seems to find Moses's actions justified, no one else does. Moses's brother Hebrews do not, and neither does Pharaoh, who, upon hearing of it, seeks to kill him (an eye for an eye?).

So Moses, the fugitive, now must flee. He finds himself in Midian—not exactly a place (Midianites were nomadic)—but a situation: Moses is in exile. In the space of the next eight short verses, Moses goes from being a single exile to becoming a married man with a family. He meets the seven daughters of Reuel (also called Jethro), who is identified as a priest of Midian; rescues them from bullying shepherds at a well; waters their flocks; gets misidentified by them as an Egyptian; receives a dinner invitation; and ends up marrying one of them, named Zipporah. The text says that Reuel gave his daughter Zipporah to Moses (Exod 2:21). She seems to have had no say in the arrangement. That is the way it was and has been for most women for most of human history. This is another example of how we must try to hear the text on its own terms without importing our modern Western moral sensibilities into our reading.

Moses is now married to a foreigner. If the promise to Abraham—given to him and his *seed*, or descendants—includes the children of this union, then *seed* must be an elastic concept. So, too, is the concept of *foreigner*, because that is exactly what Moses now considers himself. After Zipporah gives birth to a son, Moses names him Gershom, "for he said, 'I have been an alien [*ger*] residing in a foreign land'" (Exod 2:22). The family of the hero of the story is not genetically pure (as if there were such a thing). From now on, as we read the Hebrew Bible, every time there is a distinction between *us* and *them*, insiders and outsiders, the chosen people and the Gentiles, we will recall this story of mixed origins. The narrator betrays no embarrassment about it. He makes no excuses for it. It is simply a fact. The tension is right there on the surface. Moses himself now identifies as a *ger*—a foreigner, an alien, a sojourner in a foreign land.

Oddly, God has not made much of an appearance in Exodus up to this point except in the report that Shiphrah and Puah feared God, but this is about to change. In a brief notice, we learn that the Pharaoh, who pronounced the death sentence on Moses, has died—potentially a good thing—but that the Israelites are still enslaved. The narrator gives us a glimpse at their collective misery: they groaned and cried out to God (Exod 2:23). Their cry is not merely the moaning of despair; it is directed to the God that has been so invisible for so long, and as such contains a glimmer of hope: "Out of the slavery their cry for help rose up to God" (Exod 2:23). We are meant to picture God as *up* in the heavens, able to look down and see and hear what is happening on the ground below. After all this time, now we learn that God finally heard their groaning, and God, as if he had forgotten, now remembers his covenant with the patriarchs Abraham, Isaac, and Jacob (Exod 2:24). This is anthropomorphic language: God, like humans, has senses and a memory. What God remembers is the promise to Abraham, sealed in a solemn covenant ceremony and reinforced in each successive generation to Isaac and to Jacob. Now God is front and center, and so, too, is the partially fulfilled, partially unfulfilled promise. The Israelites are a multitude, but they are not a nation—and not in the promised land. And yet, God hears, sees, and remembers. There is hope.

Moses the Liberator

After that brief narrative summary, the scene shifts back to Moses, who has been tending sheep for his father-in-law, who now is called Jethro, in the land of Midian. It is in this foreign land that Moses encounters God—not in a temple, not in Jerusalem, and not even in the promised land, but *beyond the wilderness*, God comes to Moses (Exod 3:1). God's presence in the Hebrew Bible is never restricted to any particular place but may be experienced anywhere and everywhere. Here God appears in the form of a fire from a bush that burns without consuming it. God, depicted as male, identifies himself to Moses as the God of Abraham, Isaac, and Jacob, thus firmly tying this narrative to the ones in Genesis. Here in this foreign land stands Mount Horeb (called Sinai in other texts), which the narrator identifies as the mountain of God (Exod 3:1).

The dominant narrative in the Hebrew Bible is the special, particular, chosen status of the family descended from Abraham. They have been given the promise, sealed in a covenant, which has been reaffirmed generation after generation. And yet, as we have already seen, foreigners play a significant, sometimes crucial role in the way that promise is fulfilled. Joseph's brothers sell him into slavery, ironically, to Midianite traders who take him to Egypt (Gen 37:28). There he rises to power and invites his family to immigrate to avoid a famine. The Egyptians helped the chosen people to survive. A foreigner, Pharaoh's daughter, rescues baby Moses from the water and from Pharaoh's genocidal decree and raises him safely in Pharaoh's palace. Foreigners have a complicated relationship to the chosen people; they may both assist in the fulfillment of the promise and at the same time, impede it. The Hebrews have survived and multiplied, but are enslaved and suffering a long way from the land of promise.

The story now turns to the central drama of the Hebrew Bible. God rescues the Hebrew people from Egypt through Moses and his brother-assistant Aaron. God identifies himself to Moses from the burning bush, naming himself—as if for the first time—as *Yahweh*, which is most commonly translated "I am" from the verb "to be."[2] God says to Moses "I am who I am," though some scholars tell us is best translated, "I will be who I will be"[3] (Exod 3:14). What God will be is preeminently a liberator.

It seems odd to us to hear God name himself as if we had not heard that name before. But of course we have, going back to Gen 2. This is another illustration of the complex history of biblical texts. As it stands now, these narratives have been compiled and organized from sources that have had long lives before this current arrangement. Some sources have preferred one Hebrew word for God and others another. This is why modern English versions distinguish between Lord (in small capital letters), to indicate *Yahweh*; *God*, to indicate *Elohim*; and *Lord* (with lowercase letters) to indicate *Adonai*. There are other Hebrew names for God as well. The point here is that Moses is to know the liberator God as *Yahweh* and to announce that name to his enslaved people. Moses may have needed this introduction, but Yahweh is, nevertheless, the God of Abraham, Isaac, and Jacob—the God of the promise. Throughout this book, whenever you see Lord in small capital letters, it stands for *Yahweh*, Israel's God, the God of liberation. (A few times you will see Lord [small letters] God [small capital letters], which is how the NRSV indicates the Hebrew phrase *Adonai Yahweh*—but that is rare.)

From that burning bush, God announces to Moses his liberating intentions and his motivation, saying, "I have observed the misery of my people who are in Egypt; I have heard their cry on account of their taskmasters.

2. BDB, s.v. "יְהוָה."

3. See Fretheim, *Exodus*, 135.

Indeed, I know their sufferings, and I have come down to deliver them from the Egyptians, and to bring them up out of that land to a good and broad land, a land flowing with milk and honey" (Exod 3:7–8). God's motivation is compassion. He himself acknowledges seeing their misery and suffering. He has heard their cries. Why it has taken 430 years is never asked nor answered, but now, at last, God is motivated (Exod 12:40). Therefore, he says, "I have come down to deliver them." Who exactly does he announce it his intention to deliver? "My people," he says (Exod 3:7). Here the tension we are exploring is pronounced. The God who created the original groundlings in God's own image and likeness must therefore be the God of all people on earth who descended from them. And yet, somehow at the same time, God can be the particular God of one people: the descendants of Abraham. These are the ones he calls "my people."

God will not, however, accomplish this deliverance without the intermediary role played by Moses. So God tells Moses what his role will be. In this call narrative, Moses receives his commission to go to Pharaoh and ask for permission to take a religious holiday. Moses, God says, is to tell Pharaoh, "Let us now go a three days' journey into the wilderness, so that we may sacrifice to the LORD [*Yahweh*] our God [*Elohim*]" (Exod 3:18). Like the deceptions of Shiphrah and Puah, this sounds like another ruse. And anyone who knows the story, knows that the idea of a short religious holiday for the whole enslaved population is not what is going to happen. Nevertheless, these ethical concerns may be ours, but they are not the narrator's. God's promised deliverance from their misery and suffering is not going to be a temporary reprieve.

The process of receiving Pharaoh's permission to exit Egypt is long and tortured. After Moses requests a religious holiday, Pharaoh becomes angry and orders the enslaved Hebrews to continue to make the same required number of bricks, but without supplying them with straw. This makes their work harder, since in addition to making bricks they also must harvest the needed straw. When the Israelite work supervisors complain to Moses about this, Moses takes their case up with God, saying, "Since I first came to Pharaoh to speak in your name, he has mistreated this people, and you have done nothing at all to deliver your people" (Exod 5:23). This sets the stage for God to come clean with his plan to liberate the people, not just for a short holiday, but permanently; not taking them a three days' journey to worship at Mount Horeb, but to a new land. God says to Moses,

> Say therefore to the Israelites, "I am the LORD, and I will free you from the burdens of the Egyptians and deliver you from slavery to them. I will redeem you with an outstretched arm and with

> mighty acts of judgment. I will take you as my people, and I will be your God. You shall know that I am the LORD your God, who has freed you from the burdens of the Egyptians. I will bring you into the land that I swore to give to Abraham, Isaac, and Jacob; I will give it to you for a possession. I am the LORD." (Exod 6:6–8)

Though this announcement of the divine intention seems categorical, accomplishing its goal will not be instantaneous. Pharaoh's heart is hard, partly his fault and partly by divine instigation, as the narrator tells us (Exod 9:12). He does not willingly let his labor force exit his country. So begins the famous series of plagues. During this sequence, we learn of another divine motivation. God is concerned with his reputation, not just among the Israelites but also in a wider venue: all the earth. For reasons unexplained—should they be obvious to us readers?—God wants the whole world to know who he is and how powerful he is. God gives a script to say to Pharaoh just before the seventh plague of thunder and hail: "For this time I will send all my plagues upon you yourself, and upon your officials, and upon your people, so that you may know that there is no one like me in all the earth. . . . But this is why I have let you live: to show you my power, and to make my name resound through all the earth" (Exod 9:14, 16). Here the tension returns. God will deliver his people, whom he has chosen, the descendants of Abraham, but at the same time God wants every foreigner—every non-Israelite on the planet—to know that God is God and there is no other. This is a glimpse of the fact that God has concerns that go beyond his people because, at least in some sense, there is no one who is not his people. The Creator has concerns that extend to everyone who will ultimately benefit from the promise to Abraham, because in him all the families of the earth were promised a blessing (Gen 12:3).

Returning to the story, as soon as Moses is ready to depart Pharaoh's presence and await the seventh plague he says to him, "As soon as I have gone out of the city, I will stretch out my hands to the LORD; the thunder will cease, and there will be no more hail, so that you may know that the earth is the LORD's" (Exod 9:29). Again, the tension between particularity and universality is present.

An Aside About Difficult Issues

For many reasons, the Bible is a hard book to read. Besides the jarring dyssynchronies—as when Yahweh introduced his name to Moses as if for the first time—and beyond the acceptance of dishonesty—as in the ruse about taking a religious holiday—there are the far greater problems of violence in the Hebrew Bible. Some of the violence reported is what humans do, some of it they do with God's explicit assistance, as in battles won with God's help. But the most problematic for us is the violence that God does directly. Besides the flood narrative, which is depicted as a worldwide genocide, none for me is harder than the last plague, the slaughter of all the firstborn of Egypt. It is the most problematic for those who take the story literally, but it is also hard to take a narrative, even if understood metaphorically, in which God's angel of death slaughters babies, especially after God himself hardens Pharaoh's heart against letting them go. What kind of God would do that, even metaphorically? This is another example of how we modern readers of the Bible must come to terms with the distance between ourselves and these ancient texts. All that we can say in the context of this book is that these questions, though real, are outside our present scope. Nonetheless, it is important to acknowledge them as real problems.

The Mixed Multitude

Returning to the story, after the plagues convinced Pharaoh to let the Israelites go, the text says something unexpected: "The Israelites journeyed from Rameses to Succoth. . . . A mixed crowd [or mixed multitude] also went up with them" (Exod 12:37–38). Scholars agree that a "mixed crowd" or "mixed multitude" can only mean non-Israelites joined the exodus. We have noted that God had said that he would deliver his people by bringing them "up out of that land" (Exod 3:8), and now we see that the ones being delivered—in other words, the ones described as his people—include both Israelites and non-Israelites. Scholars have noted that the definition of God's people has always been both theological and biological. The two ways of being included in the people of God have always intermingled. From the original promise to Abraham, which included a blessing for all the families of the earth, to the inclusion of Moses's Midianite wife, Zipporah, the definition of the people of God has been elastic.

It is not as though these non-Israelite joiners were on the same level as biological descendants. Soon the text will give instructions for the annual remembrance of this liberation through the Passover liturgy. Foreigners are welcome to join in the celebration of Passover, but only under the condition that the males be circumcised (Exod 12:34–49). That restriction notwithstanding, it is expected that there will be non-Israelites who want to and who do celebrate Passover along with Israelites in their homes. When a circumcised foreigner is there in your home celebrating Passover with your family, how should you regard him? "He shall be regarded as a native of the land" (Exod 12:48). Non-Israelites may be regarded as natives because they were part of God's people who experienced liberation along with Israelites as part of the mixed multitude. The promise to Abraham is now taking another step toward fulfillment. The seed of Abraham is being liberated, and all the families of the earth that came with them are being blessed.

3

The Good Prostitute

THE STORY OF THE prostitute Rahab hiding the spies of Israel in her residence in Jericho is our next look at a non-Israelite's role in the story of the chosen people. Sex lurks in the shadows of this story, giving it a depth and complexity that we all notice as we read. If we were reading it as Israelites who lived long ago, at least before the Roman army's obliteration of Jerusalem in 70 CE, how would we read it? We are on safe ground to suggest that we would read this story in the context of the stories that, in the current arrangement of texts, came before. Where are we in the story? The Israelites who had been living under the oppression of Pharaoh's empire for four hundred years or so had escaped. Moses, according to the narrative in the Hebrew Bible, had confronted Pharaoh, who reluctantly agreed to allow them to all leave as an ethnically mixed multitude. But Pharaoh changed his mind and ordered his army to pursue them. Miraculously, the Hebrews, whose name *Hebrew* comes from the verb *to cross over*,[1] manage to cross over the Red (or Reed) Sea on dry ground by the skin of their teeth.

Under the leadership of Moses, they all come to Mount Sinai (or, as it is called in Deuteronomy, Mount Horeb), where Moses ascends the mountain and meets God. By God's finger, as the narrative says (Exod 31:18; Deut 9:10), Moses receives the tablets of stone containing the Ten Commandments, and subsequently, all the other commands and ordinances that comprise what forever after has been called "the law of Moses" or "the book of the law." The Hebrew word for it, *Torah*, means "guidance," "law"

1. BDB, s.v. "עָבַר."

or "instruction."[2] After receiving the law and binding themselves to it by solemn covenant, (or a treaty, but with spiritual, not just legal implications), the Israelites set out for the promised land. They are in rough, barren desert territory they call "wilderness." God sustains them on the way with a daily provision of "manna" (meaning "What is it?")[3] from heaven and several miraculous provisions of water. But when they get to the land's border they send spies who come back with a report that they are facing giants in a land that consumes its inhabitants (Num 13–14). They all lose heart, not believing that the God who promised them the land could help them defeat its inhabitants. As a consequence, they are condemned to wander in the wilderness one year for every day the spies were in the land: forty.

The book of Joshua begins after those forty years. That unfaithful generation has now died. Moses, too, has just died. Joshua, his successor, now sends out another set of spies, this time only two, to repeat the reconnaissance of the land. They cross over the border into the city of Jericho where they take cover in the residence of Rahab the prostitute.

This is not just a review of the story to catch us up to date. It is now important to take these narratives into consideration as we read everything that follows. Now, whenever anyone in any story says something or does something, the reader must now ask, "Does that conform to the laws that God himself gave to us?" For example, if someone suggested having a pork chop for dinner, the faithful Israelite would be horrified: "That's pig meat, and pigs are 'unclean' or not kosher, according to the law!" If someone suggested you would support him in a lie, a faithful Israelite would say, "No way! The law tells us 'Thou shalt not bear false witness.'"

Ancient Israel's Moral Landscape

When we think about breaking one of the laws given by God, we commonly use the word "sin." Committing a sin makes the sinner guilty (whether or not they feel guilty). Israelites, however, had a more nuanced moral world that may not be obvious to us modern readers. Remember, we are reading these texts from an ocean's distance of history and culture, so a bit of work is involved in trying to read the texts as they did. In fact, we will always probably miss a lot. But our hope is to make as much progress as possible to bridge that ocean. There were categories the Israelites had that we do not normally consider. Some acts were sinful, and led to simple guilt, like theft or murder. But other acts of law breaking led to impurity, or uncleanness,

2. BDB, s.v. "תּוֹרָה."

3. BDB, s.v. "מָן."

not guilt. Impurity, or uncleanness, was not a happy condition, but it could be remedied.

Impurity seems to have a range of severity with different consequences. Touching a corpse or a carcass made a person impure. It polluted them spiritually. The remedy specified by the law of Moses involved purifying oneself by having the "water for cleansing" sprinkled on them on the specified day (Num 19). Notice, this is not about washing dirt off, it is about symbolic sprinkling of purifying water, thus removing the condition of impurity. Remember, we are not talking about germs, the discovery of which was many centuries later. Sometimes even unintentional actions could make a person impure, such as being in the room when someone died. Sometimes impurity or uncleanness was simply unavoidable, such as having a baby or menstruating (Lev 12:2). Impurity is a real condition but different from guilt.

Other kinds of impurity, however, were more consequential, especially when it comes to sex. Some sexual infractions were so significant as to have severe consequences. The Hebrew Bible gets as graphic as it can on this subject. Some sexual acts were so abhorrent to God as to be considered "abominations" that "defiled the land." And what would the God who was giving you this land as a gift do to you if you defiled his land? Like a person who ate something disgusting, God would make the land itself "vomit you out for defiling it, as it vomited out the nation that was before you" (Lev 18:28) who did the same things and thus were vomited out.

Prostitution was something that defiled the land, according to Lev 19. In fact, prostitution was the Hebrew Bible's favorite metaphor for spiritual defilement. Both literal prostitution and spiritual prostitution could even be used in the same verse, as in Lev 19:29: "Do not profane your daughter by making her a prostitute, that the land not become prostituted and full of depravity." If a daughter literally becomes a prostitute, then the land has spiritually prostituted itself, becoming full of depravity. Notably, there is a Hebrew pun involved here: *zanah* ("prostitute") sounds like *zimah* ("depravity"). The point is, such defilement was serious.

Rahab's Otherness

It is hard for us to understand concepts such as moral purity today. It still signifies, but does so a bit below the surface outside of some conservative Christian communities. It is helpful, I believe, to look at it a bit more closely because it will help us understand what is happening in the story of Rahab. When the spies come in contact with her, they are encountering someone whose *otherness* has the capacity to make them polluted or impure on a number of levels. First, she is a foreigner, a Canaanite. Foreigners are outside the covenant relationship between God and Israel. Their foreignness is considered a high-risk danger that requires extermination (Exod 34). Treaties with nearby foreigners were prohibited by the law of Moses (Deut 7:2). The spies have crossed a border by entering foreign territory and have crossed over the threshold of a Canaanite person's residence, thus risking polluting themselves and becoming impure, even though their job necessitates it.

This Canaanite person is not just an impure foreigner; she is also a prostitute. This brings up all kinds of ambiguity. Why did these two men choose a prostitute's residence? (Why should we not call it a brothel with a single worker?) Did they select the home of a prostitute merely because it is the kind of place men can come and go without raising neighbors' suspicions? Or were they there also as patrons of the establishment? Nothing is said in the text to eliminate any possibility, leaving them all open to our curiosity. In fact, their visit was not just a quick in and out. The narrator dangles this detail for us: they stayed there through the night (Josh 2:1).

But one thing is clear to every faithful Israelite: relations with foreign women are strictly forbidden. Readers of the entire narrative to this point remember what happened at Peor where the men of Israel had sexual relations with the Midianite women. The fiasco of seduction there, including spiritual seduction, had bloody consequences—including public impalings, a plague that wiped out twenty-four thousand, and a scene of the double murder of a couple who were run through with a single spear while *in flagrante*. (Readers may also remember that Moses's wife was a Midianite woman. Is that a deliberate narrative reference or just a bug of coincidence?)

Somehow, the narrative theme of avoiding impurity—including the impurity of foreigners, even prostitutes—is subverted by more significant values. This impure foreigner, this doubly impure prostitute, instead of endangering Israel becomes the vehicle of their salvation. Once again, a foreigner is not only tolerated but is in fact appreciated as essential. If the promise to Abraham, sealed in a covenant, is to be fulfilled, the Israelites must enter and successfully conquer the promised land. One impure foreign prostitute is now in a position of either facilitating that process or, because she could easily betray them, thwarting it.

The impurity of foreignness and sexual deviance is inverted in this narrative. Inverted also is the very space Rahab inhabits. The narrator locates her residence inside the walls of Jericho. Those walls, erected as a defense against foreign invasion, become the very location of refuge for the spies. Rahab, the narrator tells us, hid the spies under stalks of flax she was drying up on the flat roof. When the king's agents alert him to the presence of foreigners in town, as his surveillance system has discovered, he sends them to Rahab's house with questions. Rahab answers them with a stratagem that reminds the reader of the way in which midwives Shiphrah and Puah subverted Pharaoh's genocidal plans: with a lie. To paraphrase Rahab's response, "Sure," she tells them, "they were here but they have gone already." (Who would be surprised that foreign men visited a prostitute?) Then she gives them a game plan to further gas-light them, saying, "When it was time to close the gate at dark, the men went out. Where the men went I do not know. Pursue them quickly, for you can overtake them" (Josh 2:5). Surprisingly perhaps, the professional agents of the king of Jericho take the spy-catching advice of a woman, and a socially marginal one at that; they run out in vain pursuit as she suggested, to no avail.

Rahab, in spite of her marginal social status in the eyes of other Canaanites, exercises self-confidence and agency. Not only does she stand up to the king's spy-catchers, she also exacts guarantees of protection for herself and her entire family from the Israelite spies. She believes that their impending invasion will be successful, but she wants to make sure her family can walk away from the slaughter when the dust settles.

Holy War: Memory or Parable?

We need to pause here and again try to hear this part of the story the way a faithful Israelite reader may have heard it. The Israelites, according to the narrator of the book of Joshua, are conducting a campaign of holy war. They are not unique in this ancient strategy but adopt it with sincere zeal. According to the doctrine of holy war, also known in the biblical tradition as "the ban," everything about the war was dedicated to God. No booty could be taken by the victors; it all had to be destroyed as it was God's. God was the guarantor of the victory, and so God got all the credit and all of the spoils. No one was to be spared. Holy war meant genocide: men, women, and children—even animals—were to be annihilated without exception. The law of Moses had said, "But as for the towns of these peoples that the Lord your God is giving you as an inheritance, you must not let anything that breathes remain alive. You shall annihilate them" (Deut 20:16–17). According to the narrator, that is the law they followed in this case too. The aftermath scene is described this way: "Then they [the Israelites] devoted to destruction by the edge of the sword all in the city, both men and women, young and old, oxen, sheep, and donkeys" (Josh 6:21).

This is hard for us to read, as it should be. It is another glaring example of the distance between ourselves today and the world that produced these texts. How anyone could conceive that God would order such wanton slaughter is hard to imagine. Nevertheless, that is how the story is told. The goal of Joshua's campaigns against the Canaanites is specific: he went after the royal cities—that is, cities ruled by kings—not with the goal of conquering and possessing them intact but to annihilate them, leaving behind a pile of rubble. The book of Joshua, scholars have recognized, reflects the concerns and ideological perspectives of northern Israel in contrast to Judah in the south. Without belaboring the details here, suffice it to say that Joshua focuses on significant events, such as the covenant-making ceremonies at the northern Israelite shrine at Shechem and on the mountains of Ebal and Gerizim. More is at stake than geography. The ideal in the north was that God would be worshiped at an open-air shrine by sacrifices made on an altar of uncut stone. That stands in marked contrast to the elaborate icon-laden temple in Jerusalem. Even circumcision needed to be performed with a raw flint knife, not a manufactured metal blade. The ideology was anti-urban. The ideal was an egalitarian, agrarian, rural utopia, rejecting a hierarchical, urban city-state. So the holy war strategy of total destruction was meant to produce an empty land where a do-over might be possible. Some have suggested that the context in which a story written this way would have been useful was in opposition to the Neo-Assyrian imperial city-state project of centuries later. If that hypothesis is correct, these holy war accounts were symbolic, functioning as parables, not meant to be taken as literal history. But in any case, what they describe is horror, not to be defended, in my opinion.

Rahab's Confession and Bargain

Returning to the story, given the ideology of holy war, how likely should it have been that the spies would agree to the bargain that Rahab proposed? She demanded a sign of good faith from them that would include safety for her entire extended family (Josh 2:11–13). Much to the faithful Israelite reader's surprise and in spite of the demands of holy war, they agree. If she would not divulge their presence, they would make sure that when the Lord gave the Israelites the land, they would all be spared (Josh 2:14). What could possibly motivate those spies to agree to a request that would violate the strict requirements given by God himself in the law of Moses to utterly destroy everything and everyone? It could only be the fact that this foreign, pagan prostitute has just delivered the most complete confession of faith in Yahweh, the God of Israel, that we have read so far. From the lips of this foreign prostitute, we hear,

> I know that the LORD [Yahweh] has given you the land, and that dread of you has fallen on us, and that all the inhabitants of the land melt in fear before you. For we have heard how the LORD dried up the water of the Red Sea before you when you came out of Egypt, and what you did to the two kings of the Amorites that were beyond the Jordan, to Sihon and Og, whom you utterly destroyed. As soon as we heard it, our hearts melted, and there was no courage left in any of us because of you. The LORD your God is indeed God in heaven above and on earth below. (Josh 2:9–11)

On the basis of this confession of complete faith—surpassing even that of the Israelites themselves, who had to wander around for forty years after the first spies' cowardly report—they promise her protection for herself and her family. The spies tell her that if no one betrays them, and if they all stay in her house, and if she identifies her home by having a red cord out the window, then they will be spared on the day of the assault. And they were spared. When the Israelites marched around the city seven times one day, after having marched around it in silence once each of the preceding six days, and after blowing the ram's horns and shouting, the city walls of Jericho came down and the slaughter ensued. Rahab's house, however, was spared the carnage and those inside were saved. They did not just walk away from the rubble to restart life elsewhere. Rather, they were welcomed into the community of Israel. "Rahab the prostitute, with her family and all who belonged to her, Joshua spared. Her family has lived in Israel ever since" (Josh 6:25). The foreigners—the whole extended family of them—became part of the mixed multitude that comprises the chosen people, the people of Israel. The Hebrews who crossed over the Red Sea and now the Jordan River had crossed over the ethnic and purity barriers constructed by their own God-given law to embrace foreigners whose actions protected their spies and enabled the Israelite victory. The promise is still intact. The ethnically exclusive provisions of the law have been transcended by higher values.

Achan's Counternarrative

As important as this story is on its own, its significance is only magnified by its juxtaposition with the story that follows. This one is less well-known. The next objective of the advancing Israelites is the nearby city of Ai, recounted in Josh 7. It begins as the Jericho story did, with spies who are sent in and come back with a favorable report. On that basis, part of the army is sent up to take Ai, which is deemed a soft target. But instead of an easy win, the

Israelites were routed and thirty-six were killed. Joshua nearly panics. News of this defeat, he tells God, will spread, emboldening their enemies who will together wipe the Israelites off the face of the earth. God replies, justifying himself to Joshua, basically saying that the Israelites got what was coming to them because they violated the strict provisions of holy war. How? Not by failing to slaughter Rahab and her family, who are not even mentioned. Rather, someone has taken booty that should have been devoted to God. Now, the reader already knows whodunit, because the narrator began this story by saying, after the success at Jericho, "the Israelites broke faith in regard to the devoted things: Achan . . . of the tribe of Judah, took some of the devoted things; and the anger of the Lord burned against the Israelites" (Josh 7:1). Joshua conducts a family-by-family interrogation until he gets to Achan, who fully confesses. Achan admitted that he was the one who sinned. He says that he took a beautiful imported mantle, hundreds of shekels of silver, and a bar of gold, and hid them in his tent (Josh 7:20–21). There is only one thing to do. Joshua knew that this brazen violation would bring trouble on them all, therefore the Lord, he said, would bring trouble on Achen. To avoid collective punishment from God, all the people stoned him, his family, and their animals to death and burned them with fire. That assuaged the Lord, the narrator informs us. He turned from his burning anger. Therefore we are told that the place is still called the Valley of Achor (Josh 7:25–26). Achor means "trouble."

This is yet again a text that horrifies us. Collective punishment that included, the text says, "his sons and daughters, with his oxen, donkeys, and sheep, and his tent and all that he had" (Josh 7:24). All were killed by stoning in which everyone participated. It is hard to conceive, hard to read, and impossible to justify by our lights. But again, some read this as a dark parable, saying in effect, "at least it never actually happened," as if imagining it as something God would sanction is better. But that is the story.

The reason this story is important on the heels of Rahab's story is the stark contrast. There is almost a mirroring of opposites seen when the two stories are read against each other. In one, a non-Israelite confesses total faith; in the other, an ethnic Israelite breaks faith. In one, a foreigner is embraced and welcomed into the community on a permanent basis. In the other, a natural-born Israelite's family is eliminated from the community permanently. What does it mean to be part of the people of Israel? It is much deeper than mere bloodlines. In fact, bloodlines alone are insufficient. The definition of the "people ['ām] of God" defies limitation to ethnic or nationalist boundaries. It can and does include foreigners or, as modern English versions translate it, "aliens" among the people of God. The city of Ai is eventually captured and burned to the ground. This time the people are allowed to keep rural plunder, general spoil, and livestock as booty after they have eliminated the people and devoted the metal objects to the treasury of Yahweh (Josh 8:27). Afterward, when they gather on Mount Ebal in solemn assembly, the author notes twice that aliens were included among them.

> All Israel, alien as well as citizen, with their elders and officers and their judges, stood on opposite sides of the ark in front of the Levitical priests who carried the ark of the covenant of the LORD, half of them in front of Mount Gerizim and half of them in front of Mount Ebal, as Moses the servant of the LORD had commanded at the first, that they should bless the people of Israel. And afterward he read all the words of the law, blessings and curses, according to all that is written in the book of the law. There was not a word of all that Moses commanded that Joshua did not read before all the assembly of Israel, and the women, and the little ones, and the aliens who resided among them. (Josh 8:33–35)

The stories of Rahab and Achan illustrate that inclusion among the "people of God" or "chosen people" is a matter, not of ethnicity, but of faithfulness. Rahab confesses exclusive faith in Yahweh, and her actions on behalf of the spies demonstrate the authenticity of her confession. By contrast, Achan is part of the natural born "seed of Abraham," but his unfaithful actions of taking forbidden booty betray his lack of authentic commitment to the God of the covenant. Achan ends up excluded from the people of God, while Rahab and her family join Moses's wife and others in the mixed multitude as recipients of the blessings on all the families of the earth.

Rahab, the former outsider turned member of "the people of God," is remembered as a heroine of faith in the New Testament, where she is mentioned three times. Matthew lists her as an ancestress of Jesus (Matt 1:5). The book of Hebrews includes her in the "hall of faith" for her protection of the spies (Heb 11:31). James says she was justified, or saved by her works when she hid the spies and provided for their escape (Jas 2:25). Some argue that people live best when they live with those of their kind alone. While there may be some general validity to this human habit, it is nonetheless part of the scriptural tradition that foreignness is no barrier to God. Repeatedly, in fact, foreigners are necessary parts of the story.

There is no question that the dominant narrative of the Hebrew Bible is a story of God's choice of a particular family. The Hebrew Bible centers on God's promise to Abraham, sealed in the most solemn of covenants, and reinforced through the generations of Isaac and Jacob. Joshua conducts a covenant-renewal ceremony, as his predecessor Moses had done one generation earlier. The law of Moses, or Torah, had strict provisions excluding non-Israelites, who were considered dangerous to Israel's fidelity to Yahweh. Israelites were forbidden from intermarriage and from making covenants with nearby foreigners. The rules of holy war, or "the ban," included the mandate to slaughter every man, woman, and child.

It is all the more remarkable, therefore, that interspersed among these narratives, laws, and prohibitions are stories offering a diametrically alternative view. There were exceptions to that strict particularism that continue to emerge with regularity. These non-Israelites—foreigners, aliens, outsiders to the covenant—are not just present; they are crucial. Their actions, like Rahab's in this case, directly support the success of the Israelites and, therefore, the fulfillment of the promise. The God who created all humans in his image shows a universal perspective that is not restricted to the descendants of one family. It is not an afterthought but a significant fact that the promise to Abraham, as particular as it sounds, also includes the phrase "and to your descendants" (literally "seed") and refers not just to some, but universally, to all the families of the earth (Gen 12:1–3).

4

Elijah and the Widow of Zarephath

LIKE A RUSSIAN NESTING doll, the narrator of this text layers stories within stories. The story of the widow of Zarephath sits inside the story of a drought, which is inside the story of Elijah's confrontation with King Ahab and Queen Jezebel, which is inside the story of the kings of Israel and Judah. The book of Kings is now part of a long story that starts in Deuteronomy and ends in 2 Kings. Deuteronomy is, for the most part, one long speech in which Moses addresses the nation from the edge of the wilderness just before they cross the Jordan and enter the promised land. The story ends tragically in Babylon, where they are in exile. Deuteronomy and this entire retrospective were written, at least in part, as a struggle to understand what happened. How could the God of all creation, who promised to bless one particular family, have let this happen?

In the ancient world, it was commonly believed that each nation had its own god. The nation was supposed to venerate its god, who would reciprocate with protection and fertility. When two nations went to war, the assumption was that two gods were fighting for their people; the stronger would win. If Israel lost and ended up exiled, did that mean Israel's God was defeated? A political crisis like exile was also a theological crisis.

The alternative explanation is to consider exile, not as defeat, but as punishment. The answer to the question "How could this happen?" was "We deserved it." Back in Deuteronomy, Moses had warned that the nation had two possible futures. One was a future of blessings. The other was a future of curses. Blessings would follow obedience and faithfulness to Yahweh, Israel's God. Curses would follow disobedience and unfaithfulness (Deut 28). How do you understand national defeat, destruction, and exile? They are the curse in operation. If the people were unfaithful, Moses had warned, "the LORD will bring a nation from far away, from the end of the earth, to swoop down on you like an eagle, a nation whose language you do not understand, a grim-faced nation showing no respect to the old or favor to the young" (Deut 28:49). And, "You shall be plucked off the land that you are entering to possess. The LORD will scatter you among all peoples" (Deut 28:63–64).

That seems to shut the door on hope for the future. But you would never spend so much time and effort to write such an epic story if you had no hope. Israel's story of God included blessings and curses, but it also included forgiveness and mercy. Moses could sometimes argue God out of his planned punishments (e.g., Exod 32:7–14). Therein lies hope.

The story of Elijah and the widow of Zarephath is part of the explanation for why "we deserve the curse," but it also provides a window of hope. Even in times of unfaithful kings, who persecuted worshipers of Yahweh—that is, times of deepest darkness—Yahweh is still the one true God. Between Yahweh and Baal there is no contest. The best way to demonstrate this is to have a contest with an obvious winner and loser. The contest between Yahweh and Baal lies in the background from the beginning but then becomes explicit in the drama on Mount Carmel between Elijah and the prophets of Baal.

King Ahab and Queen Jezebel

The story begins with Elijah, whose name means "My God is Yahweh," addressing King Ahab of Israel. The reader has been warned about King Ahab: "Ahab son of Omri began to reign over Israel; . . . Ahab son of Omri did evil in the sight of the LORD more than all who were before him" (1 Kgs 16:29–30). Ahab is twice identified as the son of King Omri. What do readers know about Ahab's father, Omri? Not much. Only that Omri did what was evil in the sight of the LORD; to the extent that we are told he did more evil than all the kings before him (1 Kgs 16:25). If this seems repetitive, it is meant to be. How did we end up in exile? After a long string of kings that led the nation astray, spiraling downward with each successive monarch. Incidentally, though the Hebrew Bible does not say much about Omri, he was so powerful that the Assyrians kept calling Israel the kingdom of Omri even after his death. But for the purposes of this narrative, it is enough to know that he was bad. His son, Ahab, was worse. How? He married Jezebel, the daughter of the king of the Sidonians. Sidon is in Phoenicia. Sidon is also where the widow of Zarephath lives. This is not a coincidence, as we will see.

Why is it such a problem to marry a foreign princess? As readers of this epic, we already know that intermarriage was prohibited by the law of Moses in Deuteronomy (7:1–6). The reason was simple: if you intermarry with people of another religion, they will likely bring that religion into your home and your land, and you may fall under its sway and start worshiping their gods. And that is exactly what King Solomon had already done, with the predicted effect (1 Kgs 11:1–8). And that is exactly what Ahab did as well. He started worshiping Baal, the Phoenician god of rain, storms, fertility, and life itself. He set up a temple with a public altar in his capital, Samaria, for Baal and his consort goddess, Asherah.

Formerly princess, now queen, Jezebel was such an ardent proponent of Baal worship that she was slaughtering the prophets of Yahweh (1 Kgs 18:4). Ahab, as king, could have stopped her but did not, so he is complicit. Elijah appeared before King Ahab and announced, "As the Lord, the God of Israel, lives, before whom I stand, there shall be neither dew nor rain these years, except by my word" (1 Kgs 17:1). The contest is on. Who is the true god who can control the rain? We will see.

Then God tells Elijah to go hide in a wadi, a streambed that fills during the rainy season but otherwise remains dry. We are not told why he needs to hide, but announcing to the king that a drought is coming, and with it, famine, would not endear you to the king and his prophet-killing wife. The point of hiding there seems to be that because the wadi will dry up quickly, it is a sign that the drought has begun. At the wadi, God sends ravens to bring Elijah food. God, Yahweh—not Baal—is in control of nature on both a large and a granular scale.

The Widow of Zarephath

When the wadi dries up, Yahweh tells Elijah to go to Zarephath, in the land of Sidon (1 Kgs 17:8). This puts Elijah in Baal's home country and the homeland of Queen Jezebel. God informs Elijah that he has commanded a widow to take care of him there. When we meet the widow, she has apparently not received the memo of that command. She is willing to bring Elijah some water, but when he asks her to prepare a meal for him, she demurs, saying, "As the Lord your God lives, I have nothing baked, only a handful of meal in a jar, and a little oil in a jug; I am now gathering a couple of sticks, so that I may go home and prepare it for myself and my son, that we may eat it and die" (1 Kgs 17:12). We are about to learn that the drought Elijah announced to King Ahab is not a local one affecting Israel alone but that Sidon, too, is rainless. Yahweh's power to withhold rain is not limited to the promised land, nor are his blessings limited to his chosen people. Elijah assures the widow that the meal in her jar and the oil in her jug will not run out until the rains come that the LORD will send (1 Kgs 17:14). Here, in Baal, the rain god's home turf, Yahweh can turn on and off the rain and keep a widow, her son, and her guest prophet alive. Baal is losing this contest at every turn.

Rain is essential for sustaining life—plants, animals, and people alike. Now we will see that it is Yahweh, not Baal, who has life-giving power. The widow's son becomes gravely ill and dies. The text describes his death by telling us that he had no breath (1 Kgs 17:17), which may sound to us like nearly but not completely dead. But the widow believes he is dead and blames his death on Elijah. Having a man of God in the house draws God's attention, she believes, and thus his awareness of her sins, for which she is punished by losing her son. She says to Elijah, "What have you against me, O man of God? You have come to me to bring my sin to remembrance, and to cause the death of my son!" (1 Kgs 17:18). Elijah responds by taking the lifeless boy up to his chamber where "he cried out to the LORD, 'O LORD my God, have you brought calamity even upon the widow with whom I am staying, by killing her son?'" (1 Kgs 17:20). This sounds accusatory, and it is, but implicit in Elijah's accusation is the acknowledgment that Yahweh has the power of life and death. If the child died, it must have been Yahweh's doing. But the prophet believes Yahweh can also restore life, so he prays three times that God would let the child's life come into him again (1 Kgs 17:21). Yahweh hears Elijah's prayer and restores the boy's breath, the breath of life.

There is more going on here than we modern Westerners are used to thinking about. It has to do with the worldview of people who lived in ancient polytheistic circumstances. When they looked at the world, they all knew that things go in cycles. There is the cycle of day and night and also the cycle of the seasons. There is a time when the earth is full of life: plants grow, flocks breed, and needed rain falls. There is also a time when the earth seems to die: plants go dormant, nothing multiplies, and the rains cease. This is a fertility cycle and survival depends on its dependability. That is why so many gods are connected to fertility. The stories of the gods, or myths, explain how it works. In the Canaanite fertility religion, Baal annually dies and descends to the underworld for a time until his female consort goddess comes to restore him to life. This explains the cycles of the seasons: the earth blooms while he is alive and the rains fall, but he dies each year as the rains cease during his time in the underworld. When Yahweh demonstrates the power to withhold rain and to restore life, this is a direct assault on the mythical pattern. Yahweh, not Baal nor his consort, has the power of life and death. This is the contest lying in the background.

When her son is restored to her alive, the widow makes this affirmation of faith to Elijah: "Now I know that you are a man of God, and that the word of the LORD in your mouth is truth" (1 Kgs 17:24).

The Contest of the Gods

Three years of drought come and go, with the result that the famine was severe in Samaria (1 Kgs 18:2). Then Yahweh called Elijah to return to Israel and to Ahab with the message that at last he will send rain on the earth. Yahweh gets to decide when it rains, not Baal. But the final showdown is yet to occur. In a bit of a role reversal, the prophet Elijah instructs King Ahab on how to proceed. He told him to make everyone gather at Mount Carmel, along with the 450 prophets of Baal and the 400 prophets of Asherah who Jezebel had been providing for (1 Kgs 18:19). Ahab obediently complies.

Elijah summons all the people of Israel to join him on Mount Carmel for the contest but first has some harsh words for them; they have, after all, shown up for Baal worship, as if that were compatible with the worship of Yahweh. Elijah mocks their divided loyalties with an either-or question: "How long will you go limping between two opinions? If the LORD is God, follow him; but if Baal, then follow him" (1 Kgs 18:21). The literal meaning of "limping between two opinions" in Hebrew is murky but likely pictures someone trying to walk unsteadily on uneven homemade crutches. In other words, he is mocking them. Some have maintained that there is humor in the Bible. There may be some here. If not humor, then at least mockery. But no one laughs. In fact, his question is met with stony silence. They did not say a word (1 Kgs 18:21).

If the civilians deserve mockery, how much more do the prophets of Baal? They all assemble as Elijah directs. Two bulls are prepared for sacrifice, one on Baal's altar and the other on Yahweh's. No one is to light the fire to burn the sacrifice; they will let the real God do that. Elijah says, "Then you call on the name of your god, and I will call on the name of the LORD; the god who answers by fire is indeed God" (1 Kgs 18:24). The people all agree to this contest. The prophets of Baal get to go first. They pray that Baal, the god of storms, would oblige them with a lightning bolt that he was so often represented as wielding. We read that they called out to Baal until noon, begging him to answer. But there was neither voice, nor an answer (1 Kgs 18:26).

Now the author gets to throw in his own mocking jab, describing their religious dance as "limping" about the altar they had made (1 Kgs 18:26). Elijah is intentionally mocking the prophets of Baal. "At noon Elijah mocked them, saying, 'Cry aloud! Surely he is a god; either he is meditating, or he has wandered away, or he is on a journey, or perhaps he is asleep and must be awakened'" (1 Kgs 18:27). They take the bait and become even more animated. "Then they cried aloud and, as was their custom, they cut themselves with swords and lances until the blood gushed out over them" (1 Kgs 18:28). That last part is always left out of the Sunday School version of the story, unsuitable as it is for children. The Hebrew Bible can be graphic. All this is to no effect: again the narrator repeats that there was neither a voice, nor an answer; no response from Baal (1 Kgs 18:29).

Finally it is Elijah's turn. He prays a prayer that has something odd about it. "O Lord, [Yahweh] God of Abraham, Isaac, and Israel, let it be known this day that you are God in Israel" (1 Kgs 18:36). While Yahweh is "God in Israel," part of the plot of the larger story is that Yahweh is God in Zarephath, in Sidon too, beyond the borders of Israel. In fact, it is crucial, if you are telling this story to exiles in Babylon, to recognize that Yahweh is God everywhere. But at this moment in the story, if the people of Israel do not recognize him at home, what chance would they have of recognizing him abroad?

Elijah's prayer continues by asking God for an answer so that the people would know that the Lord was God (1 Kgs 18:37). The text does not say that God "answered," as if Elijah could command him, but rather simply describes the answer in action: "Then the fire of the Lord fell and consumed the burnt offering, the wood, the stones, and the dust" (1 Kgs 18:38). The contest is over. The Baal altar is standing, now bloodied and uncooked, while Yahweh's altar is ablaze. The people get the point. "When all the people saw it, they fell on their faces and said, 'The Lord indeed is God; the Lord indeed is God'" (1 Kgs 18:39).

What happens next is a horror. Elijah has all the prophets of Baal killed (1 Kgs 18:40). We must try again to suspend our modern sensibilities and allow this narrative to be what it is: a story that can imagine God authorizing terrible violence. We will not try to excuse it but rather acknowledge that when this text was written, God could be conceived of this way. This part is also left out of the Sunday School version—and for good reason.

The Two Contrasting Women

Standing back and looking at these stories within stories, we see a pattern emerging. There is a stark contrast between two Sidonian women: the widow of Zarephath and Queen Jezebel. The widow is poor, powerless, and alone, while Queen Jezebel is wealthy, powerful, and surrounded by submissive people. Jezebel conducts a personal vendetta against Yahweh, while the widow honors him. The widow supplied food for Elijah, Yahweh's prophet, while Jezebel fed the prophets of Baal. Ironically, the widow is outside of Israel, but Jezebel is inside. The widow's beloved son is given life, but in the end Jezebel's pet prophets of Baal are killed. The contrast is sharp, but it has nothing to do with their status as non-Israelite foreigners. Phoenicia, where Zarephath lies, is Baal country. Nevertheless, the widow there confesses faith in Yahweh. The widow receives the blessings of sustenance during the drought-induced famine and the restored life of her son, while Jezebel's fate, described later, is to be thrown to her death from a window (2 Kgs 9).

The tension between the particular blessings promised to the descendants of Abraham and the blessings extended to all the families of the earth is a lasting tension that runs through the Bible from beginning to end. Ahab, too, meets his untimely demise at the hand of Jehu, who not only deposed and killed him but also killed Ahab's seventy sons in a gruesome purge (2 Kgs 10). Ahab and his sons were all descendants of Abraham who experienced the curse that Deuteronomy had pronounced on those who walked away from Yahweh and his law.

There is no biblical precedent for believing that the status of chosen people could ever be applied to another nation as it was to ancient Israel. While the concept of "the people of God" becomes the moniker that the church wears, it wears it not as a nation but as people from any nation who have become "followers of the Way," as the early Christians were called. That is why Paul could say specifically that in Christ, there is no Jew or Greek (Gal 3:28). No nation as a nation has the status of chosen. But, if despite this most obvious fact, one nation were to imagine themselves as somehow inheriting the status of chosen-ness, what would that mean? It would mean a concerted openness to people of other nations—in fact, to all the nations of the earth. Israel received no pass when they were unfaithful. Just the opposite. Ethnic purity was never the criterion for inclusion in what, from the beginning of the exodus, was a mixed multitude. God has never been limited to acting within or on behalf of one nation and its people exclusively. God's sphere of concern, compassion, and even intervention extends beyond the borders of Israel, beyond the bloodlines of Abraham, all the way to lowly widows in Zarephath. This alone is the glimmer of hope that exiles in Babylon can see that one day they may be able to return, rebuild, and maybe get it right this time.

5

Elisha and Naaman the Syrian Leper

THE LONG STORY THAT began in Deuteronomy on the eve of entering the promised land comes to a close hundreds of years later. The last chapter of 2 Kings ends with the surviving Israelites as exiles in Babylon. For those of us who have never lived on the losing side of a catastrophic national disaster, it is hard to imagine what that must have felt like. America has suffered some devastating circumstances, like 9/11, but our country has never fallen to an enemy invasion. We have not witnessed the destruction of our capital nor the decimation of our entire army. We have no concept of what it means to be among a relatively small number of survivors herded five hundred miles across Middle Eastern sands on caravan trade routes into exile in Babylon. Jehoiachin, the last king to reign in Jerusalem by succession, had rebelled against the king of Babylon and eventually capitulated to him. He was among the survivors of the exiles there, alive, but powerless. That catastrophe was not only military; it was also religious. The temple, "the place that the LORD [Yahweh] your God will choose as a dwelling for his name" (Deut 12:11), was a smoking pile of rubble by the last chapter, 2 Kgs 25. The high priest, the second highest priest, and the remaining officials they could find in Jerusalem were all killed. After such a total disaster, how could there be any basis of hope for the future at all? And yet, why bother to tell such a long, detailed story of the rise and fall of this nation if there was no hope at all?

No one knows for sure when this whole story came together in the final form that we have today. There have been several hypotheses about the process. We know, because of how the last chapter ends, that the final narrators knew of the Babylonian exile. Did they live to see much beyond that? We do not know but it seems unlikely; they said nothing further. They likely did not know that the Babylonians would fall prey to the Persians. Nor that the Persian King Cyrus would allow exiled people in his kingdom to return to their native lands and rebuild their temples as long as they promised to pray for him. That must have seemed like the least likely turn of events to powerless exiled people. It must have been considered miraculous. In fact, a miracle was the only thing they could have hoped for under exile.

As the narrator who told the long story of the rise and fall of the Israelite monarchy reflected on how to tell it, he apparently gathered together the miracle stories of Elisha, the man of God, knowing that they were important. By his time, the Elisha miracle stories were an ancient memory. But those memories could be useful to inspire people to keep hoping many years later, even after the disaster of exile. Keeping the hope of a miracle alive was one of the reasons the stories of Elisha the prophet are told the way they were in the book of 2 Kings. With little connection between them beyond Elisha the miracle worker himself, the narrator presents the reader with a series of miracle stories. They are of a rather private nature. They do not portend any national events, they do not effect change beyond the ones receiving the miracle, and they do not have much of a connection to an ongoing plot. But for some reason, someone felt it important to keep alive the idea that Yahweh, for his own reasons, could work miracles. By the time we get to the story of Naaman the leper, which is our focus in this chapter, Elisha has already split the Jordan river (2 Kgs 2:14), healed a poisoned water supply (2 Kgs 2:21), made bears kill forty-two boys (2 Kgs 2:24), multiplied a widow's oil (2 Kgs 4:3), restored a woman's childbearing ability (2 Kgs 4:17), brought a dead man to life (2 Kgs 4:35), neutralized poisoned food (2 Kgs 4:41), and multiplied loaves of bread (2 Kgs 4:44). And there will be more to come.

It has been suggested that the overarching theme of these stories of 2 Kings is that the course of history is determined by the degree of the king's loyalty to Yahweh, rightly worshiped exclusively in Jerusalem. Most kings fail to be loyal to Yahweh, which is why the larger story of the nation ends in the disaster of exile. Elisha's ministry spanned the reigns of several kings. In the story of Naaman, the Jewish king is not named but is most likely Joram, son of Ahab. His reign is remembered this way: "He did what was evil in the sight of the LORD, though not like his father and mother, for he removed the pillar of Baal that his father had made. Nevertheless, he clung to the sin of Jeroboam son of Nebat, which he caused Israel to commit; he did not depart from it" (2 Kgs 3:2–3). Joram does not get much attention in the story of the healing of Naaman the leper, but knowing this may help explain his exasperation upon receiving the letter from the king of Syria about Naaman's predicament.

Naaman's Story

Why would the king of Syria write to the king of Israel? A bit of background information helps us understand. Naaman, the narrator tells us, was the commander of the Aramean army (2 Kgs 5:1). Aram, also known as Syria, was a neighboring kingdom. During the end of the reign of Joram, there were frequent hostilities between Israel and the Syrians. This story may have taken place in a lull between hostilities. On one of those raids we learn that the Syrians took an Israelite girl captive. She was pressed into service by Naaman's wife. She is about to become the catalyst of the story, but before that, we learn some more details about Naaman. The narrator says he was an important, or great man, and that he was in high favor with the king (Joram) (2 Kgs 5:1). The English "high favor" translates a Hebrew idiom that literally means "to lift up the face."[1] It refers to the gesture the king would perform of extending his scepter to touch the face of a person humbly bowed before them, thus lifting up their face toward the king.

Why would Naaman have found such favor? The narrator attributes his military prowess and success, even success against Israel, to the power of Yahweh. He gained the king's favor because by him the Lord had given victory to Aram (Syria). This is the first glimpse, in this story, of the work of Yahweh beyond the borders of Israel on behalf of people who are not descendants of Abraham. The story focuses on the individual Naaman, but he is part of a much wider work attributed to Yahweh among the nations of the earth. The nation that drove Israel into exile, Babylon, was a tool in the hand of Yahweh, as was the Persian King Cyrus, who allowed the return of the exiles back to the promised land. All the nations of the earth, in the eyes of the narrators of Israel's Scripture, are part of God's plan.

The final fact that we need to know about Naaman is that, though he was a mighty warrior, he suffered from leprosy. The disease we call leprosy, Hansen's disease, is probably not the one that afflicted Naaman. Many skin diseases were called leprosy in the ancient world. The fact that Naaman was not isolated from society, even from the king of Syria, means that he had something other than the highly contagious Hansen's disease. No one around him feared that his disease would affect them, but it was significant to Naaman. He shows how important it was to him by the lavish gifts he is willing to pay to be cured. But there is no cure available to him in Syria.

1. BDB, s.v. "נָשָׂא."

Ironically, this "great man" is at a total loss to fix a problem that apparently makes him miserable enough to be willing to spend a fortune to solve.

Now the captive Israelite young girl (2 Kgs 5:2) enters the story. She says to her mistress, Naaman's wife, "If only my lord [Naaman] were with the prophet who is in Samaria! He would cure him of his leprosy" (2 Kgs 5:3). The city of Samaria was the capital of the northern kingdom of Israel and is another term for Israel, just as "Washington" sometimes means "the United States."

Without any explanation of why Naaman the Syrian should have believed her claim, perhaps out of desperation, Naaman takes that information right to his boss, the king of Syria. We are told, "So Naaman went in and told his lord [the king] just what the girl from the land of Israel had said. And the king of Aram said, 'Go then, and I will send along a letter to the king of Israel'" (2 Kgs 5:4–5).

Naaman and the Syrian king make the assumption that people of power deal directly with other people of power to get things done. They also make the assumption that people of power will be respected and treated as great people, with deference and respect. Neither one is in a position to understand that the power of Yahweh is such that human power appears as insignificant as dust on the scales, as Elisha knows and Naaman will soon learn. The Syrian king writes a letter, not to Elisha in Samaria, as the Israelite slave girl has identified, but to the king of Israel. There was no postal service in those days. If you want to send a letter, king to king, you have to use a letter carrier to do the job in person. If the letter is about a "great man" who needs to be cured of his leprosy, what better delivery agent to do the job but the great man himself. The king of Syria writes the letter and tells Naaman to deliver it in person to the king of Israel (2 Kgs 5:5). Naaman accepts the command as a good soldier and gathers the gratuities he believes will be suitable for such a healing service: "He went, taking with him ten talents of silver, six thousand shekels of gold, and ten sets of garments" (2 Kgs 5:5). The gifts Naaman brings seem like an unimportant detail, as if we needed an accounting, but the narrator is setting the stage for events that are yet to unfold.

The letter was short and to the point: "He brought the letter to the king of Israel, which read, 'When this letter reaches you, know that I have sent to you my servant Naaman, that you may cure him of his leprosy'" (2 Kgs 5:6). People of power expect people of power to use their positions to accomplish their objectives. Remember, this narrative has been written by people who have seen the demise of the monarchy of Israel from the vantage point of a Babylonian address. And long before the rump tribe of Judah landed as exiles in Babylon, they had seen the total collapse of the northern kingdom of Israel, which fell to the Assyrians centuries earlier. There are plenty of reasons to tell the story of the incompetence of kings in the face of the power of Yahweh.

This is how the mighty king of Israel reacts upon receipt of the letter: "When the king of Israel read the letter, he tore his clothes and said, 'Am I God, to give death or life, that this man sends word to me to cure a man of his leprosy? Just look and see how he is trying to pick a quarrel with me'" (2 Kgs 5:7). Tearing of one's clothing is a sign of deep mourning in ancient Israelite culture. The king is at a total loss. He may fear that the present lull in the on-again-off-again conflict with Syria is about to heat up, which he would be in no position to prevent. Far from having the power to give death or life, which he attributes to God alone, he does not even have power over a skin rash. The only positive element in this scene is that the Israelite king is humbled. Humility is the correct and only appropriate emotion before Yahweh, which Naaman will soon learn.

The narrator leaves the scene of the Israelite king's despair and turns to a scene in which Elisha, the man of God, has become aware—though we are not told how—of what is happening at court. "But when Elisha the man of God heard that the king of Israel had torn his clothes, he sent a message to the king, 'Why have you torn your clothes? Let him come to me, that he may learn that there is a prophet in Israel'" (2 Kgs 5:8).

Elisha and Namaan

The phrase "let him come to me" suggests that the king of Israel's address is not the right one to come to with a need that requires God-like power to solve. Just like the condition of exile in Babylon, healing leprosy would take a miracle. The good news is that Yahweh is a God of miracles, as the accounts of Elisha's ministry have already demonstrated. We are not told anything about how Elisha's message was received or anything about the king of Israel's reaction to it, only that Naaman acted upon it immediately. He drove his chariots right to Elisha's door (2 Kgs 5:9).

This is where the sub-topic of humility becomes a dominant motif. Elisha treats this great man no better than a passing salesman. Instead of coming out of his house to greet him personally, we are told that Elisha sent a messenger to him. Naaman would not have been accustomed to being treated with this kind of disrespect. From his perspective it gets even worse. Elisha's remedy seems both ridiculously simple and demeaning. The messenger said to Naaman that he should go, wash in the Jordan seven times, and his flesh would be restored and he would be clean (2 Kgs 5:10).

Naaman comes from a polytheistic culture. There are many gods, each with their own territory of influence, each with their own capacities. Some are good with rain, others with battle success. But behind them all is a source of power greater than any of them. This source can be destructive or protective. It could be appealed to and even coaxed into action by magical rites: potions, spells, incantations, gestures, and the like. Naaman is a believer in this meta-divine sphere as some have called it. He expects a man of God like Elisha to perform whatever ritual act is necessary to compel the Force to enact a healing. Elisha believes none of that nonsense. To him, there is only one God, one source of power over death and life, leprosy, and the fate of nations. Elisha's power is only that he is in touch with Yahweh in ways that the narrator never explains. And because he knows that it is Yahweh alone whose power is at work behind his miracles, he can take no credit for them nor can he accept any gratuity in compensation. This is why the story unfolds as it does.

> But Naaman became angry and went away, saying, "I thought that for me he would surely come out, and stand and call on the name of the Lord his God, and would wave his hand over the spot, and cure the leprosy! Are not Abanaa and Pharpar, the rivers of Damascus, better than all the waters of Israel? Could I not wash in them, and be clean?" He turned and went away in a rage. (2 Kgs 5:11–12)

A servant girl set this story in motion by informing her mistress that there was a man of God in Israel who could cure leprosy. Now another servant saves the story from disaster and Naaman from a life of leprosy by his intervention. Servants are used to being humble; they know how prideful resistance would probably be the death of them. So this servant recommends a bit of humility to Naaman, the great man.

"But his servants approached and said to him, 'Father, if the prophet had commanded you to do something difficult [literally "great"], would you not have done it? How much more, when all he said to you was, "Wash, and be clean"?'" (2 Kgs 5:13). He knows that the great man would be willing to do something "great" as would befit his station, but using a clever argument form—"If you would have been willing to do X, why not do less than X?"—he convinces him.

"So he went down and immersed himself seven times in the Jordan, according to the word of the man of God; his flesh was restored like the flesh of a young boy, and he was clean" (2 Kgs 5:14). The "young girl" was the catalyst for this story, which reaches its climax when Naaman's skin is described using the same words in the masculine form: his flesh is that of a "young boy."

Now we reach the point of this story. Naaman is a foreigner. He is not a descendant of Abraham, not part of the chosen people, not even a monotheist. But this foreigner has just experienced the power of Yahweh to heal and restore, to give life to skin that was dead. Naaman comes to the realization that his former belief in the power of the meta-divine realm manifested in the many gods of the Syrian pantheon is misplaced faith. He blurts out a confession of faith that is far more thoroughgoing than any that the Israelite King Joram could have made.

"Then [Naaman] returned to the man of God, he and all his company; he came and stood before him [Elisha] and said, 'Now I know that there is no God in all the earth except in Israel'" (2 Kgs 5:15). He dutifully offered Elisha his gratuity, which the man of God declined saying, "'As the LORD lives, whom I serve, I will accept nothing!' He urged him to accept, but he refused" (2 Kgs 5:16).

Naaman's reply seems odd to us at this distance from the ideas and concepts of our world:

> Then Naaman said, "If not, please let two mule-loads of earth be given to your servant; for your servant will no longer offer burnt offering or sacrifice to any god except the LORD. But may the LORD pardon your servant on one count: when my master goes into the house of Rimmon to worship there, leaning on my arm, and I bow down in the house of Rimmon, when I do bow down in the house of Rimmon, may the LORD pardon your servant on this one count." (2 Kgs 5:17–18)

The ancient concept that Naaman expressed seems to be that Yahweh could only be worshipped correctly in the land of Israel. Because he wants to worship Yahweh but must return to his own land, he takes some representative portion of Israel back with him in the form of two mule-loads of Israelite soil. He no longer believes in the Syrian god, called Rimmon here, but as a man under command, he must accompany his superior officer at worship. (The name Rimmon, Hebrew for "pomegranate," is probably a parody of *Ramman*, the title of Hadad, the Syrian Baal, god of storms and rain.)[2] Elisha apparently understands his motives and his dilemma, and accepts his solution saying simply, "Go in peace" (2 Kgs 5:19).

2. BDB, s.v. "רִמּוֹן."

Gehazi's Story

It would be great if the story ended there. Tragically it doesn't. Elisha has an understudy named Gehazi (which means "avaricious") who chases down Naaman and makes up a story about Elisha changing his mind about the gifts because the guests he has received need support. We will not belabor that story, only to mention that Gehazi's greed produced the result that Naaman's leprosy "clings" to Gehazi and his descendants forever. Just as the story of the nation of Israel ends in disaster, so did this story, at least as far as Gehazi is concerned. Disregarding Yahweh has consequences. As in the case of the Israelite Achan who tried to abscond with the banned spoils of Jericho, who then lost his standing among the chosen people (and his life), so now Gehazi the Israelite has leprosy, while the foreigner Naaman, like Rahab before him, is blessed.

Once again the Hebrew Bible shows that it is not merely ethnicity that defines the people of God, but faithfulness to Israel's God, Yahweh, that matters.

Yahweh's power has never been restricted to Israel nor to the Israelites alone. His power to heal extends beyond Israel's borders—to the widow of Zarephath and Naaman the Syrian. Both of these foreigners make confessions of faith, as did Rahab. The mixed multitude that Moses led out of Egypt continually encountered foreigners who were capable of embracing the true and living God, Yahweh.

Some maintain that there is something about ethnicity, language, and country of origin that impart an indelible quality making people of other ethnicities ineligible for full membership among "the chosen people," usually defined as "us." This kind of nationalism may sound reasonable on the surface, but it runs counter to the biblical narrative that finds foreignness no barrier whatsoever to full inclusion in the community of the faithful. The tension in the Hebrew Bible continues. Yes, the descendants of Abraham have a particular place; they know God as Yahweh. As such, Yahweh is not only the God of Israel but is universally the Lord of heaven and earth. Thus, God's concern is not only to bless the descendants of Abraham but, through them, to bless all the families of the earth.

6

Other Nations' Promised Land

God promised the land of Canaan to the patriarchs—Abraham, Isaac, and Jacob—at least eighteen times in the book of Deuteronomy. The land of Canaan was a gift given to Israel by God. This land grant was part of the promise to Abraham, renewed in succeeding generations. According to the biblical narrative, the Israelites knew that they were not indigenous to the land and would not possess it because they were superior in number or power, but solely because their God, Yahweh, had promised it (Deut 7:7). The fact that the Israelites were not the only people to whom God had given land will be the subject of this chapter. But we first need to set the stage and consider issues that this text brings up.

Getting to the promised land has been a long, difficult journey. After escaping hundreds of years of slavery in Egypt, and after a whole generation spent wandering in the wilderness, the Israelites have finally arrived. They have reached the outskirts of the land. But it was not an empty land. As they entered the territories adjacent to Canaan, they met various groups of inhabitants settled there. The story of what happened in those encounters is described more than once. There is a version in Num 20 as well as Deut 2.

We noted that the Bible is best described as a library of books rather than a single book. As such, the Bible was not the product of one individual or even one community with a unified perspective. It was not even composed in one place or in one generation. Some have described the Bible as a conversation between people with similar but not identical perspectives. The primary goals of these ancient writers sometimes seem more oriented toward making theological points rather than reporting literal history. That different books tell the story differently is not news; rabbis of old have wrestled with differences for centuries. It may be a surprise to modern people who come to these texts with the mistaken assumption that they will conform to our current notions about how history "should be" written. The ancient world, of course, had no such standards for "history." The ancient rabbis did not even call Joshua, Judges, Samuel, and Kings "histories" but rather referred to them as the "former prophets." That should put a different spin on our expectations. This next account is one of those places that shows different perspectives. The issue is how the Edomites treated the Israelites as they were nearing their territory, approaching the land of Canaan on their journey out of the wilderness.

In Num 20:18 we read, "But [the king of] Edom said to him [Moses], 'You shall not pass through, or we will come out with the sword against you.'" This is Edom's reply to Moses's request that the Israelites be allowed to pass through Edomite territory in peace, assuring him that "We will not pass through field or vineyard, or drink water from any well" (Num 20:17). Even after Moses insisted that the Israelites would pay for anything they needed, even water for their livestock, the Edomites, in this version, were belligerent. The king of Edom said, "You shall not pass through" (Num 20:18). This was no idle threat: the Edomite army came out en masse against the Israelites. Edom did not allow Israel to pass through their territory. Israel had to find an alternate route (Num 20:20–21). Israel averted warfare only by staying well away from Edom's territory.

A different perspective of Israel's encounter with the Edomites is told in Deut 2. Deuteronomy, you will recall, is mostly the long speech of Moses, delivered on the banks of the Jordan just before the Israelites entered the promised land of Canaan. In it, Moses reviews the events that led up to this moment. He recalls the people they encountered along the journey. He begins with the Edomites. He reviews how they got to the land of the Edomites, whom he refers to as the Esau's descendants (Deut 2:4). They had been skirting Mount Seir, but Moses told the people that God instructed them to pass through the territory of the Edomites, their kindred (Deut 2:4).

But instead of being combative and resistant, Moses reports Yahweh saying that the Edomites would fear them (Deut 2:4). Fear can precede violence, but God wants to avoid conflict, so Moses quoted God as saying, "So, be very careful not to engage in battle with them, for I will not give you even so much as a foot's length of their land, since I have given Mount Seir to Esau as a possession" (Deut 2:4b–5). Instead of conflict, and instead of making an offer of payment for the food they may need from them—the offer rejected in Numbers—God predicts, "You shall purchase food from them for money, so that you may eat; and you shall also buy water from them for money, so that you may drink" (Deut 2:6). Moses summarizes the conclusion of their encounter with the Edomites, saying that they passed by their kin, again calling them Esau's descendants (Deut 2:8). In this account of the meeting of the Israelites with their relatives, the Edomite descendants of Esau, there was no threat of violence and no rejection of the offer of compensation.

We have noted the differences in the two accounts. We will never know which is more faithful to literal history (or if either account recounts actual events), but again we notice that the Bible is not attempting to be a modern literal history. It is rather history told as theology—history in the service of theology, a sacred story. Again, these differences have long been observed and were most likely known by the first people who let them stand beside each other without attempting to harmonize them. It simply was not a problem in the ancient world. This is another reminder that when we read the Bible, we are reading an ancient text that conforms to ancient standards. Knowing this will help us not make the mistake of over-literalism.

God's Gifts of Lands

Let us get back to the main issue: when Moses was recalling how the people got to the Jordan River, ready to cross into the land, and recounted their past experience with the Edomites, he quotes God as saying, "I have given Mount Seir to Esau as a possession" (Deut 2:5). This introduces a new concept. Israel was not unique when it came to gifts of land from Yahweh. God had also given Mount Seir to Esau's descendants, the Edomites, as a possession. Being the chosen people who have been the recipients of God's gracious gifts may be a blessing, but it is not necessarily an exclusive one.

The Edomites were not the only other people whose land was a gift from God. As they proceeded through the wilderness of Moab, Moses recalls that God had warned them, "Do not harass Moab or engage them in battle, for I will not give you any of its land as a possession, since I have given Ar as a possession to the descendants of Lot" (Deut 2:9).

Remarkably, the chosen people, who had inherited the special blessing of promises from God, including the gift of land, narrated accounts of God also gifting other people with land. It is all the more remarkable to consider that by the time these narratives were put into the form that we have them, many years had passed between the events they describe and the final editor's time. The astounding part is not that a long time had passed but rather the history of the Israelites' relationship with these two nations. There was bad blood, to say the least. There was open hostility, the memory of wars with both Edom and Moab, and betrayals and resentment toward the Edomites particularly.

The memory of conflicts went back to the stories of David's campaigns against Edom, which included accounts of slaughtering eighteen thousand Edomites and conquering them on one occasion (2 Sam 8:13–14; the title of Ps 60; 1 Chr 18:12). David's general Joab led the campaigns and at one time is reported to have killed every Edomite male—obviously an overstatement (see 1 Kgs 11:15–16). That massacre prepared the way for the permanent animosity that followed. The prophet Amos summed up the history of hatred many years later, saying, "For three transgressions of Edom, and for four, I will not revoke the punishment; because he pursued his brother [the Israelites] with the sword and cast off all pity; he maintained his anger perpetually, and kept his wrath forever" (Amos 1:11). The entire book of the minor prophet Obadiah is one long poem excoriating Edom. When the Babylonians were conquering Israel, the Edomites took advantage of the situation and joined the plunder. Obadiah says, "For the slaughter and violence done to your brother Jacob [i.e., Israel], shame shall cover you [Edom], and you shall be cut off forever. On the day that you stood aside, on the day that strangers carried off his wealth, and foreigners entered his gates and cast lots for Jerusalem, you too were like one of them" (Obad 1:10–11).

Animosity against the Moabites was also intense. Numbers 22–24 tells the story of the Israelites' encounter with the Moabites as they were making their way through the wilderness. The Moabites, the text says, feared them, so Balak, the king of Moab, enlisted the services of Balaam to curse them so that they could be defeated. Balaam was unable to curse the Israelites (the story involves the talking donkey), so King Balak's plan was thwarted, but his attempted curse and desire for conquest stands. Moreover, it was Moabite women who seduced Israelite men to have sexual relations with them and to bow down to their gods. The narrator tells us, "Thus Israel yoked itself to the Baal of Peor, and the LORD's anger was kindled against Israel" (Num 25:3). That event became infamous and was recalled many years later by Nehemiah (13:2) and in 2 Pet 2:15. There were other conflicts and massacres exchanged between Moabites and Israelites described in the Hebrew Bible. Psalm 83 calls on God to execute vengeance against Israel's enemies, including both Moabites and Edomites.

After all of this animosity, you would think that the editors of the final form of Deuteronomy might have eliminated the offhand comments about God gifting land to their enemies, but they let them stand. Israel considered themselves God's chosen people and their land a gift of God. But they also knew that God's concern and care for people extended beyond their borders. God was also able to give land to other people, even to their enemies.

Conditions on the Gift

There is more to this story about land as a gift of God. By telling the story of how they entered the land of Canaan, which they were not native to, the Israelites acknowledged that their successful conquest was God's doing. But the promise of land and the successful conquest were conditional. Just because God promised the land and enabled them to possess it did not mean that the Israelites had some kind of guarantee of permanence. Continued existence in the land of promise entailed obligations. The book of Leviticus tells the Israelites that the reason God was enabling their successful conquest was to drive out the former inhabitants because of their idolatrous defilement of the land. The text is graphic, even shocking: "Do not defile yourselves in any of these ways, for by all these practices, the nations I am casting out before you have defiled themselves. Thus, the land became defiled; and I punished it for its iniquity, and the land vomited out its inhabitants" (Lev 18:24–25). If the Israelites were to maintain possession of the land, they had the obligation to be faithful to Yahweh and his laws (the law of Moses). Leviticus continues, "But you shall keep my statutes and my ordinances and commit none of these abominations, either the citizen or the alien who resides among you (for the inhabitants of the land, who were before you, committed all of these abominations, and the land became defiled); otherwise the land will vomit you out for defiling it, as it vomited out the nation that was before you" (Lev 18:26–28).

Far from being a guarantee of special treatment, the very fact of being God's chosen people put special obligations on Israel to be faithful and obedient. The prophet Amos, speaking for God, makes this explicit, saying, "Hear this word that the LORD has spoken against you, O people of Israel, against the whole family that I brought up out of the land of Egypt: You only have I known of all the families of the earth; therefore I will punish you for all your iniquities" (Amos 3:1–2). Faithful obedience was not just a religious concern but also an ethical one, as Amos makes clear: "Thus says the LORD: For three transgressions of Israel, and for four, I will not revoke the punishment; because they sell the righteous for silver, and the needy for a pair of sandals—they who trample the head of the poor into the dust of the earth, and push the afflicted out of the way" (Amos 2:6–7). Selling the righteous and the needy refers to debt slavery. The low price of a "pair of sandals" reduces the value of a human life to the negligible range. The graphic picture of the heads of poor people being trampled into the dust is meant to horrify and shock the reader. God's concern for faithful obedience extended far beyond the religious sphere. It encompassed the economic sphere of life as well. According to Amos, "Therefore thus says the Lord

God [Adonai Yahweh]: 'An adversary shall surround the land, and strip you of your defense; and your strongholds shall be plundered'" (Amos 3:11). In other words, the unfaithful, disobedient people will lose the land that had been promised to them. They, like the inhabitants they dispossessed, will be "vomited out" of the land because of their unrighteousness and injustice.

Amos ends with a vision of a future day of restoration when Israel will once again return to the land. But that future hope of return from exile would come only after the catastrophe of destruction. Many people, Amos predicts, will die in battle (Amos 9:10). The survivors will go into exile as captives (Amos 9:4).

The Complications of Being Chosen People

The tension between particularism and universalism, between being a chosen people and God's will to bless all the families of the earth, runs throughout the Bible. Israel is given the promised land of Canaan, but non-Israelites have also been given land by Yahweh. Being chosen as God's particular people is itself complicated. Instead of a blanket guarantee of success, Israel learned that it could incur greater punishments for failing to remain faithful. "You only have I known of all the families of the earth; therefore I will punish you" (Amos 3:2). In spite of this, there are some today who claim that America has inherited Israel's status as a chosen nation. That claim is surprising, given that there is no basis in Scripture for any people or any nation to consider themselves God's new chosen people or nation. In the New Testament, this status of chosen-ness is applied to the church, but that application is specifically non-national. First Peter says "You are a chosen race, a royal priesthood, a holy nation, God's own people" (1 Pet 2:9). But instead of making a new national entity as Israel of old was, this new status given to believers makes them "aliens and exiles" to their culture (1 Pet 2:11). Instead of having special privileges, God's people should be prepared to endure what he calls a fiery ordeal as they are sharing Christ's sufferings (1 Pet 4:12–13).

Importantly, anyone who might want to take on the moniker of God's chosen people or who maintain that their nation is God's new promised land might want to take this warning. Being chosen entails obligations to faithful obedience. God cares about righteousness and justice. It is the fact of being chosen and blessed that lays special obligations on God's people. According to the biblical record, failure to be faithful to those responsibilities has severe consequences. Israel was brutally defeated and went into exile in Babylon.

The God who made a covenant with Abraham and promised his descendants blessings, including the land of Canaan, also promised to bless all the families of the earth. God was able to give land to others as well, including Israel's archenemies, Edom and Moab. Nationalism carries with it a sense of special privilege and even uniqueness, but these features are vexed in the Bible. To be specially privileged is also to be held responsible. To be uniquely blessed is also to be uniquely obligated. In Scripture, to be chosen is to have obligations of faithfulness to the Source of blessings. Faithfulness includes both the religious and socio-economic parts of life. It is faithfulness that makes a follower of Jesus "the light of the world[, a] city built on a hill" (Matt 5:14), not simply arriving on the shores of a continent you intend to make your new home. That was the assertion that John Winthrop made to the colonists in his sermon of 1630. He proclaimed that God had made a covenant with the Massachusetts Bay colonists—an assertion he pulled out of thin air. He was not a theologian or even a clergyman, but the colony's governor. There is simply no basis for any nation to claim special covenant status with God *as a nation*. That role has been, according to the New Testament, given to the church, who are collectively the new Israel, chosen "in Christ" in whom "there is no Jew nor Greek" (Gal 3:28). The tension, however, still remains. Though the church "in Christ" inherits the promise, nevertheless it proclaims, "For God so loved the world" (John 3:16) and he "is not willing that any should perish" (2 Pet 3:9).

7

Ruth the Foreigner

THE BOOK OF RUTH is subversive. Many people have read it as a simple, happy tale of a gentle widowed woman (Ruth) who, out of loyalty to her mother-in-law (Naomi), leaves her native land of Moab, journeys back to Bethlehem, and finds a clever way to vouchsafe her future. People love Naomi's speech to her mother-in-law and even read it at weddings, as if it is about romantic love. Ruth pledges to Naomi,

> Do not press me to leave you
> or to turn back from following you!
> Where you go, I will go;
> Where you lodge, I will lodge;
> your people shall be my people,
> and your God my God.
> Where you die, I will die—
> there will I be buried.
> May the LORD do thus and so to me,
> and more as well,
> if even death parts me from you! (Ruth 1:16–17)

But Ruth is far from a simple, happy, gentle tale. First, it is a story about women whose men have died acting with agency in a man's world. One of them, Naomi, is a native of the land of Israel. But the other, Ruth, is a foreigner. Her foreignness is essential to the plot. The fact that she is from the land of Moab, and is therefore a Moabite, is mentioned fourteen times in this little book of only four short chapters. The narrator tells us that she is from Moab, and many of the characters in the book inform each other of her Moabite ethnicity. The author wants us to keep her status as a foreigner to the chosen people front and center as we read this story.

The story has a simple plot at the start. An Israelite family from Bethlehem faces a famine, so they pack up and move to the neighboring country of Moab. The family consists of the father, Elimelech, his wife, Naomi, and their two sons, Mahlon and Chilion. The narrator mentions that they are "Ephrathites from Bethlehem in Judah" (Ruth 1:2). *Ephrathites* sounds like *Ephriamites*, a tribe different from the tribe of Judah. This could be intentional wordplay. Throughout this little story there are many ambiguities and plays on words meant to evoke deeper or alternative meanings. Later, we will see that events that took place among Ephriamites add one of many layers of danger to the story.

Names are important in this story. The family is from Bethlehem, which means "house of bread" or "food,"[1] but, ironically, there is a famine. The father's name, Elimelech, means "God is king" or "My God is king."[2] But God did not look like he was being king in those days. The author begins the book by setting the story "in the days when the judges ruled" (Ruth 1:1); there was not yet a king in Israel. What was happening, according to the book of Judges, "in the days when the judges ruled"? As the book of Judges approaches its conclusion, there is a line that is repeated, with variation, that says, "In those days there was no king in Israel," and sometimes adds, "All the people did what was right in their own eyes" (Judg 17:6; 18:1; 19:1; 21:25). And indeed, the book describes a lawless time that included gang rape, murder, civil war, and other horrors. If "everyone did what was right in their own eyes" because "there was no king in Israel," then the reader is led to think that a king would bring order out of that chaos and things would be better. As it turns out, Ruth ends up the great-grandmother of King David, Israel's greatest king. So a happy ending to the chaotic time when the judges judged (Ruth 1:1)? Or is that another clever ambiguity? We are left to ponder it, given King David's story and the tragic account of the entire monarchy that follows.

To Moab and Back

So Mr. "God is king," when there was no king, has a wife named Naomi, a word associated with the word "pleasant."[3] Her life is far from pleasant as we will see. Their two apparently grown sons are auspiciously named Mahlon

1. BDB, s.v. "בַּ֫יִת."
2. BDB, s.v. "אֱלִימֶ֫לֶךְ."
3. BDB, s.v. "נָעֳמִי."

and Chilion, which come from the words for "sickness" and "consumption."[4] They both abruptly die. Before they die, they both marry Moabite women, Orpah and Ruth. Elimelech also dies in Moab. Now there are three women, each of them widowed. Naomi decides that there is nothing left for her to do but to return to her native soil, "for she had heard in the country of Moab that the Lord had considered his people and given them food [literally "bread"]" (Ruth 1:6). She urged both daughters to stay behind in Moab and find new husbands there. Neither wanted to separate; both wept, but Orpah finally agreed, turned around, and left. Orpah can mean "back of the neck,"[5] the last thing Naomi saw of her. Ruth, whose name is associated with the word "friend" or "companion,"[6] decides to stay with her mother-in-law and return to Bethlehem. She announces her decision in the poetic speech quoted above (Ruth 1:16–17).

On their return, the town's women observe them coming and ask each other if this is Naomi, Mrs. Pleasant. She replies, "Call me no longer Naomi [pleasant], call me Mara [bitter], for the Almighty has dealt bitterly with me" (Ruth 1:20). Notice how Ruth's foreignness is emphasized in the simple description of their return. "So Naomi returned together with Ruth the Moabite, her daughter-in-law, who came back with her from the country of Moab. They came to Bethlehem at the beginning of the barley harvest" (Ruth 1:22). With no husband to protect her and with a foreign, widowed daughter-in-law in tow, her prospects seem bleak.

At least the famine is over, and the time of the barley harvest has come. Naomi starts a conversation with Ruth about their situation. She tells Ruth that she has a near relative, kin to Elimelech, a prominent wealthy man named Boaz. Boaz is a pun on "in him is strength."[7] It is also the name of one of the pillars in the temple Solomon would later build (yes, they named pillars) (1 Kgs 7:21). Strong Boaz is, as some have suggested, a pillar of the community. Upon hearing that news, Ruth jumps at a plan. "And Ruth the Moabite said to Naomi, 'Let me go to the field and glean among the ears of grain, behind someone in whose sight I may find favor'" (Ruth 2:2). Notice again that Ruth's Moabite status is highlighted, as if by now we do not already know. It is there for a reason. The reason is danger. Not only is Ruth an unprotected widow, she is also a foreigner, which puts her at risk. Her suggestion that she glean in the fields of Boaz includes several things we need to know to enter the world of this ancient text.

4. Bledstein, "Female Companionships," 131.
5. Linafelt, "Ruth," 2.
6. BDB, s.v. "רוּת."
7. BDB, s.v. "בֹּעַז."

First, she was right to expect to be allowed to glean in a field during harvest time. The narrator does not tell us how she, as a Moabite, might have expected to have gleaning rights. There is scant evidence that any other nations had that custom. But Israel did. Perhaps Naomi told her, or maybe the poor in neighboring counties knew and even envied the practice. Israel's gleaning customs came from the law of Moses. Leviticus 19:9–10 says, "When you reap the harvest of your land, you shall not reap to the very edges of your field, or gather the gleanings of your harvest. You shall not strip your vineyard bare, or gather the fallen grapes of your vineyard; you shall leave them for the poor and the alien: I am the LORD your God." (See also Deut 24:19.) The word *alien* means non-Israelite, an immigrant or perhaps a slave. The poor were given the right to the leftovers of the harvest. In the case of Ruth, she expected to go behind the reapers and collect what they missed.

Danger and Protection

Ruth's suggestion to glean behind the reapers in Boaz's field includes a detail that heightens the danger for Ruth. She suggests that she glean "among the ears of grain" (Ruth 2:2). The word for "ears of grain" is *shibboleth*.[8] That word alone evokes memories of a bloody civil war between Israelite tribes in the "time when the judges ruled." The war was between the tribes of Ephraim and Gilead. Remember the off-handed description of Elimelech's family as "Ephrathites"? That seemingly insignificant detail may have been included to obliquely echo the story of that civil war. The story goes like this: During the war, the Gileadites controlled the fords of the Jordan River. Whenever one of the Ephraimites wanted to cross over, the text says, the Gileadites asked him to say "Shibboleth," but, being unable to pronounce the *sh* sound, the Ephraimites would say "Sibboleth" (Judg 12:6). This is why *shibboleth* has come into English meaning "password." The Ephraimites had trouble making the *sh* sound, as modern Finns do today. The word was an ethnic identity marker. In this civil war, saying that word wrong had bloody consequences. We read that if the Ephraimite soldier could not say "shibboleth," the Gileadites would kill him. The author says forty-two thousand of the Ephraimites died there (Judg 12:6). When Ruth suggests she gleans to collect the "shibboleths" (*shibbolim* is the Hebrew masculine plural) the original Israelite reader shudders. Being an ethnic outsider, as was "Ruth the Moabite," could have lethal consequences.

8. BDB, s.v. "שִׁבֹּלֶת."

Moabites, like Ammonites, had a history with ancient Israel that stayed with them. Deuteronomy, part of the law of Moses, holds them guilty of two unforgivable crimes. Moses says, speaking in the LORD's name,

> No Ammonite or Moabite shall be admitted to the assembly of the LORD. Even to the tenth generation, none of their descendants shall be admitted to the assembly of the LORD because they did not meet you with food and water on your journey out of Egypt, and because they hired against you Balaam . . . to curse you. You shall never promote their welfare or their prosperity as long as you live." (Deut 23:3–6)

Both crimes occurred when, according to the narrative, the tribes of Israel were making their way toward and into the land of Canaan, passing through neighboring lands on the way. They would typically ask for water and food to buy as they went. But the Ammonites had refused them and came out to fight them. Apparently, the Moabites were held guilty of the same crime, although the story in Num 20 says nothing about their participation in refusing support or fighting. But once having joined the two in common memory, they were both severely penalized in perpetuity.

The second crime Moses found the Moabites guilty of was hiring a soothsayer named Balaam to curse the Israelites. In the ancient world people believed that curses contained spiritual power. They took them with utter seriousness. So when, as Num 22 recounts, the Moabites, out of fear of the Israelites, hired Balaam to curse them, they were guilty of a grave offense. As the story goes, Balaam accepted their payment and tried to curse the Israelites several times from Mount Peor, but the LORD turned his curses into blessings. Nevertheless, the Moabites intended the curse, so they were perpetually guilty.

Moses only mentions these two crimes, but the Israelites held the Moabites guilty of a third infraction: the events at the "Baal of Peor." This, too, took place during the wilderness period. There was a shrine to the Canaanite fertility god "Baal" (literally "lord" or "master")[9] on Mount Peor in Moab. The region is called Shittim, meaning "acacia trees."[10] Numbers 25:1–3 says, "While Israel was staying at Shittim, the people began to have sexual relations with the women of Moab. These invited the people to the sacrifices of their gods, and the people ate and bowed down to their gods. Thus Israel yoked itself to the Baal of Peor, and the LORD's anger was kindled against Israel." The Moabites were held guilty of seducing the Israelites into both sexual indiscretion and idolatry. The sexual nature of this infraction sets

9. BDB, s.v. "בָּעַל."

10. Bush, *Ruth/Esther*, 297.

the stage for the ambiguity around what Ruth did later when she showed up surreptitiously and freshly bathed on the threshing floor where Boaz, after feasting and drinking, lay sleeping. What would you expect a Moabite to do to ingratiate herself to this powerful man in that situation? Merely uncover his feet? The author has clouded the scene in ambiguity and possible double entendre, leaving the Israelite reader, wary of the ways of Moabite women, to wonder.

Now we can better understand why Ruth's Moabite ancestry is so important to the story. The Israelites had a bone to pick with the Moabites, one carried with them for hundreds of years and into exile in Babylon (Neh 13:1). An unprotected female Moabite may have been a target. Naomi understood the danger. After Ruth returned from the first day of gleaning, she met Boaz, who was impressed with her and sent her home with a load of grain. Naomi advised Ruth to avoid the male harvesters in preparation for her return to glean again. She said it would be better that Ruth stay with Boaz's young women, otherwise she might be molested (Ruth 2:22). Boaz, too, understood the danger: "Then Boaz told Ruth, 'Now listen, my daughter, do not go to glean in another field or leave this one, but keep close to my young women'" (Ruth 2:8).

Boaz the Redeemer

After the nighttime meeting at the threshing floor, Ruth asks Boaz to spread his cloak (or wing) over her, which he interprets as a marriage proposal. Ruth explains her request by saying, "for [or, indeed] you are next-of-kin [or redeemer]" (Ruth 3:9). There is a provision in the law of Moses for the next-of-kin to intervene on behalf of his relative to buy back or "redeem" land they have had to sell because they have "fallen into difficulty" (Lev 25:25). If a near relative redeems your land in this way, they would be called your redeemer. Land redemption carries with it no obligation to marry. Ruth makes two requests to Boaz: that they marry and that he act to redeem Naomi's family land. Boaz is ready to comply with both requests. The marriage is his decision to make, but the right of land redemption has one complication. Boaz is aware that a man who is an even closer relative of Elimelech has the right of first refusal. So the two men met at the city gate, where legal questions were settled in front of responsible witnesses.

Boaz informs the next of kin that the land is available to be redeemed and gives him the opportunity to buy it. The man accepts and says he will buy (redeem) the land. However, it appears that Boaz wants to marry Ruth and redeem the family's land, so he employs a strategy to discourage the next of kin from accepting his right of redemption. What he says to the man is, however, not clear.

Mr. What's-His-Name and Boaz

Over the centuries, when rabbis discovered written texts they believed needed to be corrected, they added marginal notes to indicate how the text was to be read aloud in the synagogue. Their respect for the written text was so high that they did not feel comfortable correcting it, but preferred to make their suggested corrections in the margins. This is known as the distinction between what is written (*ketiv*) and what is to be read (*qere*) in the synagogue.[11] According to the marginal note's correction added to Ruth 4:5 (which is followed by many modern translations), Boaz says to the next-of-kin, "The day you acquire the field from the hand of Naomi, *you* are also acquiring Ruth the Moabite, the widow of the dead man, to maintain the dead man's name on his inheritance." The legal rationale for that statement has been significantly debated. Alternatively, if we take the uncorrected written text, Boaz says, "The day you acquire the field from the hand of Naomi, *I am* acquiring Ruth the Moabite, the widow of the dead man, to maintain the dead man's name on his inheritance." That makes perfect sense. Boaz announces that whoever buys the land, he intends to marry Ruth. The children of that marriage would then inherit the land. This makes the unnamed next-of-kin decline the offer, clearing the way for Boaz to redeem it.

The fact that this next-of-kin is unnamed is significant. When Boaz first met him at the gate, many of our English texts has him saying, "'Come over, friend; sit down here.' And he went over and sat down" (Ruth 4:1). But he did not call him "friend" in Hebrew, but rather a nonsense rhyming name "peloni almoni,"[12] used when a person's identity is deliberately concealed, just as we might say "John Doe." Every other character in the book of Ruth has a name heavy with significance. That the next-of-kin—a man who did not want to redeem his near relative's land for her benefit—has a name lost to history is telling.

But something is missing from this whole negotiation. At no time does anyone raise the objection that a good Jewish man like Boaz should marry a foreigner, especially a despised Moabite. In the law of Moses, foreign marriages were strictly forbidden (Deut 7:1–4). It was taken for granted by that law that foreign women would do what the Moabite women did to the

11. Bush, *Ruth/Esther*, 297; Linafelt, "Ruth," 68.

12. Bush, *Ruth/Esther*, 297; Linafelt, "Ruth," 65.

Jewish men at Mount Peor: seduce them to bow down to Baal, thus committing idolatry. We notice that Ruth's ethnicity is yet again emphasized. It is almost as if "the Moabite" has become her last name. She wears her foreignness publicly and constantly. No one, however, objects to the marriage. Ruth is a widow, along with her sister, and both of them had married Jewish men. The narrator passes over the religious illegality of those marriages without a moment's hesitation.

The final irony of this forbidden interethnic marriage is that it produces a son, who the women of the town named Obed (worshiper).[13] Obed had a son named Jesse, who had a son named David, who became Israel's greatest king. So it is that David, the greatest king of Israel, has a Moabite grandmother. This datum was not suppressed as shameful but remembered in the Jewish tradition, probably because it was written up in the book of Ruth. The memory of this union was known all the way up to the time of Matthew's Gospel, whose genealogy of Jesus includes the same information: "And Salmon the father of Boaz by Rahab, and Boaz the father of Obed by Ruth, and Obed the father of Jesse, and Jesse the father of King David" (Matt 1:5–6).

Subversive Ruth

The book of Ruth subverts the nationalist perspective of resentment and hostility toward foreigners at every turn. The Jewish written tradition kept the historical memory of their reasons for hating the Moabites very much alive: the sexual and religious seduction at Mount Peor, the withholding of food and water as they were entering the land, the hiring of Balaam to curse them. Despite all this—and despite the law against marrying foreigners and the law forbidding Moabites from the temple in perpetuity—this Moabite woman saves the whole Davidic line from extinction. According to the Hebrew Bible, David would go on to unite the twelve-tribe confederacy into a cohesive nation capable of defending itself against attack. David's life, however, was complicated, to say the least. His affair with Bathsheba and the arranged murder of her husband was not its finest hour. Nor was the rebellion of his son Absalom that nearly ended his monarchy. Perhaps this story, set in the days when there was "no king in Israel, and everyone did what was right in their own eyes," is a cautionary tale about what to wish for. Some people in those days, like Boaz, did the right thing, even without a king. Maybe "God is my king" was not just the meaning of Elimelech's name but also the manner in which Boaz lived. Boaz embraced a foreigner who

13. BDB, s.v. "עוֹבֵד."

was not a member of the chosen people and praised her for her willingness to put herself at great risk for the sake of her mother-in-law Naomi, whose life ended up being pleasant after all. If, after everything, even Moabites can be included as essential to the story of Israel, then it must be clear that God's purposes include all the families of the earth, as the promise to Abraham affirmed.

8

Jonah and the Assyrian Mission

THERE IS NO WHALE in the story of Jonah. The text calls the beast that swallowed the prophet a "large fish" (Jonah 1:17). That is one example of how the story we were read in our children's Bible storybooks diverges from the Bible's version. The children's version misses the point of the story by a large margin. We will examine the story carefully to understand the message we are meant to take away from it. This is not a happy story of the miraculous rescue of a reluctant prophet and the happy salvation of a nation. This is a tragedy about a man who completely misunderstood the God he was sent to proclaim. If you have not recently read the story, now would be a good time to pause and take it in. It's four short chapters that can be read quickly. In brief, God called Jonah, an Israelite prophet, to preach to the people of the city of Nineveh, which was eventually famous as the capital of Assyria, a hated enemy nation. Jonah, instead, books passage on a ship bound for Tarshish—in the opposite direction. But a huge storm at sea prompts the non-Israelite sailors to interrogate Jonah, who admits he is the cause of the storm, as he is running from God. He asks them to throw him overboard, which, reluctantly, they eventually agree to, and the storm subsides. Instead of death by drowning, Jonah is swallowed by a large fish, from which he authors a poetic plea for deliverance. The fish deposits him alive on shore, where God repeats his call to go to Nineveh to preach a message of impending judgment. When the king of Nineveh hears of it, he orders all the people and animals to repent by fasting and wearing sackcloth. God saw it and relented from his planned judgment. Jonah, meanwhile, went out to wait and watch for the announced calamity, but when it did not come, he was angry. God confronted Jonah's anger and gave him an object lesson to try to teach him about mercy. In the end, we never hear of Jonah's conversion. We are left to assume he remained a frustrated bigot.

Perhaps it is saying too much to suggest that Jonah completely misunderstood God. It would be more faithful to the Bible's witness to say that Jonah partially misunderstood God, because different biblical authors emphasize different aspects of God's character. The book of Jonah, which describes the mercy of God, now sits between the books of Obadiah and Nahum, both of which celebrate in graphic detail the wrath of God against his enemies—that is, against Israel's enemies; they are one and the same. Obadiah celebrates the destruction of Edom. "[The Israelites] shall burn them [the Edomites] and consume them, and there shall be no survivor" (Obad 1:18). Nahum delights in the annihilation of Nineveh: "I am against you, says the Lord of hosts, and will lift up your skirts over your face; and I will let nations look on your nakedness and kingdoms on your shame" (Nah 3:5). There is then a wrath-mercy-wrath sandwich in these three short little books. The conclusion that "mercy triumphs over judgment" (Jas 2:13) is still a long way off. In any case, the author of the story of Jonah was pointing in that direction, not in the form of a theological assertion, as in James, but in narrative form. Jonah would rather have Obadiah and Nahum's kind of wrathful God. But that characterization would be at least incomplete, according to Jonah's anonymous author.

Who Was Jonah ben Amittai?

Jonah ben (literally "son of") Amittai, according to the narrative, was a prophet whom God called to go to the city of Nineveh in Assyria to announce impending judgment. Who was Jonah? We do not know much about him. In 2 Kgs 14:25 we read of a person named Jonah ben Amittai who prophesied about the coming enlargement of northern Israel under King Jeroboam II (793–753 BCE). Otherwise, nothing is known of him. If this is the same Jonah, then he lived many years before the nation of Assyria attacked the northern kingdom of Israel and carted off the survivors into exile, never to be heard from again. The character Jonah has such animus toward Assyria, represented by the city of Nineveh, that it seems to many that the author lived after that calamity. Nineveh was both the capital of Assyria and a symbol of its power, but not until the reign of Sennacherib (705–681 BCE), which was long after the conquest of Israel in 722 BCE. Perhaps the author lived after those days? He clearly expected his readers to understand Jonah's hard feelings against the Ninevites and probably to sympathize with them. Why, then, would the author make the main character Jonah, when

Jonah ben Amittai lived long before the Assyrian conquest? Some suggest that his gleeful prophecy of Israelite territorial expansion pointed to his character as an Israelite nationalist. This sort of person would not have been happy to see a foreign nation get a reprieve from God's judgment. That hypothesis seems as good as any, but we will never be certain.

Jonah's name can mean either "dove" or "oppressiveness."[1] Is it meant to be symbolic? A dove, as a symbol of the nation, was a notoriously fickle bird, according to Hosea 11:11, flitting back and forth between Assyria and Egypt. Jerusalem is accused of being an "oppressive" (same word) city whose "prophets are reckless, faithless persons" (Zeph 3:1, 4). Perhaps both meanings are intended to produce a double entendre. Jonah is a fickle prophet who faithlessly runs from his call in the beginning and who resents God's mercy in the end.

The narrative itself is told with some literary artistry. Scholars have noted the elements of parody and satire in the story. It opens with a storm at sea during which pagan sailors desperately try to save the life of Jonah, crying out to the God that Jonah is attempting to avoid, and making vows and sacrifices to Yahweh. The satire is comical at times. At the command of the king of Nineveh, the people were to repent by fasting and wearing sackcloth, the symbol of mournful repentance. The king also commanded them to make the animals fast and wear sackcloth. Readers are meant to picture a comic scene of shepherds running frantically around to try to prevent rag-wearing sheep, goats, and cattle from grazing. There are fantastic elements, like the whole episode of being swallowed by the fish and delivered to a safe shore. And, in the middle of the book, we find Jonah's prayer of repentance, apparently composed during his time inside the large fish, in structured Hebrew poetry. A magical plant grows up in a day to shade Jonah, then dies as quickly. These and other elements suggest that this story is not a literal, historical narrative, but rather a parable, similar to the ones Jesus told. Readers are free to make up their minds about that.

Jonah's Decent

Though the children's storybook version is a happy story, the book as we have it tells a tale of descent into darkness. The story begins in the daytime on dry land as God calls Jonah to go to the great city of Nineveh, to announce God's judgment against it because "their wickedness had come to God's attention" (Jonah 1:2). You would think that an Israelite prophet might enjoy an assignment to announce judgment on his enemies, but getting that close

1. Sweeney, *Twelve Prophets*, 361.

to *those* people is too much for Jonah, who goes "down" to Joppa. He found a ship and not only "went on board" as the NRSV says (Jonah 1:3) in English, but literally went "down" into the ship. The word appears again as Jonah goes "down into the hold of the ship" (Jonah 1:5). Without saying "down," we read that Jonah sinks further into sleep. After he admits his downward spiritual path as a prophet who refused his divine call, the downward direction continues. The desperate sailors throw him overboard to sink into the sea. His prayer for deliverance depicts him as sinking all the way down to the "roots of the mountains . . . down to the land whose bars closed upon me forever" (Jonah 2:6), at the bottom of the dark, watery world. You literally cannot get any lower or darker than that.

Ethnic Identity

Ethnic identity plays a big role in this story from the start. The ship on which Jonah attempted to run from God was piloted by non-Israelite sailors. They are not worshippers of Israel's God, Yahweh. In fact, as the storm at sea intensified, the sailors were afraid, and each prayed panicked prayers to their respective gods (Jonah 1:5). They each had their gods to pray to. They assumed Jonah might have his own God to pray to as well, and when they found him asleep in the storm, the captain said to him, "What are you doing sound asleep? Get up, call on your god! Perhaps the god will spare us a thought so that we do not perish" (Jonah 1:6). Polytheists can be all-inclusive when it comes to gods.

Though they were pagans from an Israelite perspective, they were highly moral. Believing, as most people in the ancient world did, that a god causes all events, they decided to cast lots to see who was responsible for bringing the storm. The lot fell to Jonah. They interrogated him, saying, "Tell us why this calamity has come upon us. What is your occupation? Where do you come from? What is your country? And of what people are you?" (Jonah 1:8). The author wants us to know that ethnicity is a significant concern for them. And yet, will it determine their actions toward Jonah? We will see.

His answer was interesting, and we will get to it in a minute. In short, Jonah admitted he was the cause of the storm and suggested that they throw him overboard. However, it is essential to consider what the sailors did and did not do when they heard his story. They did not just say, "Oh well, what are you going to do with these foreigners? Toss him over and be done with it." Instead, wishing to avoid taking a human life, no matter of what ethnic origin, the men rowed all the harder to try to get the ship back to land. Their noble efforts were in vain. The storm only grew worse (Jonah 1:12). Even pagans valued the significance of human life. They had no wish to take a life, even one whose presence threatened their own. The author paints a word picture of people who are not chosen, not children of Abraham, and have never heard a word of the law of Moses, yet they maintain a high moral standard regarding the value of every human life. Jonah, by contrast, having been instructed in the law of Moses, even a prophet whose profession it is to speak the words of Yahweh, does not, disappointingly, value all human life in the same way. He longs for the destruction of life that he prophesied.

The situation on board the ship in the storm was desperate and worsening. The sailors finally concluded that Jonah's God, Yahweh, had sent the storm to punish him, and that Yahweh alone could reverse it. So they cried out to Jonah's God that he not punish them for fulfilling Jonah's wish; after all, they acknowledged that Yahweh had put them in this predicament by "hurling" a storm against them. They prayed, "Do not make us guilty of innocent blood; for you, O Lord, have done as it pleased you" (Jonah 1:14). So they "hurled" Jonah into the sea. "Then the men feared the Lord even more, and they offered a sacrifice to the Lord and made vows" (Jonah 1:16). Notice they were first called sailors. Now they are called men, sharing a common humanity with the Israelite prophet.

Returning to the way Jonah answered the sailor's interrogation about who he was, what he did, and his ethnicity, Jonah said he was a Hebrew (Jonah 1:9). Jonah ben Amittai was a prophet of Israel, so he could have said, "I am an Israelite." You may recall that, according to the biblical narrative, after King Solomon's death the nation split into two and never reunited. From then on, the northern ten tribes retained the name "Israel," while the two remaining tribes eventually became known as "Judah" (the twelfth tribe, Benjamin, was absorbed by Judah), from which the name "Jew" originates. In 722 BCE, many years after the time of Jonah ben Amittai, the northern kingdom of Israel was attacked and conquered by the nation of Assyria, which had made Nineveh its capital. Those northerners never recovered. They were lost to history. Their Judean (or Jewish) brothers to the south were nearly wiped out also, but they escaped by the skin of their teeth when the Assyrians left off conquering them to deal with trouble back home. We can imagine how the Judeans must have felt about the Assyrians after all that. Hatred would not be an overstatement. The Jonah of this story similarly hated the Assyrians of Nineveh and wanted nothing more than the judgment he had proclaimed against them. That is one strong reason for thinking that the story was written long after the time of Jonah ben Amittai, after the horrors of 722 BCE. The author assumes that his readers shared Jonah's animosity toward Assyrians.

The name "Hebrew" is full of possibilities. It could merely come from their ancestor Eber (Gen 10:21). "Eber" means "one who crossed boundaries,"[2] which is interesting, given the fact that the nation became a nation by crossing the boundary of the Red Sea from Egypt, and then crossing the Jordan river into the promised land of Canaan. A compelling question of this story is whether they can also cross ethnic boundaries and embrace people as humans who are not descended from Abraham and Eber. Ironically, the non-Israelite sailors seemed to have been able to put ethnicity aside in their concern for Jonah's life. Will Jonah cross the boundary and value the lives of Assyrians whom God has forgiven? That is the question the story leaves dangling.

Jonah in Nineveh

After the large fish that God designated, or appointed, swallows Jonah and spits him out on shore, God calls Jonah a second time. This time Jonah obeys the call. He goes to Nineveh, that "great city," and proclaims that in forty days, Nineveh would be overthrown (Jonah 3:4). Ironically, the pagan Assyrians "believed God; they proclaimed a fast, and everyone, great and small, put on sackcloth" (Jonah 3:5). That is, they repented. This was first a people's movement. They were sincere. When news reached the king, he, too, repented and decreed, a bit late to the game, that they should all do what they were already doing, and that the animals too should fast and don sackcloth, as silly as that sounds. He told them, "All shall turn from their evil ways and from the violence that is in their hands" (Jonah 3:8). After 722 BCE, violence was what Assyrians were best known for, especially to the Hebrews of the Southern Kingdom.

The king then revealed his motive for commanding repentance, saying, "Who knows? God may relent and change his mind; he may turn from his fierce anger, so that we do not perish" (Jonah 3:9). The king of Assyria would not have read a copy of Torah, the Hebrew Bible, so he could not have known what every Israelite knew about God. It was what Jonah knew as well and said explicitly to God, "You are a gracious God and merciful, slow to anger, and abounding in steadfast love, and ready to relent from punishing" (Jonah 4:2).

This description of God, in one form or another, occurs at least ten times in the Hebrew Bible and is alluded to in many other places as well. It has achieved almost the status of a creed according to Hebrew Bible scholars. In other words, every Israelite knows that God has several characteristics. God

2. BDB, s.v. "עָבַר."

can be both judgmental and merciful. God's mercy is appealed to over and over by the Israelites who are experiencing hardship, difficulty, and danger. They cry out to God for help, and remind God of God's self-description. On Mount Sinai, God appeared to Moses "in the cloud" (Exod 34:5) and revealed himself. The text says,

> The Lord passed before him, and proclaimed,
> "The Lord, the Lord,
> a God merciful and gracious,
> slow to anger,
> and abounding in steadfast love and faithfulness,
> keeping steadfast love for the thousandth generation,
> forgiving iniquity and transgression and sin,
> yet by no means clearing the guilty,
> but visiting the iniquity of the parents
> upon the children
> and the children's children,
> to the third and the fourth generation." (Exod 34:6–7)

Here, God included both of his characteristics of judgment and mercy. But sometimes, when this foundational text is cited, mercy seems to triumph over justice, as in Ps 145:8–9, which says,

> The Lord is gracious and merciful,
> slow to anger and abounding in steadfast love.
> The Lord is good to all,
> and his compassion is over all that he has made.

This psalm recounts God's characteristic of mercy but leaves out the judgment. Interestingly, this is the form Jonah cites as he watches the judgment fail to arrive against his enemies, the Assyrians of Nineveh. After his proclamation of impending doom, Jonah "went out of the city and sat down east of the city, and made a booth for himself there. He sat under it in the shade, waiting to see what would become of the city" (Jonah 4:4). When judgment did not come, the text says, Jonah became angry (Jonah 4:1). In his anger he lashed out against Yahweh: "He prayed to the Lord and said, 'O Lord! Is not this what I said while I was still in my own country? That is why I fled to Tarshish at the beginning; for I knew that you are a gracious God and merciful, slow to anger, and abounding in steadfast love, and ready to relent from punishing'" (Jonah 4:2–3). Jonah and all those who read the Hebrew Bible knew that it is in God's prerogative to be merciful, even after threatening judgment. Moses several times pleaded with God to relent from punishing the people, and sometimes God "repented" (KJV) or "changed his mind" (NRSV) about punishing his people (e.g., Exod 32:14).

Jonah knew that God had the capacity to show mercy, and that is what he feared the most. He wanted his enemies to experience God's wrath. The author, probably having known of the Assyrian invasion of Israel in 722 BCE and the total destruction of their relatives, presents a reluctant prophet who had no intention of forgiving their enemies and who did not want God to, either. How deep does such animus go? Jonah ended his screed against God like Job, cursing his own life. "And now, O LORD, please take my life from me, for it is better for me to die than to live" (Jonah 4:3). That is the ultimate absurdity of nationalistic bigotry. In the end, death is preferable to life if living includes embracing the "other."

An Object Lesson

You may think that God would have had it with this prophet, who, after running from him, accused him of malfeasance. However, this merciful God wanted to help Jonah evolve ethically, morally, and spiritually, so he prepared an object lesson for him. Jonah has gone out of the city to wait for its demise under a "booth," or temporary shelter, probably made of cloth. It is a shelter, to some degree, but it is no match for the Middle Eastern sun as it beats down in the middle of the day.

God's object lesson involved a fast-growing vine or bush of some kind (its variety is undetermined), a plant-killing worm, and a hot wind. God is described as the one who "designated" (or "appointed") a bush, a wind, and a worm—just as he had previously "appointed" the "large fish" to do his bidding.

Here is how the lesson begins: "The LORD God appointed a bush, and made it come up over Jonah, to give shade over his head, to save him from his discomfort; so Jonah was very happy about the bush" (Jonah 4:6). Jonah is self-absorbed. His concern is solely for his own well-being.

The lesson continues. "But when dawn came up the next day, God appointed a worm that attacked the bush, so that it withered. When the sun rose, God prepared a sultry east wind, and the sun beat down on the head of Jonah so that he was faint and asked that he might die." He said that it would be better for him to die right then and there (Jonah 4:7–8). This is Jonah's second death wish. The first was when he asked the sailors to throw him overboard. There will be a third. To curse one's own life—to despise the precious gift of life—is a slap in the face of the God who breathed life-giving oxygen into the original earthlings on the sixth day of creation. God would have been justified at this point in bringing his wrath down on Jonah. But the God who defined himself as "a God merciful and gracious, slow to anger, and abounding in steadfast love and faithfulness" (Exod 34:6) shows mercy to Jonah yet again.

God engaged Jonah in a dialogue about the bush, hoping the object lesson would sink in. Here is the dialogue: "But God said to Jonah, 'Is it right for you to be angry about the bush?' And he said, 'Yes, angry enough to die'" (Jonah 4:9).

Jonah is not getting it, so God makes the meaning of the object lesson explicit: "Then the LORD said, 'You are concerned about the bush, for which you did not labor and which you did not grow; it came into being in a night and perished in a night. And should I not be concerned about Nineveh, that great city, in which there are more than a hundred and twenty thousand persons who do not know their right hand from their left, and also many animals?'" (Jonah 4:10–11).

That was Jonah's third repetition of his death wish. The lesson was about concern. Jonah could be very concerned, but only about himself. God, in contrast, was trying to show why his concern for all of life, including the Assyrians of Nineveh, was justified. Unlike Jonah, who did nothing to grow the bush, God is the maker of every person in his image and likeness. God even takes into consideration the enormity of damage against humans that the destruction of such a great city would be. He is even concerned for the welfare of all those repentant animals. God's concern is for all the families of the earth, as his promise to Abraham indicated. To heighten his reasons for compassion, God is even able to take into account the fact that the Ninevites have had no prior knowledge of God or the Torah or what repentance entails. To God, they are the equivalent of ignorant children who do not yet even "know their right hand from their left" (Jonah 4:11). God's concluding question, "Should I not be concerned?" (Jonah 4:11) is an indictment. Yes, God should be concerned. And so, by implication, should Jonah.

That is where the story ends. The last time we heard from Jonah, he was a miserable nationalist who wanted nothing more than the annihilation of his nation's hated enemy. Though God mercifully spared his life, and though Jonah knows God's characteristic of mercy and forgiveness, his nationalistic fervor has left him a person who wants to argue that God should not be God. This is a tragedy. It is like the tragedy of all of those who, in the name of nationalism, are unable or unwilling to understand that God's concern is for all the families of the earth. The Assyrians were eventually conquered by a coalition of the Babylonians and the Medes in the seventh century BCE; however, northern Israel never recovered from the damage they suffered in 722 BCE. The Babylonians were subsequently conquered by the Persians, who allowed the exiled Judeans to return to Judah and rebuild their homeland. The chosen people were back in their land. The tension between God's particular care for his chosen people and his broader concern for all the families of the earth continues, lesson after lesson.

9

"My Name Shall Be Great in All the Earth"

God's particular choice to bless the family that descended from Abraham and his desire to bless all the families of the earth is one of several tensions that run through the Hebrew Bible, or Old Testament. For example, we have just seen the way the book of Jonah explores the unresolved tension between God's judgment and God's mercy. Another tension is that Yahweh is the God of Israel but is also the God of the entire world. In the ancient world people generally understood that gods were local. Each people or nation had their own god or set of gods. They were expected to take up the cause of their nation in defense and to provide for its fertility.

Yahweh, according to the Bible, is both a national God whom the people of Israel worshiped and the Creator of every human being in his image. The creation story in Gen 1 was not the first story written, but it takes pride of place in the current order of books, or the "canon," so that we read the entire Bible with an understanding of God's global character. As the God of the entire earth, the authors of the Bible often worry about God's reputation beyond the borders of Israel. We will look at several of these texts. They are all written by the people who descended from Abraham for the people who descended from Abraham. However, remarkably, the authors seem to assume that their fellow Israelites, who received these texts, would share their concern. It would be terrible if the God of all creation got a bad reputation among the nations that Israel interacted with. For monotheists, the God of the whole world, unlike national or tribal gods, had an international reputation to be protected.

Malachi

We will begin with the prophet Malachi, whose name means "My (God's) messenger."[1] Malachi started his prophetic book by announcing God's involvement in elevating Jacob, meaning Israel, over Esau, meaning Edom. The result of that divine intervention on the international stage would be that God would be known internationally: "Great is the LORD beyond the borders of Israel!" (Mal 1:5). God's reputation was crucial because the God of Israel was the God of the world. This theme will be developed further as we will see.

Malachi lived during the post-exilic period. That means that he lived during the time in which the Jewish community, which had been living in exile in Babylon for decades, had now returned. They say that an expectation is a disappointment waiting to happen. The returnees were a disappointed group of people. They had high expectations about what a return to the land would be like, but they were not coming true. Had God let them down?

Jeremiah

They came by their high expectations honestly. As miserable as it must have been to live as an exile, after seventy years or so, people got settled. If they heeded the advice of Jeremiah, given in his letter to the exiles in Babylon, then they were indeed settled. Jeremiah wrote,

> Thus says the LORD [Yahweh] of hosts, the God of Israel, to all the exiles whom I have sent into exile from Jerusalem to Babylon: Build houses and live in them; plant gardens and eat what they produce. Take wives and have sons and daughters; take wives for your sons, and give your daughters in marriage, that they may bear sons and daughters; multiply there, and do not decrease. But seek the welfare [shalom] of the city where I have sent you into exile, and pray to the LORD on its behalf, for in its welfare [shalom] you will find your welfare [shalom]. (Jer 20:4–7)

If you are Jeremiah, how do you get people whom you have encouraged to settle in to want to make the arduous journey back and start over? Jeremiah's solution was to prophesy that the return would be glorious days of restored prosperity (Jer 30:1). They would live lives of security and peace without fear of enemy attack (Jer 30:10). Their captors, the Babylonians, would fall to defeat because God was uniquely "with" his people. "For I am

1. Ross, *Malachi Then and Now*, 55.

with you, says the LORD, to save you; I will make an end of all the nations among which I scattered you" (Jer 30:11). Jeremiah pictured the returnees coming back home with singing and radiant faces celebrating abundant harvests of wine and oil. They would be almost like Adam and Eve, living in an abundant garden, dancing and making merry.

> Hear the word of the LORD, O nations,
>   and declare it in the coastlands far away;
> say, "He who scattered Israel will gather him,
>   and will keep him as a shepherd a flock."
> For the LORD [Yahweh] has ransomed Jacob,
>   and has redeemed him from hands too strong for him.
> They shall come and sing aloud on the height of Zion,
>   and they shall be radiant over the goodness of the LORD,
> over the grain, the wine, and the oil,
>   and over the young of the flock and the herd;
> their life shall become like a watered garden,
>   and they shall never languish again.
> Then shall the young women rejoice in the dance,
>   and the young men and the old shall be merry.
> I will turn their mourning into joy,
>   I will comfort them, and give them gladness for sorrow.
> I will give the priests their fill of fatness,
>   and my people shall be satisfied with my bounty,
>   says the LORD. (Jer 31:10–14)

Who would not have high expectations? And Jeremiah was not alone in this effort to coax the exiles to return with promises of abundance. The prophet Isaiah speaks for God, who is encouraging his angelic hosts to help the returning exiles, saying to them, "Comfort, O comfort my people" (Isa 40:1). How should they comfort the exiles? With the promise that even the long journey back would be made easy because "every valley shall be lifted up and every mountain and hill be made low; the uneven ground shall become level, and the rough places a plain" (Isa 40:1–5). Therefore, says Isaiah, get going! "Go out from Babylon, flee from Chaldea [Babylon], declare this with a shout of joy, proclaim it, send it forth to the end of the earth" (Isa 48:20).

Ezekiel

The prophet Ezekiel weighed in as well. He had a dream in which the nation of Israel, in its rump captive state, was like a valley of dry bones. But in his vision God caused the bones to start rattling and coming together, and on the bones sinews and flesh began to appear until God breathed new breath into them and they came alive again. God said to Ezekiel, "These bones are the whole house of Israel. They say, 'Our bones are dried up, and our hope is lost; we are cut off completely.' Therefore, prophesy, and say to them, Thus says the Lord God [Adonai Yahweh]: I am going to open your graves, and bring you up from your graves, O my people; and I will bring you back to the land of Israel" (Ezek 37:11–12). Once back in the land, Ezekiel promised that they would have a new version of the once great King David and that God would "make a covenant of peace with them; it shall be an everlasting covenant with them; and I will bless them and multiply them, and will set my sanctuary among them forevermore. My dwelling place [temple] shall be with them; and I will be their God, and they shall be my people" (Ezek 37:26). And what will the worldwide effect of this regathering be? "Then the nations shall know that I the Lord sanctify Israel, when my sanctuary is among them forevermore" (Ezek 37:26–28). It will be worldwide acknowledgment that Yahweh, Israel's God, had done something magnificent.

Many of the settled exiles made up their minds to travel on foot the 550 miles from Babylon to Jerusalem to return, restart, rebuild, and experience these promised blessings, peace, and prosperity. The experience did not live up to the hype. They did not return to an empty land. When they got there, the locals, called "the people of the land," were not so happy to give way to new arrivals. They resisted their efforts to rebuild. According to Ezra, the people of the land made the returnees discouraged, and even fearful of rebuilding by bribing the officials to thwart their plan (Ezra 4:4–5). The returnees set about the task of rebuilding the wall of Jerusalem and the temple. Nothing was easy, and nothing was grand. In fact, upon seeing the Second Temple, the people's disappointment was palpable. The prophet Haggai asked them, "Who is left among you that saw this house in its former glory? How does it look to you now? Is it not in your sight as nothing?" (Hag 2:3). This Second Temple did not hold a candle to the former Temple of Solomon. The reaction of the religious leaders, upon seeing the new modest temple, was telling: "But many of the priests and Levites and heads of families, old people who had seen the first house on its foundations, wept with a loud voice when they saw this house" (Ezra 3:12).

Sloppy Religion

The expectation-fueled disappointment led to less-than-enthusiastic worship practices. God had, in their eyes, let them down. Malachi took it upon himself to criticize their sloppy observance of religious obligations. The law of Moses specified that animals offered in sacrifice needed to be healthy and whole (Exod 12:5). The quality and value of the sacrifice were directly calibrated to the level of honor it showed. You were only to bring the best sacrifice to honor God; how could you not? But that was not what was happening. Malachi said that God, like a father or the master of slaves, deserves to be honored by his sons and servants. But the priests, instead of honoring God, have despised him. How? "When you offer blind animals in sacrifice, is that not wrong? And when you offer those that are lame or sick, is that not wrong? Try presenting that to your governor; will he be pleased with you or show you favor? says the Lord of hosts" (Mal 1:8). The governor—since Judea was now only a province of Persia, ruled by a governor—let alone God, would not accept such dishonorable sacrifices. God had the right to utterly reject such sacrifices. "Oh, that someone among you would shut the temple doors, so that you would not kindle fire on my altar in vain! I have no pleasure in you, says the Lord of hosts, and I will not accept an offering from your hands" (Mal 1:10).

What was the fire in Malachi's belly? It was that God had an international reputation that was threatened by the dishonorable religious practices of the day. In the following sentence, Malachi says, "For from the rising of the sun to its setting my name is great among the nations . . . says the Lord of hosts" (Mal 1:11). Malachi's criticism of lax religious practices continues for the rest of chapter 1. He takes no prisoners. The rhetoric is brutal: "If you will not listen, . . . I will rebuke your offspring, and spread dung on your faces" (Mal 2:3). The bottom line is summed up as Malachi quotes God directly saying, "I am a great King, says the Lord of hosts, and my name is reverenced among the nations" (Mal 1:14).

Moses

Malachi is not an outlier. Instead, he builds on a tradition that goes back to Moses. According to the book of Exodus, the "Hebrew" people, as they were known during their enslavement in Egypt, cried out to God to relieve them of their suffering. God was known as the particular God of the Hebrews, the one they relied on for liberation. Moses was God's solution. When he confronted Pharaoh, famously saying, "Let my people go" (Exod 5:1), Pharaoh resisted. In response, God brought a series of ten plagues upon the Egyptians: frogs, gnats, flies, boils, and even water turned to blood (Exod 7–9). The point of the plagues was twofold. They were meant to pressure the Pharaoh to let the Hebrew people go, but that was not all. They were also meant to make a point about the scope of God's universal divinity. Notice the tension that the text celebrates between God as the particular God of the Hebrews and God as the universal God of the world, as Yahweh instructs Moses to confront Pharaoh yet again.

> Then the LORD said to Moses, "Rise up early in the morning and present yourself before Pharaoh, and say to him, 'Thus says the LORD, the God of the Hebrews: Let my people go, so that they may worship me. For this time I will send all my plagues upon you yourself, and upon your officials, and upon your people, so that you may know that there is no one like me in all the earth. For by now I could have stretched out my hand and struck you and your people with pestilence, and you would have been cut off from the earth. But this is why I have let you live: to show you my power, and to make my name resound through all the earth.'" (Exod 9:13–16)

The God of the Hebrews, who is in the process of liberating them in particular, wants Pharaoh, the head of the world's one great superpower at the time, to know that "there is no one like me in all the earth." Yahweh is not just one among many tribal-ethnic deities. He is without precedent, the God over all the families of the earth, as the promise to Abraham insisted.

This case is not even unique in Exodus. The plagues finally produced their desired effect, and Pharaoh reluctantly let the Hebrew people go free. They journeyed into the wilderness and camped at the foot of Mount Sinai. Moses went up the mountain to meet with God while the people waited below. It was not a short meeting. The text says Moses delayed his descent (Exod 32:1). How long a delay? We are not told, but long enough for the people waiting below to become impatient. It is hard for us to get our heads around what happened next. This is one example of how historically distant we are from the world of the Bible. Without trying to belabor an explanation, suffice it to say that the people pooled their jewelry and pressured Moses's brother Aaron to make a golden calf for them to worship—a "worship" that involved a lot of scandalous behavior that the Bible cryptically describes this way: "The people sat down to eat and drink, and rose up to revel" (Exod 32:6). A "revel" sounds to us a lot like a rave.

When Moses arrived on the scene, he was not amused. Neither was God. God told Moses, "I have seen this people, how stiff-necked they are. Now let me alone, so that my wrath may burn hot against them and I may consume them" (Exod 32:9). Moses was horrified at this plan. What would have been the point of all those plagues if God were to finish them off then and there? What would have been the point of dividing the waters of the

Red Sea for them to walk into freedom on dry ground? What would become of the promise to Abraham? And most of all, what would the Egyptians think? What would become of God's global reputation?

> But Moses implored the LORD his God, and said, "O LORD, why does your wrath burn hot against your people, whom you brought out of the land of Egypt with great power and with a mighty hand? Why should the Egyptians say, 'It was with evil intent that he brought them out to kill them in the mountains, and to consume them from the face of the earth'? Turn from your fierce wrath; change your mind and do not bring disaster on your people. Remember Abraham . . . how you swore to them by your own self, saying to them, 'I will multiply your descendants like the stars of heaven, and all this land that I have promised I will give to your descendants, and they shall inherit it forever.'" (Exod 32:11–13)

Moses's invocation of the Abrahamic promise was effective: "And the LORD changed his mind about the disaster that he planned to bring on his people" (Exod 32:14). This is one of those remarkable examples of God changing his mind. Part of the motivation for the change, besides the promise to Abraham, was God's global reputation. What would the Egyptians say? It mattered.

That was not the last time Moses had to plead with God not to destroy his people, as we learn in Num 14. When they came at last to the border of the land of Canaan, they sent spies into the land to reconnoiter it. They came back with a bad report (Num 14:36). They said they felt like "grasshoppers" (Num 13:33) compared to the mighty Canaanites. This made the people panic. How could they have come all this way to die by the sword? Rebellion ensued. They were ready to stone Moses and Aaron to death, select a new leader, and head back to Egypt. Moses went to God about it, but God was ready to give up on them. God said to Moses, "How long will this people despise me? And how long will they refuse to believe in me, in spite of all the signs that I have done among them? I will strike them with pestilence and disinherit them" (Num 14:11–12).

Moses's reaction was like before; he appeals to God, not so much on humanitarian grounds, but based on the damage that would be done to God's reputation among the Egyptians and "the nations"—that is, God's global reputation.

> Moses said to the LORD, "Then the Egyptians will hear of it, for in your might you brought up this people from among them, and they will tell the inhabitants of this land. . . . Now if you

> kill this people all at one time, then the nations who have heard about you will say, 'It is because the LORD was not able to bring these people into the land he swore to give them that he has slaughtered them in the wilderness.'" (Num 14:13–15)

Moses then invokes the same formula that Jonah quoted to supply even more motivation for God to relent and show mercy. Moses said,

> And now, therefore, let the power of the LORD be great in the way that you promised when you spoke, saying,
> "The LORD is slow to anger,
> and abounding in steadfast love,
> forgiving iniquity and transgression,
> but by no means clearing the guilty,
> visiting the iniquity of the parents
> upon the children
> to the third and the fourth generation."
> Forgive the iniquity of this people according to the greatness of your steadfast love, just as you have pardoned this people, from Egypt even until now. (Num 14:17–19)

God relented, the people survived, and God's global reputation was preserved intact.

These are only a few examples of the tension that the biblical text celebrates between God's particular care for his chosen people and God's concern that his reputation as the God of the world remain unblemished. Here's a quick roundup of a few more examples.

Persistent Concern for God's Reputation

When Moses gave the Law, or Torah, to the people, he had an eye on how their obedience would be perceived by "the peoples," or nations, around them. Moses said, "You must observe [these statutes] diligently, for this will show your wisdom and discernment to the peoples, who, when they hear all these statutes, will say, 'Surely this great nation is a wise and discerning people!'" (Deut 4:5–6).

We all have heard the story of how the young David killed the giant Goliath with his slingshot. The Philistine army faced off against the Israelite army under King Saul. For days, they were frozen in place. The Philistines had suggested that instead of a whole-army battle, they should have a battle between two representative champions. They put up their giant. But Israel had no equivalent giant champion. Day after day, Goliath would go out and taunt the Israelites. When young David finally persuaded King Saul to allow him to be Israel's champion, Goliath, feeling insulted that a mere boy should come out against him, "cursed David by his gods" (1 Sam 17:44). David replied with his taunts, predicting that he would successfully kill the giant (let's leave the specific graphic description out of it), "so that all the earth may know that there is a God in Israel" (1 Sam 17:46). Goliath had cursed David by his God, Yahweh, so David wanted to ensure that God's reputation before "all the earth" would remain unsullied. The tension is again on full display. Yahweh will help his particular chosen people, but his global reputation will be established.

When David's son Solomon succeeded him as king, he began a series of monumental architectural projects, according to 1 Kings, that included building a magnificent temple in Jerusalem. When it was finally completed it was a wonder. Solomon led the dedication of the temple, which included a long prayer of consecration. Solomon predicted that the glory and fame of this temple would attract people from foreign lands to come and pray to the God this temple was meant to house. Only Solomon, in his prayer, was careful to acknowledge that God could not be contained in any temple, no matter how grand. In his prayer, he repeated seven times that no building could house God, with sentences like this: "But will God indeed dwell on the earth? Even heaven and the highest heaven cannot contain you, much less this house that I have built!" (1 Kgs 8:27). God's name would dwell there, if not God, per se. Nonetheless, foreigners, most of whom were probably polytheists, would want to come and pray, most likely imagining that Yahweh, like their own gods, was present in the temple. Solomon thought that would be fitting, because it would help establish God's global fame. He prayed, "When a foreigner . . . comes and prays toward this house, then hear in heaven . . . so that all the peoples of the earth may know your name and fear you" (1 Kgs 8:41–43).

The psalmist said, "May God be gracious to us . . . that your way may be known on earth, your saving power among all nations" (Ps 67:1–2).

The prophet Isaiah said, in the name of God, "Turn to me and be saved, all the ends of the earth! For I am God, and there is no other" (Isa 45:22–23).

The prophet Ezekiel could even say that God's saving acts on behalf of his chosen people had a deeper purpose with global implications. "But I acted for the sake of my name, that it should not be profaned in the sight of the nations" (Ezek 20:9), and, "It is not for your sake . . . that I am about to act, but for the sake of my holy name. . . . I will vindicate the holiness of my great name . . . then the nations will know that I am the LORD" (Ezek 36:22–23).

All of these texts illustrate that God's concern for his reputation in the entire world was not a minor sidenote, but a continually repeated theme. There remains an unresolved—because unresolvable—tension: yes, Yahweh is Israel's God. Yahweh is their God and they are his people in a particular way. Nevertheless, Yahweh is the Creator God, the maker of heaven and earth and of every person in God's image. Therefore, it is never enough to say that Yahweh is Israel's God and leave it there. It must also be said that Yahweh is always the God of all the families of the earth, whether they know it or not. But they should know it.

We hear people today claim that America has inherited the status of God's new chosen people. The idea that a modern nation can co-opt that status has no basis in Scripture. The closest it comes is the claim that those who are in Christ by faith have become grafted onto the Israelite vine and have become children of Abraham by faith, not by nationality. We will examine this in more detail later. But even if the idea of being God's chosen were to be granted for the sake of argument, it must also be acknowledged that God has never been and will never be the pet of one nation. God's willingness to bring down judgment on his own chosen people should be enough to dispel any notions that God gives special guarantees to anyone. God chose Abraham and his descendants, calling them to faithful obedience and punishing their disobedience, according to the Bible. Even the status of chosen-ness did not mean automatic privilege if the people became lax or unfaithful. Perhaps those who want to claim a new status as God's chosen should reconsider these implications. God will always be the God of all the families of the earth, with the result that, as he said, "My name shall be great in all the earth."

10

Jeremiah and the Ethiopian

An African proverb says when elephants fight, it is the grass that suffers. In conflicts between the powerful, it is the weak who get hurt. The elephants in this story are the empires of Egypt and Babylon. The grass is Judah. This story is about Judah when the grass was getting trampled by the elephants. Judah was the rump nation that remained standing after the division of the kingdom of Israel between the northern ten tribes and the two southern tribes. After the destruction of northern Israel at the hands of the Assyrians, the tribes of Judah and tiny Benjamin alone were all that remained of Israel. Benjamin was left just a territory in Judah, with Jerusalem as its capital. A map of the Fertile Crescent shows Egypt to the west, Mesopotamia (modern Iraq)—now controlled by the Babylonians (who conquered the Assyrians)—to the northeast, with little Judah sitting vulnerably in between. As Egypt and Babylon competed for regional dominance, Judah, caught in the middle, was a mere distraction.

A mere distraction unless you were Judean—in that case, you were aware of the clash of the elephants to your northeast and west, and you were constantly wondering which to align with against the other. Choose wrong at your peril. But choosing wrong seemed to be what Judah did best.

Enter the prophet Jeremiah. He had an opinion on the matter, and it differed from the king and the leading nobles. King Zedekiah of Judah thought Egypt would end up on top. Jeremiah said Babylon (also called Chaldea) would win. The conflict between these two men and their geopolitical analyses is the central conflict of this story.

This story is about heroism, bravery, and integrity in the context of palace intrigue, mortal danger, and duplicity. Let us set the stage. The

Judeans have been hearing about the steady march of the Babylonians. The Babylonian army has already entered their land, conquering cities, burning, looting, killing, and deporting people as it goes. That was the way of ancient empires.

How did we get here? Jeremiah was born in the last generation of independent Judah, before the Babylonians came. He would live to witness Judah's fall to the Babylonians, the destruction of the temple and the palace, and the deaths of thousands of his fellow Judeans, including King Zedekiah and his sons. He would witness the forced deportation of most of the survivors and their exile into Babylonian captivity. He was to survive that catastrophe, only to be forcibly herded off to Egypt, where we would not hear from him again. That he survived at all depended on the intervention of an African man named Ebed-melech. This is his story.

How do we know Ebed-melech's story at all? Because the descendants of the community that endured the Babylonian defeat and exile remembered Jeremiah's words and deeds. He had, after all, warned that the path that the king and his nobles were taking would end disastrously, as it did. In other words, in what we now call the exilic Jewish community in Babylon and their descendants who were able to return, many considered Jeremiah a prophet. The book of Jeremiah is their record of his words and actions, still regarded as meaningful and relevant, even in exile and after exile. We will see why Jeremiah's message about the end of Judah was still relevant to the exiles and the returnees.

The elephant tumble between Egypt and Babylon had no clear winner at first. Nor is it clear how anyone in a small in-between nation like Judah knew what was going on internationally. There were probably spies, rumors, and reports from traders. But how current could they be? How reliable were they? A caravan carrying news of an army invasion could be weeks, if not months, old by the time word reached Jerusalem. We do not know how Jeremiah or anyone got their information. And yet they knew enough—and more—as the danger grew closer.

The story of Ebed-melech's intervention that saved Jeremiah's life only makes sense in the context of Judah's pitiful plight, sandwiched between the empires of Egypt and Babylon and their struggle for world domination. To simplify the back-and-forth between Egypt and Babylon, with Judah in the middle, it may be helpful to think of it in terms of a stage play in several acts. This is not to trivialize it: it was war and war is always a horror. But explaining it can test the patience of all but the most interested ancient history buffs. As a play in four acts, here is how the drama developed.

The play's audience takes their seats already knowing that Judah has become a vassal of Babylon (Jer 34). A vassal is subject to the terms and conditions of the suzerain, or dominant power, who typically exacts an impossibly heavy tribute tax. The tax is so burdensome that vassals often rebel, refusing to pay and seeking help from allies. But submitting to the humiliating tribute is the only alternative to being conquered with brutal violence. At this point, Judah has been invaded and has submitted. The Babylonian king Nebuchadnezzar sacked the current king, carting him off in chains along with ten thousand others, the officials, the surviving warriors, the people who were useful, the artisans and the smiths (2 Kgs 24:14). This was the first of several deportations. Nebuchadnezzar also invaded the temple and palace. "He carried off all the treasures of the house of the LORD, and the treasures of the king's house; he cut in pieces all the vessels of gold in the temple of the LORD" (2 Kgs 24:13). He then installed another as king and changed his name to Zedekiah (2 Kgs 24:17). As the curtain rises, Nebuchadnezzar has installed King Zedekiah. For his part, Zedekiah is not happy with the arrangement. He has his hopes set on Egyptian support to overthrow Babylonian rule.

The First Act: Egypt Advances, Babylon Retreats

At first Egypt is winning. According to Jer 35–37, this is only going to turn out to be a temporary advantage, but no one knows that at the time. Judah is desperate for Egypt to win. In this first act, Babylon lays siege to Jerusalem to starve them out. Judah's king Zedekiah, under pressure, desperately hopes for Egyptian military aid. Egypt sends an army from the south (likely under Pharaoh Hophra, ca. 588 BCE), prompting Babylon to temporarily lift the siege to go deal with the Egyptians (Jer 37:5–11). This emboldens King Zedekiah and his court. Jeremiah has been warning that Babylon will win, but his warnings appear misplaced and are ignored; he is imprisoned for "demoralizing the nation." He tells the people that Egypt is unreliable (Jer 46); Babylon is God's chosen instrument of judgment. Judah's trust in Egypt is not just political folly but theological rebellion (Jer 2:18; 37:7–10). At this point, Jeremiah seems to be rooting for the wrong nation. Why would he not want the Egyptians to prevail and help rid the Judeans of the Babylonian menace? In short, Jeremiah looks like a traitor who wishes to demoralize the troops with his predictions of doom.

At first, Egypt looked like it was going to help Judah win. When the Egyptian army approached, Babylon backed off its assault on Judah. But Egypt was not able to prevail. Their advance stalled; their army soon withdrew.

The Second Act: Babylon Regroups, Egypt Fades

In the second act, according to Jer 37:11–21, Babylon resumes the siege. Jeremiah is arrested as he tries to visit territory outside Jerusalem. En route he is accused of desertion and is imprisoned under miserable conditions, but continues to prophesy Babylon's victory. King Zedekiah, oddly wavering, consults him secretly, but refuses to surrender to Babylon. Zedekiah will ask for Jeremiah's consultation several times, even his prayers, as if he respects him as a true prophet, while ignoring his advice. Still hoping Egypt might return, Zedekiah won't declare full loyalty to Babylon or resist openly. Babylon regains the advantage. Egypt disappears from the action. Judah is confused and indecisive, and its courtiers, or royal advisors, appear divided. Sometimes they try to protect Jeremiah and his scribal secretary Baruch by hiding them, but at other times they conspire to kill the prophet. The text does not make it clear, but it could be that early supporters of Jeremiah were deported in the first wave of the siege, leaving only his enemies as the remaining courtiers. It is hard to tell.

The Third Act: Babylon Dominates

According to Jer 38:1–13, Jeremiah tells the people that resisting Babylon is suicidal and urges surrender. "Thus says the LORD: Those who stay in this city shall die by the sword, by famine, and by pestilence; but those who go out to the Chaldeans shall live; they shall have their lives as a prize of war, and live. Thus says the LORD: This city shall surely be handed over to the army of the king of Babylon and be taken" (Jer 38:2–3). The courtiers accuse him of treason. "The officials said to the king, 'This man ought to be put to death, because he is discouraging the soldiers who are left in this city, and all the people, by speaking such words to them. For this man is not seeking the welfare of this people, but their harm'" (Jer 38:4). With the king's permission they took Jeremiah and threw him into a waterless, muddy cistern to die.

Surprisingly, an Ethiopian court official, Ebed-melech, goes to King Zedekiah and argues for Jeremiah's rescue. Somehow he receives royal permission, and Jeremiah is hauled out of the cistern. Zedekiah again consults Jeremiah, who repeats his call to surrender, promising that they will live if they do (Jer 38:17). Zedekiah seems to believe his prediction, but fears that if he supports capitulation to Babylon, his own officials will kill him. So he does nothing. Babylon is now in full control. Jerusalem is surrounded. Egypt is absent. Judah is paralyzed, with King Zedekiah vacillating.

The Fourth Act: Babylon's Victory

In Jer 39:1–18 we learn of the Babylonian victory. In 586 BCE the Babylonian army breaches the walls of Jerusalem. King Zedekiah attempts to flee but is captured. His sons are executed before his eyes; then he is blinded and taken to Babylon (Jer 39:6–7). Jerusalem is burned; the temple is destroyed. Yet Jeremiah is spared, and Ebed-melech is promised protection, underscoring divine vindication.

Ebed-melech's Intervention

Who was Ebed-melech? His name simply means "servant of the king."[1] He is called a Cushite in Hebrew (Jer 38:7) which the NRSV correctly translates as Ethiopian. But the term actually refers to his skin color, which is black. Jeremiah emphasized Ethiopians' skin color, asking poetically, "Can the Ethiopian change his skin, or the leopard his spots?" (Jer 13:23). The English versions, following the Greek translation (LXX) also call Ebed-melech "a eunuch" (Jer 38:7). Eunuchs were employed in the monarch's service, true, but the word can also simply mean "official," which is probably meant here. There is no indication as to how this African became an official to the king. His family could have been in the land for several generations. In any case, he has free access to the king, who not only listens to him but also acts on his advice. He was a trusted advisor in spite of his foreign African origins.

We are not told anything about Ebed-melech's religious views at this point in the story. All we know is that when he heard that Jeremiah had been left in the cistern to starve to death, he decided to act. His decision was a huge risk. Jeremiah's arrest had been for disloyalty—in fact, for treason. He was accused of weakening the troops' fighting spirit, perhaps contributing to a potential loss. The courtier advisors had King Zedekiah in a corner. If the king refused their demand to have Jeremiah killed, he, too, might end up assassinated in a coup. So he acquiesces and allows them to carry out the sentence. This means that if Ebed-melech supports Jeremiah, he supports a traitor. Ebed-melech is risking his life. But this courageous man did what no one else did. He went to the king and said, "My lord king, these men have acted wickedly in all they did to the prophet Jeremiah by throwing him into the cistern to die there of hunger, for there is no bread left in the city" (Jer 38:9). The king and his court had their own bread supply, but the city was already on the brink of starvation. No one could have taken food to Jeremiah at night to keep him alive. If the king did not intervene, he would die.

1. BDB, s.v. "עֶבֶד מֶ֫לֶךְ."

The text goes into great detail about how Ebed-melech accomplished the rescue. He received the king's permission to get some help from several men. The text reads, "So Ebed-melech took the men with him and went to the house of the king, to a wardrobe of the storehouse, and took from there old rags and worn-out clothes, which he let down to Jeremiah in the cistern by ropes. Then Ebed-melech the Ethiopian said to Jeremiah, 'Just put the rags and clothes between your armpits and the ropes.' Jeremiah did so. Then they drew Jeremiah up by the ropes and pulled him out of the cistern" (Jer 38:11–13). Why the rags? We do not know how long he had been down there without food, but we can only assume that Jeremiah was so emaciated at that point as to be skin and bones. Ebed-melech was likely concerned that the ropes against his bare body would cut into his skin, perhaps causing further injury. His wise, compassionate solution was to pad the ropes with rags. He was successful and Jeremiah's life was spared. He was not released from house arrest, but at least he was alive.

After Jeremiah's rescue, King Zedekiah again called him in for a consultation. After sentencing him to death and then ordering his rescue, the king still had some hope that, as a prophet, Jeremiah could give him a positive message. But Jeremiah's warning did not change. With the courage of a man who had already faced death, he repeated to the king,

> Thus says the LORD, the God of hosts, the God of Israel: If you will only surrender to the officials of the king of Babylon, then your life shall be spared, and this city shall not be burned with fire, and you and your house shall live. But if you do not surrender to the officials of the king of Babylon, then this city shall be handed over to the Chaldeans, and they shall burn it with fire, and you yourself shall not escape from their hand. (Jer 38:17–18)

That is what happened. The siege began in the ninth year of Zedekiah's reign, January 588 BCE, and lasted until July 587 BCE. The Babylonian army breached the wall, sacked and burned the city, the palace, and the temple. The king fled and was captured. The last thing he saw was the execution of his sons, then his eyes were put out and he was chained and deported to Babylon. The army sacked the city, but the order was given to protect Jeremiah. "King Nebuchadnezzar of Babylon gave command concerning Jeremiah through Nebuzaradan, the captain of the guard, saying, 'Take him, look after him well and do him no harm, but deal with him as he may ask you'" (Jer 39:11–12). We are not told why Jeremiah was given special treatment. It seems plausible that Babylonian spies had learned that he had advocated surrender and therefore treated him as an ally.

So the independent existence of Judah came to an end. Jeremiah was taken to a staging area where the surviving Judeans were gathered in preparation for their deportation to Babylon. He was free but, at this moment, still in official custody in the court of the guard. From there he pronounced an oracle about his rescuer, Ebed-melech:

> The word of the LORD came to Jeremiah while he was confined in the court of the guard: Go and say to Ebed-melech the Ethiopian: Thus says the LORD of hosts, the God of Israel: I am going to fulfill my words against this city for evil and not for good, and they shall be accomplished in your presence on that day. But I will save you on that day, says the LORD, and you shall not be handed over to those whom you dread. For I will surely save you, and you shall not fall by the sword; but you shall have your life as a prize of war, because you have trusted in me, says the LORD. (Jer 39:15–18)

This is the first indication that Ebed-melech "trusted in" Yahweh. This African's life was spared. Not only was he spared, but by this public announcement, Jeremiah was holding him up as an example for Israel. Trusting God's word through the prophet leads to life. Failure to listen to and trust the prophet's words leads to death. Ebed-melech trusted and will live.

The Lessons Learned

Why was this story remembered and treasured by the community that experienced this calamity? What good is an object lesson about shutting the barn door after the cows have escaped? Why rub it in? Judah did not heed the word of God through the prophet, and they were defeated. Now there is no chance of a do-over. What good is an example of someone like Ebed-melech who did the right thing after the opportunity to follow his example had passed?

The answer may be in how the Jewish community that survived the Babylonian defeat and exile looked at the story. By the end of the story, Babylon is the world's sole superpower. They have been unstoppable. But even Babylon did not rule forever; a coalition of Medes and Persians later defeated them. The community that survived and their descendants knew that fact. The Persians had even allowed them to return and rebuild the temple and the walls of Jerusalem. However, the returnees were not an independent nation. They were not free "Judeans" but residents of the Persian province of Yehud.

The book of Jeremiah ends with Babylon as the reigning power and the people in exile. Though the future judgment against Babylon has been announced in Jeremiah, and its future destruction predicted, by the end of the book that has not yet happened. The community that treasured Jeremiah's message read Babylon as a metaphor. They were still in a kind of exile, even if the literal name of their overlord was Persia, not historical Babylon. They were able to say, "This text speaks to us."

There is an interesting part of this story we have not yet told. Jeremiah dictated a text through his secretary, Baruch (Jer 36). Baruch transmitted this text to the officials, who eventually read it to King Zedekiah. It repeated Jeremiah's insistence that they surrender to Babylon. As each section of the scroll was read to the king, he took a knife, cut off that section from the rest of the scroll, and tossed it in the fire to be burned. Repeatedly, the text says that the king would not "listen." Jeremiah was not present, but the text was speaking. After the scroll was burned, Jeremiah dictated a second scroll, "But neither he nor his servants nor the people of the land listened to the words of the LORD that he spoke through the prophet Jeremiah" (Jer 37:2). The act of not "listening" literally means they did not heed the words. The words were not verbal, but present as a written text. In this way, the prophet Jeremiah was not present to the descendants of the exiles, but his written text was present, and they heard it speaking to them. They were still in exile. Persia was the new Babylon. In this case, they had a chance to heed the words of the prophet. They could learn from the example of Ebed-melech and put their faith in Yahweh.

The Hebrew Bible tells the story of the chosen people, the descendants of Abraham, and how God preserved them through days of horror, war, the collapse of the nation, and the destruction of the temple. But they were not without the prophetic word to guide them. They had the text of Jeremiah to listen to because a foreigner named Ebed-melech acted with heroic courage in the face of mortal danger and rescued Jeremiah. Consequently, he was blessed with life and held up as an example of true faith. The blessing Ebed-melech received illustrates again that the promise to Abraham entailed God's will to bless all the families of the earth. Any nationalist vision that would exclude foreigners or people of color from the community is at odds with the witness of this text and so many more. The lengthy detail about how Ebed-melech arranged for Jeremiah's safe retrieval from the cistern slowed down the story to lengthen our attention focused on this African's role in the story. The public pronouncement of blessing on Ebed-melech enhances his prestige as an example, in contrast to the quisling king and his faithless courtiers. The chosen people needed the lesson from a foreigner. The question we are left with is whether or not we, too, will heed its message.

Part 2

The New Testament's Vision of Inclusion

11

Jesus's Near-Death Experience

If you were to ask anyone on the street in the land where Jesus ministered how they felt about their homeland, they likely would have said, "We are still in exile." They were not literally in exile in Babylon anymore, but neither were they free. They were living in their homeland, but under Roman occupation. Troops were everywhere. Physical, sexual, and financial abuse was common. Public crucifixions were common, too, and were meant to be a deterrent to would-be liberation movements.

In Jesus's time, the memory of the day the Roman troops came en masse, killing thousands, was still painfully present. That massacre happened around the time Jesus was born. King Herod the Great had just died. He had been a client-king to the Romans, supporting their occupation while trying to ingratiate himself with the Judeans by gestures like enlarging the Jewish temple in Jerusalem. At his death in 4 BCE, revolution broke out in every quarter of the Jewish homeland, including in the city of Sepphoris, close to Nazareth. (Some have speculated that as a carpenter, Jesus may have worked on the rebuilding of Sepphoris.) From there, a would-be messiah figure had emerged who led a rebel group that took up arms against the Romans. They were all crushed with typical Roman brutality. Everyone in Jesus's circle would have known victims. Atrocities are not quickly forgotten. For them, the exile continued. They dreamed of liberation, release from this kind of bondage. They longed for the day they could come out of this dark period of imprisonment into the light again; it would be like the blind receiving their sight.

Expectations were high that on some future day, the exile would end and they would be released from captivity. A new liberation would happen.

After all, they had only been under Roman occupation for the last 90 years or so. Before that, the Jews had enjoyed a period of independence that lasted approximately 150 years. It could happen again. In those days, a rebel movement, nicknamed the Maccabean Revolution, successfully liberated Judea from earlier imperial masters. ("Maccabee" was the personal epithet of the revolution's leader, Judas Maccabeus. It may well have meant *hammer* from the Aramaic *maqqəḇa*, a nod to Judas's battle tactics.)[1] The Maccabees overthrew their Seleucid (Greek) overlords. No one forgot. In Jesus's day, mothers and fathers were naming their sons for the heroes of that liberation struggle, including Mattathias (Matthew), Jonathan (John), Judas, and Simon.

Those parents expected the Roman occupation to end because the prophets of the Hebrew Bible said it would. Prophets like Isaiah imagined that someone would arrive "to proclaim liberty to the captives." He would say,

> The spirit of the LORD GOD is upon me,
>   because the LORD has anointed me;
> He has sent me to bring good news to the oppressed,
>   to bind up the brokenhearted,
>   to proclaim liberty to the captives,
>   and release to the prisoners;
>   to proclaim the year of the LORD's favor,
>   and the day of vengeance of our God;
>   to comfort all who mourn. (Isa 61:1–2)

"Liberty" and "release" were what the people longed for. "Vengeance" against the Romans went along with it. Isaiah predicted both were coming. The only questions were when and how?

Qumran's Expectations

The Qumran separatists were probably identified as the Essenes. Josephus, an ancient historian, says that the Essenes were one of the three sects of Jewish "philosophy" alongside the Pharisees and Sadducees. Whether or not the Qumran separatists were Essenes, they believed the day of liberation was coming, but with a twist that most Judeans would not like. The twist was that God's vengeance would not be limited to the Romans. It would be directed at all the ungodly, unfaithful, evil people. They believed that the ungodly included almost everyone, Jews and Romans alike, except for

1. Nordling, *Religion and Resistance*, 3.

their small sect of the righteous few. For them, the only legitimate king of Israel would be one from David's line. The current king was not. The only legitimate high priest would descend from Aaron's line. The current high priest, appointed and swapped out repeatedly by the Romans, was not. So the government was illegitimate, and the temple and its sacrifices were an abomination to God. This sect rejected both. They moved out to the desert around the Dead Sea and formed their own community at Qumran. There, they practiced multiple daily baptisms for purification and diligently transcribed texts from the Hebrew Bible. They also produced their own texts, some specifying rules for their common life. The texts they transcribed and produced are now collectively called the Dead Sea Scrolls. Many believe that the Qumran sect was the Essenes. No one knows for sure.

The Qumran separatists were Bible people through and through. They studied the Hebrew Scriptures daily. They had two axioms by which to interpret it: (1) that they were living in the end times, and (2) that all of the blessings of those end times were meant for them and them alone, and none of the end times curses against evil people applied to them. The curses were for everybody else. They also had some views that may seem strange to us but were popular at the time. They believed that in the end, a heavenly character called Melchizedek would lead the heavenly armies of God in a great, determinative battle. They came by this idea in part by their interpretation of Ps 110, in which God identifies a person as his instrument, saying, "The Lord has sworn and will not change his mind, 'You are a priest forever according to the order of Melchizedek'" (Ps 110:4). What will this newly named Melchizedek do? Execute vengeance on God's enemies. The psalm continues, "He will shatter kings on the day of his wrath. He will execute judgment among the nations" (Ps 110:5–6).

This Melchizedek was more than a mere human. He was considered almost divine, at least angelic. He was the one, according to Ps 81:1, who "has taken his place in the divine council; in the midst of the gods he holds judgment." He would not only conduct God's vengeance, but he would also be the one to announce the good news of liberation and release to the captives. He would preside over the final Jubilee, the year of liberation, "the year of the Lord's favor." For this aspect of his role as the great "proclaimer," they turned to the texts about the year of Jubilee (Lev 25 and Deut 15) and to Isa 61.

Jesus's Take

This brings us to our point; Isa 61 is also the text Jesus quoted from in his inaugural sermon in Nazareth (Luke 4), the one that almost got him killed:

> The Spirit of the Lord is upon me,
> because he has anointed me
> to bring good news to the poor.
> He has sent me to proclaim release to the captives
> and recovery of sight to the blind,
> to let the oppressed go free,
> to proclaim the year of the Lord's favor. (Luke 4:18–19)

By claiming this prophecy was fulfilled that day (Luke 4:21), Jesus was identifying himself with the figure in Isaiah, the one who would announce divine liberation—that is, with Melchizedek. To the people of Nazareth, this likely sounded like confirmation of their hopes. Was he about to rally the faithful, arm them, and prepare to overthrow the Romans? Would he announce the final Jubilee year of the Lord's favor?

Jesus had other plans. He wasn't aligned with the militant separatists of Qumran. He stood in the tradition of the Hebrew prophets—those who critiqued Israel's political and religious leaders and envisioned God's mercy extending far beyond national boundaries. It should be clear that the Qumran separatists had no room in their theology for critique. They were the righteous ones who deserved God's favor, period. However, the prophetic tradition in Israel included numerous examples of scathing criticism of Israelite society when warranted. Prophets like Amos began their book picturing God as a roaring lion. First, the lion roars in judgment against the nations surrounding Israel and Judah. He gets closer and closer, and finally pounces on them directly. The lion roars against his own people for their unfaithfulness and violence. Other prophets like Jeremiah criticized the ruling elites and the false prophets of his day: "For from the least to the greatest of them, everyone is greedy for unjust gain; and from prophet to priest, everyone deals falsely" (Jer 6:13). When God's chosen people got it wrong, the prophets of Israel criticized them.

From Jesus's perspective, the Qumran separatists were getting it wrong in some respects. They had an in-group/out-group perspective. Who were the "poor," "captive," and the "blind" to whom Isaiah was promising rescue? The Qumran separatists said it was, metaphorically, them. They had moved out to that desert community, living in self-induced poverty, and saw themselves as the "blind" people, held "captive" in the darkness of Roman occupation that needed their sight restored by a victorious battle. By contrast,

Jesus shows that the words meaning poor, captive, blind, and oppressed do not apply exclusively to any in-group but, on the contrary, apply to those to whom God wishes them to apply. He agreed with Qumran's axiom (1)—these were the end times, "today"—but not with axiom (2). Instead, God's favor could be extended to whomever God wished to extend it to, not merely to the in-group of pure people at Qumran.

To make matters worse, the Qumran community considered people with literal physical ailments outsiders. They alone were pure enough as the "true Israel" of the end times to fight the final battle against the forces of evil. Forbidden from the fight were "the halt, blind, lame, and those of impure or injured body" (as one of their scrolls, the Rule of the Congregation, says).[2] But these were the very people Jesus brought God's healing grace to.

Jesus, Foreigners, and Judgment

To make the point that God could extend his favor or grace to whomever he wished, Jesus reminded the people of Nazareth of two biblical stories. Elijah, he said, wasn't sent to help any Israelite widow during the famine but rather one in the village of Zarephath, in Sidon (1 Kgs 18). Likewise, Elisha had not healed an Israelite leper but Naaman, the Syrian (2 Kgs 5). Those stories are recounted here in chapters 4 and 5.

The message was clear: God's grace, like his fame, extends beyond Israel's borders to non-Israelites. This enraged his audience in Nazareth, who had embraced Qumran's double axioms, except that they included themselves among the righteous whom God would set free, probably on the basis of their identity as descendants of Abraham. Luke records their reaction: "They got up, drove him out of the town, and led him to the brow of the hill . . . so that they might hurl him off the cliff" (Luke 4:29). In other words, they attempted to murder him. Jesus escaped—how, Luke doesn't say.

There was another reason the Nazareth synagogue congregation-turned-mob was angry with Jesus. When he quoted Isa 61, he stopped short of finishing verse 2, leaving out an important phrase. It was the one about God's coming vengeance. When Jesus quoted, "To proclaim the year of the Lord's favor" (Luke 4:19 = Isa 61:2a), he omitted, "and the day of vengeance of our God" (Isa 61:2b). If "today" was the beginning of the end, how could the final battle be fought and won without an outpouring of God's vengeance?

The people of Nazareth were not alone. The lack of present vengeance was also a problem for John the Baptist. According to Luke's Gospel, John

2. Sanders, "From Isaiah 61 to Luke 4," 90.

appeared in the wilderness, offering "a baptism of repentance for the forgiveness of sins" (Luke 3:2). He believed that he was "the voice of one crying out in the wilderness" (Luke 3:3), preparing the way for one who would come after him. When that one came, he would bring God's judgment. "Even now the ax is lying at the root of the trees" (Luke 3:9), ready to be picked up and wielded in judgment. John said that he was baptizing in water only, but "one who is more powerful than I is coming; I am not worthy to untie the thong of his sandals. He will baptize you with the Holy Spirit and fire" (Luke 3:16). The fire of judgment was what he expected.

But the fire of judgment was not what Jesus was all about, which confused John. Luke records John's puzzlement at the incomplete ministry of Jesus. When he was in prison, he sent two of his disciples to ask Jesus, "Are you the one who is to come, or are we to wait for another?" (Luke 7:20). Jesus's answer went right back to his inaugural sermon quotation from Isaiah: "He answered them, 'Go and tell John what you have seen and heard: the blind receive their sight, the lame walk, the lepers are cleansed, the deaf hear, the dead are raised, the poor have good news brought to them. And blessed is anyone who takes no offense at me'" (Luke 7:22–23).

John the Baptist thought that the end times meant not only the day of the announcement of "good news to the poor" but also judgment on God's enemies. According to Luke, Jesus's vision included an *already* element of fulfillment—namely, the proclamation of "good news"—and a *not yet* future time of consummation. At that future time there would be judgment, but not yet. Jesus had a two-stage view of God's plan, or eschatology, rather than a one-stage view, as at Qumran and popularly at Nazareth.

John got one thing right that Jesus picked up on, which broke with Qumran. John rejected the insider-versus-outsider perspective of Qumran in one important respect. He dismissed the popular notion that simply being a descendant of Abraham gave anyone an insider's pass. When he was calling people to baptism, he warned them, saying, "Do not begin to say to yourselves, 'We have Abraham as our ancestor'; for I tell you, God is able from these stones to raise up children to Abraham" (Luke 3:8).

Not everyone could accept John's message. To some, that was heresy. The "chosen people" were believed to be blessed as a guarantee. Some, including tax collectors, received the message, but others did not. Jesus said, "But by refusing to be baptized by him [John], the Pharisees and the lawyers rejected God's purpose for themselves" (Luke 7:30). The people of Nazareth also rejected that part of the message. It was the moment when Jesus cited God's work beyond the circle of insiders, descended from Abraham, and included outsiders, like the widow of Zarephath and Naaman the Syrian, that they became a lynch mob.

Jesus's sermon at Nazareth in which he said that the prophecy in Isaiah was fulfilled in his ministry is called his inaugural sermon. That is because it comes so early in Jesus's ministry, just after his baptism and time of temptation. It comes even before he goes to Capernaum to heal people, such as Peter's mother-in-law, a story that follows the Nazareth sermon. That is odd because Jesus says to the people of Nazareth that they would say to him, "Do here also in your hometown the things that we have heard you did at Capernaum" (Luke 4:23). According to Luke's ordering of events, Jesus had not yet done anything in Capernaum. However, Luke placed the story of Jesus's experience that day, including both the sermon and the hostile reaction to it, at the head of any other public ministry event to make it inaugural. It set the tone and announced the themes of everything that would follow. For Luke, in other words, to understand Jesus correctly you have to see him through the lens of the events that took place at Nazareth. Jesus is the Spirit-anointed proclaimer of good news, God's favor, the fulfillment of Jubilee; he must be seen that way. As such, he is the one to extend God's grace to people who had been marginalized, the blind and the lame, and to those who were not descendants of Abraham.

We will look at the way Jesus's ministry touched people who were not descendants of Abraham in future chapters. For now, though, it is important to take a step back and consider the implications of this narrative. In our day, some claim that we Americans have inherited the status of God's chosen people. As such, some have suggested that the descendants of white Europeans uniquely have the gifts and values needed to lead our unique democracy. They make the case that it is natural and right for people to live together with those like them, meaning other white Christians of European descent. Therefore, it is right to be an American Christian nationalist. In this respect, they resemble the views expressed by the Qumran separatists and by the Nazareth bigots. By doing so, they put themselves at odds with Jesus's fundamental teaching. Jesus, even though his primary audience was people descended from Abraham, was not a bigoted nationalist. Quite the opposite: Jesus acknowledged that the door to God's favor had been opened to non-Israelites from time immemorial. The Hebrew Scriptures made that clear. There could be no claim, even from fellow Judeans, for any exclusive right to God's favor. How much more should this be clear to people who are not descendants of Abraham? White Christians in America are overwhelmingly Gentiles. Nor is there any basis in Scripture to lay claim to the status of chosen-ness with the sole exception of being in Christ through faith, not nationality. From the beginning of the Hebrew Bible and repeatedly in story after story, the message is clear: God's mercy can extend beyond the ethnic and national borders of even his chosen people. As he promised to Abraham, God's will is to bless all the families of the earth.

Luke will go on to write his second volume, the book of Acts, in which God's favor extends to Gentiles. Luke will recount the experiences of the early church and then the ministry of Paul, which we will examine in future chapters. We will see that what Jesus preached at Nazareth came true. God's favor is not limited ethnically in any way. The good news of release from captivity is for everyone.

12

Jesus and Non-Israelites

JESUS, ACCORDING TO LUKE, inaugurated his ministry by being controversial. In his hometown synagogue, he burst everyone's bubble. They were proud of his newfound fame. Here he was, a hometown boy, one of their own, who was becoming famous. Certainly he would be on their team. Maybe he could even lead a new movement to free them from Roman oppression. After all, his parents had named him Joshua, after the great military leader that led the battles to conquer the promised land from the Canaanites. (*Jesus* is the English version of *Joshua*.) Hopes were high in the little village of Nazareth. Jesus was being praised by everyone (Luke 4:15).

But something he did made them so mad they tried to kill him. He did this intentionally. He predicted he would get pushback from them, saying, "Doubtless you will quote to me this proverb, 'Doctor, cure yourself!' And you will say, 'Do here also in your hometown the things that we have heard you did at Capernaum'" (Luke 4:23). In other words, the party will be over soon. Jesus expected it. He went on to say that no prophet was accepted in the prophet's own hometown (Luke 4:24).

What was the controversy Jesus provoked? He was not going to carry their nationalist flag. He brought up two stories from the Hebrew Bible, one about Elijah and the other about Elisha. In both cases, the whole point was that God used the prophets to bring blessings to non-Israelites. For Jesus, the point was clear: God's circle of concern started with his chosen people, but did not end there. The blessing promised to Abraham (Gen 12) was also extended to all the families of the earth (Gen 12:3). That is what Jesus believed and wanted his hometown friends and family to know, right from the start. He knew they would not like it, but those were his convictions.

Jesus came by his convictions honestly. He began his adult life as a disciple of John the Baptist. He even submitted to baptism by John—a fact that the Gospel writers felt uncomfortable with; their various accounts of it play it down further and further. It was probably embarrassing for the early Christians that John baptized Jesus, and not vice versa, but the facts were known, so they told the story. Besides the stories of the Hebrew Bible, like the ones Jesus alluded to in the Nazareth synagogue, he received encouragement to think beyond the borders of ethnic Israel from John's preaching too.

John the Baptist was "Mr. Sincerity." He was sincere in his beliefs and demanded his followers' sincerity. He was unhappy with the aristocrats controlling the temple and the purity police Pharisees. For John, it had to be more than talking the talk. It had to be a life lived according to ethical imperatives, like "Whoever has two coats must share with anyone who has none; and whoever has food must do likewise" (Luke 3:11). These were the visible "fruits" of true repentance. John demanded, "Bear fruits worthy of repentance" (Luke 3:8). Having the right bloodline was not enough for John. He said it as plainly as he could: "Do not begin to say to yourselves, 'We have Abraham as our ancestor'; for I tell you, God is able from these stones to raise up children to Abraham" (Luke 3:8). You are not under special protection as a descendant of Abraham; you are under special obligation. John, of course, got all of this from the Hebrew prophets. As a disciple of John, Jesus would have heard this kind of preaching.

Jesus and the Centurion

Jesus put this perspective into practice in his own public ministry. Just as it would be impossible to understand Dr. Martin Luther King Jr. by reading his sermons and speeches without knowing the context of the American civil rights movement of the 1960s, it is only possible to understand Jesus with his context in mind. His homeland, Judea, was under military occupation. There was no peace, only pacification. Rome brooked no rivals. Rebel movements, like the revolts of 4 BCE upon the death of King Herod the Great, were suppressed with brutal force. Soldiers were everywhere, and abuse was commonplace.

But not all were equally oppressive. Apparently, there was a centurion who held the Jews in high esteem. Jews were famous for their good family lives and clean living. Judaism was a curiosity to the Romans, who had difficulty understanding it. Jews, who did not believe in the Roman pantheon of gods, appeared to be practically atheists. But their lifestyles and the antiquity of their beliefs could be respected. And so it was that a certain

Roman officer, a centurion, had a concern about a severely sick slave. We have accounts of this meeting in Luke and Matthew (Luke 7 and Matt 8). Luke has more details about the meeting than Matthew, though they agree word for word on the main points. They have shared a common source for this and other narratives. One of the details Luke supplies is that the Jewish elders brought the centurion to Jesus. Another detail is that they assumed Jesus did not know him, and wanted to make sure he did not reject him on the basis that he was from the oppressor community. They informed Jesus, "He is worthy of having you do this for him, for he loves our people, and it is he who built our synagogue for us" (Luke 7:4–5). He had used his wealth to sponsor their meeting place.

When Jesus agreed to go to the centurion's home, he came out to meet Jesus, saying, "Lord, do not trouble yourself, for I am not worthy to have you come under my roof; therefore I did not presume to come to you. But only speak the word, and let my servant be healed" (Luke 7:6–7). This Roman believed that if Jesus had spiritual authority, it must have been analogous to the Roman army chain of command. A Roman general doesn't have to be on the front lines; all he has to do is give orders. It must work the same in the spiritual realm. The centurion explains, "For I also am a man set under authority, with soldiers under me; and I say to one, 'Go,' and he goes, and to another, 'Come,' and he comes, and to my slave, 'Do this,' and the slave does it." (Luke 7:8). In a world in which healers often used human touch in their healing arts, this centurion believed that Jesus could heal at a distance.

Jesus's reaction was revealing: "When Jesus heard this, he was amazed at him" (Luke 7:9). We could assume that it must have taken a lot to amaze Jesus, but this enemy-Roman just did. Jesus wanted to make sure the lesson was not lost on anyone: "And turning to the crowd that followed him, he said, 'I tell you, not even in Israel have I found such faith.'" This is the highest praise Jesus ever gave anyone, and he said it about a Roman, in contrast with his fellow Israelites. If, as John the Baptist said, God could make children of Abraham out of stones if he wished, he could also put faith into the heart of the enemy. The slave whose grave illness was the catalyst for this exchange was reported to be fully healed (Luke 7:10).

Jesus and the Torah Scholar

Jesus was not a trained rabbi, but the Gospels show that he was deeply familiar with the Hebrew Bible. He quoted it and alluded to it throughout his ministry. He was also capable of challenging some of its settled ideas. The ethical vision of the Hebrew Bible was in the background of Jesus's mind when he took it to the next level. When, according to the Gospel of Luke, a Torah scholar came to Jesus, "wanting to justify himself," claiming to have kept the greatest commandments, the love of God and of neighbor, he asked Jesus, "And who is my neighbor?" (Luke 10:29). This is a crucial question for anyone who believes that our ethical responsibilities are limited to our neighbors. The question is, who is in and who is out? Who am I ethically obligated to care for, and who is outside the circle of my moral obligation? Who is, and who is not, my "neighbor?" Many of the ethical mandates of the Hebrew Bible refer to your "neighbor." Leviticus goes furthest, saying, "You shall love your neighbor as yourself" (Lev 19:18).

Who is my neighbor? Jesus's answer was to tell a parable. We know it as the parable of the good Samaritan. Jesus did not give it a title; if he had, it would not have been "The Parable of the Good Samaritan." No one would have listened beyond that title. No Samaritan was good in the eyes of that community. The reasons were many and deep. There is no need to belabor them here. Suffice it to say that the animosity was intense and ran both directions. The modern equivalent might be to think of the Samaritan the way Jews in Israel today think of Hamas. The New Testament admits that "Jews have no dealings with Samaritans" (John 4:9). A Samaritan was in no way a neighbor.

The central character in Jesus's story was a Jewish man. He starts a journey from the Jewish capital, the home of the Jewish temple, Jerusalem. On his way, he is attacked by robbers who stripped him of his clothing, violently beat him, and then went away, leaving him half dead (Luke 10:30). If anyone saw him in that condition, what would they know, and what would they not know? They would know that he was in bad shape and needed help; that is obvious. They would also know that helping him would involve getting his blood on them. If you are beaten "half dead," you are bloody. They would not know if he were already a corpse; half dead looks a lot like dead.

If he were stripped of his clothing and could not speak, neither could you know his ethnicity. No ethnic dress, no accent; was he a Jew or a Samaritan? You could not know.

In Jesus's parable, two men see him, recognize that he needs help, but refuse to help him. They have one thing in common: they both work at the temple. One is a priest, the other a Levite. While there is no explicit law saying "do not touch blood," priestly law implies that touching blood is a matter of ritual danger, especially outside sacrificial contexts. If the victim is dead, then touching a corpse also makes you ritually impure and unable to assume your temple duties immediately. They had reasons to pass by without helping. Or at least, they had excuses.

But someone did stop and help, whom Jesus identified as a Samaritan. At risk to himself (how could he be sure the robbers had left?), the Samaritan came to his rescue. Why? Because when he saw him he was moved with compassion (Luke 10:33). We would say he felt empathy. Not only did the Samaritan dress his wounds, pour a salve of oil and wine on them, but he also put him on his own donkey, brought him to an inn, and took care of him (Luke 10:34). He did not stop there. He put himself at financial risk by giving the innkeeper a blank check. "The next day he took out two denarii, gave them to the innkeeper, and said, 'Take care of him; and when I come back, I will repay you whatever more you spend'" (Luke 10:35). Did the Samaritan know his ethnicity? Not for sure, but the road from Jerusalem to Jericho is in Jewish territory; you could assume he was Jewish.

This despised out-group person, this non-neighbor Samaritan, not only went way out of his way to rescue this victim, but he did so probably assuming that he was helping a Jew. No one hearing this parable would have missed that. Jesus is purposefully setting up an ethical dilemma if you have an in-group/out-group limitation on your understanding of moral responsibility.

To the question that the Torah scholar asked Jesus, "Who is my neighbor?" Jesus responded with a question in return. "Which of these three [the priest, Levite, or Samaritan], do you think, was a neighbor to the man who fell into the hands of the robbers?" (Luke 10:36). The question is not "Who is my neighbor?" but "Who was a neighbor to him?" Who had the ethical insight that the boundary between *care* and *no-care* lies within the heart of each of us? Whom do we have the capacity to call neighbor? Whom do we have the moral courage to care about and to care for?

The Torah scholar, to his credit, got the point. While his question revealed the limitations of his previous moral vision, he was willing to expand that vision after hearing the parable. Why? We are not told, but as an expert in the Hebrew Bible, he knew well that the call to love the immigrant, or stranger, is frequent. He knew about empathy. He knew about the prophetic vision of inclusion that imagined a future day when foreigners would be included in temple worship (Isa 56:3). He must have realized that Jesus was merely taking the neighboring ethic to its next logical conclusion. The purity concerns of the priest and the Levite may have been religiously legitimate, but they were ethically secondary to the responsibility to help another person in need. And the person who made that point was not one of "the chosen," but a Samaritan.

This may be a conversion story. The Torah scholar, instead of walking away in disgust that the hero of the parable was a Samaritan, answered

Jesus's question correctly. Who was a neighbor to the victim? "The one who showed him mercy. Jesus said to him, 'Go and do likewise'" (Luke 10:37).

Jesus and the Canaanite Woman

The story of Jesus healing the demon-possessed daughter of a Canaanite woman at a distance is remarkable for numerous reasons, but also complicated. First, this account has two versions, one in Mark 7 and the other in Matt 15. There are differences between the two that are difficult to reconcile. This illustrates one of our problems when trying to understand Jesus as presented in the Gospels. Should we find a way to work out the differences and smooth out the story? This would be to recover the original event behind the Gospel texts. Or should we examine the differences to see how each Gospel writer made unique points for their communities?

Sometimes when a story or teaching varies between Gospels, some suggest that the differences may be accounted for by the fact that Jesus likely taught the same lessons or parables on multiple occasions. That may account for some variation between the Gospels. However, some events with variations between the Gospels could only have happened once. These include Jesus's birth and baptism, Peter's confession at Caesarea, Jesus's resurrection, and others. The story of Jesus healing the Canaanite woman's daughter is a one-time event. We will note the differences between Mark's and Matthew's versions, but we will also see how their agreement makes this story both startling and significant.

The gist of the story is this: Jesus and his disciples travel to a region beyond the borders of Galilee, described as the region of the city of Tyre (Mark) or Tyre and Sidon (Matthew, and some manuscripts of Mark). Both versions start with that announcement of the location. Jesus is in predominantly Gentile territory. Mark also refers to this region as the Decapolis, or the Ten Towns (Mark 7:31). Josephus, an ancient Jewish historian, says that this was a Gentile area, whose inhabitants were "notoriously our bitterest enemies."[1] Why did Jesus and company go there? We only have hints. Mark tells us that he entered a house hoping no one would know he was there (Mark 7:24). Maybe Jesus needed a break from the crowds and thought his reputation was less well known there? If so, he was mistaken. Mark says next, "Yet he could not escape notice." Did they go there intentionally to begin the Gentile mission, as scholars refer to it? That seems weirdly unlikely, especially based on the conversation Jesus has with the Canaanite woman. And yet, he is there, in Gentile territory; you have to wonder what they

1. Josephus, *Ag. Ap.* 1.13.

expected would happen there if not direct contact with Gentiles in need? Anyway, that is exactly what happened.

Jesus is quickly discovered by a local woman identified as "a Gentile, of Syrophoenician origin" (Mark 7:26) or as "a Canaanite woman" (Matt 15:22). They mean the same thing, but by calling her a Canaanite, Matthew may be emphasizing her heritage as the historical people whom the Jews had to battle to gain possession of the promised land. Mark notes that she is a "Gentile"—as if her location as a local needed that explanation—also emphasizing her non-Jewish status. She is a pagan from the Jewish perspective, a polytheist, not a monotheist as the Jews are. Her foreignness and otherness are being emphasized in the strongest of terms.

She has a daughter who is suffering and needs Jesus's help. Mark tells us the daughter has a demonically unclean spirit (Mark 7:25). Matthew lets the woman speak for herself. "[She] came out and started shouting, 'Have mercy on me, Lord, Son of David; my daughter is tormented by a demon'" (Matt 15:22). Calling Jesus "Son of David" begs a question: what did she know of Jesus? She knew enough to ask him to heal her daughter. Did she already consider him a messiah figure? That would be unlikely, but addressing him as she did leaves us wondering. Calling Jesus "Lord" is ambiguous and is probably the equivalent of "sir." She respects him, even as she engages him.

We should not rush past the fact that this Gentile woman just did something extraordinary. She, an unknown, unrelated woman, approached a man in the home where he was staying, without invitation. In that culture, this was an affront to his honor. Remember, this was an honor-shame culture. To disregard a man's honor was to shame him. A rebuff from Jesus would have been expected, and that is what she got. Matthew and Mark differ on details. Matthew says she was repeatedly calling out to Jesus, irritating the disciples who suggest that he should send her away, (Matt 15:23) while Jesus remains silent. When Jesus finally replies to her pleadings, he answers with the expected rebuff. "I was sent only to the lost sheep of the house of Israel" (Matt 15:24). She might have replied, "Then what are you doing here in this Gentile region?" But she didn't. Instead, still in Matthew's version, "she came and knelt before him, saying, 'Lord, help me'" (Matt 15:25–26).

Again, she receives a rebuff. "He answered, 'It is not fair to take the children's food and throw it to the dogs'" (Matt 15:26). In Mark, Jesus's reply is a bit different: "Let the children be fed first, for it is not fair to take the children's food and throw it to the dogs" (Mark 7:27). Notice the word *first*. Feeding the children first does not mean only feeding them, just that they come before the dogs, who get the leftovers.

What are we to make of that reply? Is Jesus calling her a Gentile dog? Yes, he is. The "children" at the table would then be the Israelites. Matthew has Jesus saying that he was "sent only to the lost sheep of the house of Israel," and Mark has the children eating "first" while the dogs under the table wait for the scraps. Both of them agree that Jesus rebuffs her with an insult. And even though the word for "dogs" is diminutive—maybe meaning house pets—it is an insult. The dogs get the scraps while the children get the meal. Jesus was making a distinction between "the lost sheep of the house of Israel" whom he was sent "only" to (Matthew), or at least "first" to (Mark).

If the story ended there, the conclusion would be that the Jew-Gentile distinction was thoroughgoing in Jesus's mind, and he had no intention of providing healing mercy to a Gentile dog. But the story does not end there. After the insult, the woman will not be dissuaded. Mark records her riposte this way: "But she answered him, 'Sir, even the dogs under the table eat the children's crumbs'" (Mark 7:28). Matthew's version varies only slightly. She is saying in effect, "So I'm a dog. Fine. Then treat me like a dog and give me the children's crumbs. A crumb from you will be enough for my daughter."

Jesus was outplayed in this game of wits, and he knew it. In spite of his previous protests about ministering to a Gentile, her answer impressed him so much that he changed his mind. Mark does not mention Jesus noticing her faith explicitly, but Matthew does: "Then Jesus answered her, 'Woman, great is your faith! Let it be done for you as you wish.' And her daughter was healed instantly" (Matt 15:27). In spite of the utterly shameful effrontery of this pagan character, Jesus concedes her the debate.

Now we begin to wonder if Jesus's journey into Gentile territory had a method in its madness after all. Both Mark, early in the ministry of Jesus, and Matthew at the end, open the door to Gentiles as equal partners in the kingdom of God. Mark tipped his hand to Gentile inclusion when, in the passage that precedes this story, he said that Jesus declared "all foods clean"—thus undermining the kosher purity distinction between clean and unclean food (Mark 7:19). Matthew will end his Gospel with Jesus commanding his disciples to "go therefore and make disciples of all nations" (Matt 28:19). Luke, too, affirms this global mission, quoting Jesus as saying, "Repentance for the forgiveness of sins should be proclaimed in his name to all nations, beginning from Jerusalem" (Luke 24:47).

Jesus and Other Gentiles

There are more stories we could tell. John has one about Jesus meeting the Samaritan woman at the well, who not only embraced Jesus as Messiah but also became an evangelist to her whole Samaritan town (John 4:1–42). This illustrates Jesus's understanding of his inclusive mission when he said, "I have other sheep that are not of this fold. I must bring them also" (John 10:16).

Jesus's parable of the wicked tenants is told in Matt 21:33–46, Mark 12:1–12, and Luke 20:9–19. In all three, the original tenants in the vineyard, a common symbol for Israel in the Hebrew Bible, here meaning the leaders, are wicked to the point that the vineyard is taken from them and given to others.

Luke tells the story of Jesus healing ten lepers, only one of which returned to thank him. Suddenly, that story becomes a sharp barb against nationalism as Luke adds the observation "and he was a Samaritan" (Luke 17:11–19).

As a matter of timing, Jesus did go first to "the lost sheep of the house of Israel," as Mark said, but even when he was geographically inside the "house of Israel," he brought God's healing mercy to people like the Roman centurion's servant. Eventually, he left the geographical "house of Israel" in Galilee and crossed the border into the Gentile territory of the Decapolis, where a pagan Canaanite's daughter received restoration. The blessings promised to the children of Abraham are extended to all the families of the earth, all of whom should be considered "neighbors."

13

The Two Sides of the Lake

When is bread not just bread, and wine not just wine? Anyone familiar with Christianity will tell you that the Lord's Supper, or Eucharist, is symbolic of Christ's body and blood. Jesus made that clear (Mark 14:22). Other symbols in the Gospels may also be familiar, like the fig tree Jesus cursed for being fruitless at a time when, the Gospels tell us, it was not the time for figs. In the story, Jesus cursed the fig tree, then went to the temple and predicted its future destruction, and then came out to find the cursed tree had withered. The fig tree symbolized the temple. Some have called this an acted parable (Mark 11:13–20).

Less obvious symbols include calling the freshwater Lake Galilee a "sea." There is a Greek word for lake, but Mark uses the word meaning "sea." The sea, in the Hebrew Bible, is symbolic of a place of danger and threat, even chaos. Nevertheless, God is described as powerful enough to master the sea. Psalm 107 represents both the sea's threatening danger and God's power to bring it to a silent calm:

> Some went down to the sea in ships,
> doing business on the great waters;
> they saw the deeds of the Lord,
> his wondrous works in the deep.
> For he commanded, and raised the stormy wind,
> which lifted up the waves of the sea.
>
> Then they cried to the Lord in their trouble,
> and he delivered them from their distress,
> he made the storm be still,
> and the waves of the sea were hushed. (Ps 107:23–25, 28–29)

We are going to see how Mark uses the symbolism of the sea as dangerous and threatening, as the disciples crisscross it with difficulty, and how Jesus handles the difficulties he initiates by suggesting they cross to the other side (Mark 4:35). We will see that crossing the sea to the "other side" is symbolically significant.

Our focus will be on Mark's version of the story of Jesus. Each Gospel tells Jesus's story from its own unique perspective and with its own unique aims. Mark describes the sea crossings in deliberately structured ways that make a powerful point that Matthew or Luke did not make in the same way. Many people have tried to plot the sea crossings that Mark described, with limited success. Some have given up trying to make sense of them, concluding that Mark did not know the geography of the towns around the lake. Others believe the storyline became scrambled along the way. Still others have realized that the sea crossings can be read symbolically, making perfect sense of them. That is what we will explore. The sea was real, and cross it they did, but Mark tells the story of those crossings in a deliberate way to tell a story far more significant than paddling against the wind on a rough lake.

By the time we get to the stories of sea crossings to the "other side," Jesus has already led his disciples on a ministry of teaching and healing throughout the towns of Galilee. He is getting famous, generating crowds wherever he goes. The crowds come from all the places his reputation has gone, including Idumea, and the cities of Tyre and Sidon—that is, Gentile areas (Mark 3:7–8).

Jesus is also coming under increased opposition by the religious establishment, represented by the scribes, experts in the law of Moses, and Pharisees, the self-appointed purity police of the time. Why the opposition? Jesus has broken with the established religious traditions in significant ways. He has offered forgiveness of sins without the use of the temple, priests, or sacrifices (Mark 2:5). He and his disciples have not been observing days of fasting (Mark 2:18–20). Jesus has repeatedly healed on the Sabbath and even allowed his disciples to pick grain to eat on the Sabbath (Mark 2:23–27). Jesus's vision was that people could have an intimate and immediate relationship with God, not requiring the intervention of temple liturgies or personnel. It was an alternative vision of God's will for people that prioritizes human need over ritual observance. He called his vision the kingdom of God. It is like new wine, requiring new wineskins (Mark 2:22). He will be taking his disciples to predominantly Gentile areas of Galilee, where he will extend God's healing mercy to a Canaanite woman's daughter and a deaf Gentile man. Now, he is about to teach that inclusive vision by words and actions, by which he is creating an alternative community. It will not be easy.

Mark likes to tell stories in pairs that illuminate each other. Sometimes the stories are interconnected. For example, en route to the home of Jairus, the leader of the synagogue, to heal his daughter, Jesus is interrupted by a hemorrhaging woman who secretly touches his clothing to seek healing (Mark 5:21–32). The story makes him pause his journey to Jairus's house. The woman is healed, but in the meantime, word comes that the daughter has apparently died. The delay seems to have caused a disaster. But Mark has told those stories together, just like the fig tree and the temple episodes, to be mutually illuminating. He does it by paralleling elements in both stories. Jairus's daughter is twelve years old; the woman has been hemorrhaging for twelve years. Jairus is of high status, the woman is of low status—a contrasting parallel. Jairus's daughter dies but is raised from the dead. The hopeless woman is given the title "daughter" by Jesus, raising her to a new life of hope and restoring her to her community.

Mark will do the same kind of mutually illuminating paralleling of events on either side of the sea. We will see that one side of the sea, the western side, is Jewish. The "other side," the eastern side, is Gentile. Remember, these are symbolic sides, not geographically literal. The crossing from one side to the other is difficult. Storms at sea threaten to thwart the crossings. The disciples' unbelief threatens to undermine the lesson of the crossings. They do not get the point that Jesus is expanding the kingdom community to include both Jews and Gentiles. We should not be quick to judge them for finding this lesson hard to the point of almost unbelievable. Some have described the hostility between Jew and Gentile, which was culturally pervasive in that time, to be the quintessential example of all human hostility. Solving that was going to be a stormy affair. That struggle will continue on into the life of the early church, as we will see later.

But that is the point of the crossings back and forth. Mark is showing that Jesus's mission must include Jews and Gentiles; people from both sides of the lake. Mark tells the story this way, forty years after Jesus walked the earth, and after the disastrous Jewish war and destruction of the temple, to assure his mixed Jewish and Gentile congregation that they together comprise the kingdom of God. We will see how the symbol of a single loaf of bread gets involved in this story too. The inclusive community of Jews and Gentiles in Mark's church can gather to break bread from a single loaf as equal members of the mystical body of Christ in the kingdom of God.

The First Sea Crossing

At Jesus's direction, even though it is already evening and darkness is not far off, a harbinger of trouble ahead, they climb aboard the boat to head to the "other side" (Mark 4:35). A storm blows in. Mark's description is graphic: "A great windstorm arose, and the waves beat into the boat, so that the boat was already being swamped" (Mark 4:37). But Jesus was asleep, unaware of the danger they were in. That detail is essential. The struggle perceived as life-threatening to the disciples, the crossing to the other side, is not at all a threat to Jesus. The disciples awaken Jesus with the allegation that he is unconcerned about the mortal danger they perceive. "Teacher, do you not care that we are perishing?" (Mark 4:38). Jesus "woke up and rebuked the wind, and said to the sea, 'Peace! Be still!' Then the wind ceased, and there was a dead calm" (Mark 4:39). The echoes of Ps 107 ring out: "Then they cried to the LORD in their trouble, and he delivered them from their distress, he made the storm be still, and the waves of the sea were hushed" (Ps 107:28–29). The power of God, present when Jesus is present, overcomes the dangerous, threatening sea. The presence of Jesus makes the crossing to the other side smooth sailing, instead of the last boat ride of their lives that they had imagined.

If we were not reading this story symbolically, Jesus's response to their fear would seem harsh, if not severe, and even misdirected. "He said to them, 'Why are you afraid? Have you still no faith?'" (Mark 4:40). How could they have expected to have faith when he was asleep and they were being swamped? But read symbolically, as an indication of the extreme difficulty of accepting, even on faith, that there could be such a thing as an inclusive community of Jews and Gentiles, the story makes perfect sense. Attempting to create a reconciled humanity would certainly mean encountering a challenge as big as a storm at sea. It would take faith in God's power to overcome the difficulties involved.

They landed at the country of the Gentile people Mark calls the Gerasenes (Mark 5:1). At the start of his ministry on the Jewish side of the sea, Jesus's first act was an exorcism in Capernaum (Mark 1:21–28). Note that his first act on the Gentile side of the sea was also an exorcism. The Gentile nature of the region is clear: the demon-possessed man lives among the tombs in an area where they raise pigs—doubly impure from a Jewish perspective (see Isa 65:4). At Jesus's command, the demons, whose collective name is legion, are cast out of the man and into a herd of swine. The symbolism of the whole story is rich. To highlight the obvious symbols, a legion is a unit of Roman soldiers, and pigs are not herd animals. The main point is that just as Jesus successfully confronted the forces of evil at Capernaum in

Jewish space at the start of his ministry there, he does the same in Gentile space in his initial contact.

The First Feeding

When they return to the Jewish side of the lake, Jesus restores the daughter of the synagogue leader just as he has the daughter of the Canaanite woman, another parallel of acts on behalf of Jews and Gentiles. Soon they need a break from ministry, so he takes his disciples to a deserted place. As before, crowds discover him. After teaching them all day, Jesus notices it's getting late, and no one has had supper. The disciples suggest that Jesus send the crowds away to find food in the surrounding villages. Instead of agreeing, Jesus tells them that they should give them something to eat (Mark 6:37). Mark has told us that Jesus felt compassion for the people who were "like sheep without a shepherd" (Mark 6:34), but perhaps the disciples did not share his feelings. Jesus draws them in, implying that they are responsible for providing food. They demur. "Are we to go and buy two hundred denarii worth of bread [literally "breads"] and give it to them to eat?" (Mark 6:37). A denarius was a day's wage for a worker, so the disciples were indicating an enormous expense. Jesus then asks them, "How many loaves [literally "breads"] have you?" They reply, "Five, and two fish" (Mark 6:38). Jesus told the disciples to organize the crowd, which they do into groupings of hundreds and fifties. We can only wonder why Jesus chose such groupings. Some speculate that they symbolize the size of early churches with which Mark was familiar. The story continues, "Taking the five loaves [literally "breads"] and the two fish, he looked up to heaven, and blessed and broke the loaves, and gave them to his disciples to set before the people; and he divided the two fish among them all" (Mark 6:41). Many have observed that Jesus used the same four verbs that later would describe the last supper, the initial Eucharist: *took*, *blessed*, *broke*, and *gave* (Matt 26:26), adding to the church symbolism.

The result for the people was all of them ate and to the full (Mark 6:42). The result for the disciples was that "they took up twelve baskets [pointedly using the Hebrew word for *basket*, not the Greek word] full of broken pieces and of the fish" (Mark 6:43). The number twelve appears again, here on the Jewish side of the lake. Just as there are twelve tribes of Israel and twelve disciples, so there are twelve baskets of leftovers after these five thousand men (plus women and children?) had eaten.

The Second Sea Crossing

Immediately, Mark tells us, Jesus made his disciples get into the boat without him for another journey to the other side (Mark 6:45). Why would Jesus have to "make" his disciples embark on another sea journey to the other side? Their evident reluctance is part of the meaning of these crossings. Reaching out to Gentiles is not in their nature. But they acquiesced while Jesus went up a mountain to pray. For this journey to the other side, the disciples are in the boat alone, without Jesus. We know that it is already late in the day, but Mark tells us again that they were still out on the sea in the evening (Mark 6:47). Another evening trip, with darkness approaching.

This trip is also a struggle. Mark tells us that Jesus could see that they were having a hard time rowing in a strong headwind (Mark 6:48). Jesus is aware that the journey to an inclusive community is hard. It is a strain, and feels like rowing against the wind. Jesus, master of the waters of chaos, walks out on the water toward the boat. Just as God "passed by Elijah" (Exod 34:6) and Moses (Exod 33:20) so that they could glimpse the divine, so Jesus initially walks past them. They are terrified, not recognizing Jesus, mistaking him for a ghost until he calms them, saying, "Take heart, it is I; do not be afraid" (Mark 6:50). Mark's next sentence describes their reaction and places blame on them. "And they were utterly astounded . . . their hearts were hardened" (Mark 6:51–52). Being blamed for having a hard heart is extremely harsh. It would make no sense if we were not taking this story symbolically. But if this is a metaphor for their reluctance to cross to the Gentiles, a hard, perhaps nationalist heart, could explain it. Should they have known better? Mark supplies a reason for their resistance: "For they did not understand about the loaves [literally "breads"]" (Mark 6:52). When Jesus is present, not only is the storm calm and the adverse winds become manageable, but there is plenty for everyone. But so far, the only ones fed were on the Jewish side. That is about to change.

They land on the Gentile side at Gennesaret. It may be surprising to read that Jesus meets both Pharisees and some of the Torah scribes who had come to find him, all the way from Jerusalem (Mark 7:1), on that side. If they came all the way from Jerusalem, then they were on a mission to find and confront Jesus. Mark sets this confrontation on the Gentile side of the lake to make a point. One of the primary obstacles in the way of Jewish and Gentile communal inclusivity is the Jewish purity laws and customs. The Pharisees and scribes confront Jesus and his disciples about violating those purity laws (laws of Moses) and customs (of the Pharisees, like hand washing). Mark details some of the Pharisees' customs about "washing" of dishes as well as hands that went way beyond the laws of Moses. Mark calls those customs "the tradition of the elders" (Mark 7:3). By the way, the Pharisees' hand washing had nothing to do with cleanliness; it was ritual sprinkling, the equivalent of prayer before meals.

Jesus considers their opposition mere hypocrisy and openly points it out, citing another custom they follow that breaks the command to honor your father and mother (Mark 7:9). That custom involved vowing to give money to the temple that should have gone to support aging parents. This example illustrates his point. Their customs have become more significant to them than obeying the law, which was meant to truly help aging parents. For Jesus, the "tradition of the elders" was being used to undermine the law of Moses to the detriment of aging parents.

Jesus is going to go even further. He is about to radically break with all of the kosher food laws of the Hebrew Bible. "Then he called the crowd again and said to them, 'Listen to me, all of you, and understand: there is nothing outside a person that by going in can defile, but the things that come out are what defile'" (Mark 7:14–15). In case the reader missed the point, Mark adds, parenthetically, "Thus he declared all foods clean" (Mark 7:18). In spite of pages and pages of laws in the Hebrew Bible about which food sources are clean and unclean, Jesus abrogates them (for example, Deut 14:3–21). On what basis? Food is only food, to be digested and then flushed away. But the heart is another matter. "It is what comes out of a person that defiles. For it is from within, from the human heart, that evil intentions come . . . evil things come from within, and they defile a person" (Mark 7:20–23). Jesus included a short list of "evil things" that come from the heart, including "slander," speaking evil of another person. Like the way Jews spoke about Gentiles and the reverse.

This controversy, which began with the purity issue of washing hands and then extended to all kosher food laws, was set here on the Gentile side of the lake to make a point. Purity laws, including kosher laws, were an enormous obstacle to Jewish-Gentile relations. Jesus was dismantling that obstacle. His vision of the kingdom of God was inclusive, and no law, human or divine, or custom was justified as a reason for resistance.

The Second Feeding

Though we have already told the story of Jesus healing the Canaanite woman's daughter, chronologically it happens next, followed by the healing of a Gentile deaf man. Now we come to the second feeding miracle, while we are still on the Gentile side of the sea. Again Jesus observes the hungry crowd and expresses compassion for them, just as he had for hungry people on the

Jewish side. Again the disciples seem, if not entirely unconcerned, at least helpless: "How can one feed these people with bread here in the desert?" (Mark 8:4). And once again, Jesus asks about the supplies on hand: "How many loaves [literally "breads"] do you have?" (Mark 8:5). This time the number is seven. In the Bible, seven is the number for perfection and completion. What is perfectly complete? That will become clear soon. Again, the crowds sit and again, using the same four eucharistic verbs, Jesus "took," "blessed" (or "gave thanks"—same meaning), "broke," and "gave" the bread to his disciples (Mark 8:6), who now are responsible for distributing it. After four thousand people ate and were satisfied, seven baskets (this time using the Gentile word for *basket* rather than the Hebrew word, as before) were left over. Now everyone on both sides, Jews and Gentiles, has been fed to the full. As the number seven suggests, the inclusive community is complete. They depart in the boat back to the "other side," back into Jewish territory.

The Difficult Lesson of the Two Feedings

On the way home, instead of encountering a storm of wind and water, the disciples get a storm of emotion from Jesus. Mark sets up the story by telling us, "Now, the disciples had forgotten to bring any bread [literally "breads"]; and they had only one loaf [literally "one bread"] with them in the boat" (Mark 8:14). Jesus's mind seems to still be on the opposition he was experiencing so, without context, he told them "Watch out—beware of the yeast of the Pharisees and the yeast of Herod" (Mark 8:15). Yeast was a metaphor for evil, but the disciples think Jesus is referring to bread, as odd as that seems. They explained Jesus's warning to each other: "They said to one another, 'It is because we have no bread [literally "breads"]" (Mark 8:16). On a symbolic level, the disciples do not yet understand that the completed community of Jews and Gentiles is now one single bread, one loaf. They still think they need to make a distinction between the two, with two separate but equal breads, or loaves of bread. This irritates Jesus. "And becoming aware of it, Jesus said to them, 'Why are you talking about having no bread [literally "breads"]? Do you still not perceive or understand? Are your hearts hardened? Do you have eyes, and fail to see? Do you have ears, and fail to hear?" (Mark 8:17–18). Why was he so angry? He had just performed two feedings before them, one on each side of the sea. Each had leftovers. The one on the Jewish side had a symbolically significant twelve baskets of leftovers, while there were a symbolic seven baskets on the Gentile side. There was more than enough for everyone, Jew and Gentile alike. They only needed one bread.

If this interpretation seems strained or allegorical, the next moment should make it clear that Jesus, as Mark tells it, wanted them to appreciate the symbolism of those two feedings. Jesus quizzes them to help them understand the meaning. "When I broke the five loaves for the five thousand, how many baskets full of broken pieces did you collect?' They said to him, 'Twelve.' 'And the seven for the four thousand, how many baskets full of broken pieces did you collect?' And they said to him, 'Seven.' Then he said to them, 'Do you not yet understand?'" (Mark 8:19–21). Mark is asking the reader if we understand the symbols. One bread alone is needed for the one inclusive community of Jews and Gentiles together.

Events on either side of the lake have been paralleled to show a balance of God's concern for Jews and Gentiles. The difficulty of embracing this inclusive vision is fully acknowledged. Crossing over to the other side is hard; in fact, stormy. It involves getting out on a boat on the dangerous waters of the sea. It shakes settled categories to the point of feeling life-threatening. But Jesus's presence in the boat, or on the water, makes all the difference. Jesus's teaching that the human heart is the issue, not ritual purity or boundary-maintaining food restrictions. Evil hearts produce all kinds of sins, including slander, speaking evil against others. That has no place in the new wineskin where this new wine awaits the eucharistic sharing of the common bread and cup. The disciples' nationalistic reticence to receive the message of inclusion gets the harshest rebukes Jesus ever uttered. It is an act of hard-hearted, deaf, blind faithlessness that refuses to accept the other as a full participant in the reconciled community. For Jesus, there is no other option. The blessings of Abraham must be extended to all the families of the earth.

14

The International Great Commission

In the first Gospel, Mark, there is no Great Commission. Maybe it was not necessary. In one sense, the outreach to Gentiles was already a done deal. By the time Mark was written, Paul had established churches in cities throughout the Mediterranean. But the question is, did Jesus authorize that Gentile mission?

Matthew's Gospel ends with the Great Commission to "go therefore and make disciples of all nations, baptizing them in the name of the Father and of the Son and of the Holy Spirit and teaching them to obey everything that I have commanded you" (Matt 28:19–20). In most ancient manuscripts, Marks' doesn't end this way; its conclusion is both abrupt and negative, ending with the word "afraid." There is no resurrection appearance of Jesus. Rather, the women who went to the tomb find it empty and, "As they entered the tomb, they saw a young man, dressed in a white robe, sitting on the right side; and they were alarmed" (Mark 16:5). The young man in white (an angel?) tells them that Jesus has risen and that they should "go, tell his disciples and Peter that he is going ahead of you to Galilee; there you will see him, just as he told you" (Mark 16:7). But they do not go tell anyone anything. Mark ends on this dark note: "They went out and fled from the tomb, for terror and amazement had seized them; and they said nothing to anyone, for they were afraid" (Mark 16:8). At some point in history, finding this story incomplete, someone added a few more verses including a Great Commission. "Go into all the world and proclaim the good news to the whole creation" (Mark 16:15). Almost no one believes that was original, even if a genuine ending has been lost. Others think the ending works as is. There are some signs of hope in the text. It was sunrise when they went to the tomb, so maybe that is a hint that a new day is dawning. Also, the man in white predicted they would meet Jesus back in Galilee, where it all started. In any case, the Gospel in the most authoritative manuscripts has no Great Commission.

Mark and the Gentile Mission

However, Mark provides many indications that Jesus authorized a Gentile mission. We just saw that Mark constructed his story showing Jesus's outreach to non-Israelites, balancing his ministry on both the Jewish and Gentile sides of the sea. Jesus himself is shown to have begun the Gentile mission by his ministry to Gentiles. There is also another indication that Jesus approved a mission outreach to Gentiles. It comes in a passage about what to expect in the future. Bad times are coming, Jesus warns his disciples: "Beware; for they will hand you over to councils; and you will be beaten in synagogues; and you will stand before governors and kings because of me, as a testimony to them" (Mark 13:9). But in the context of those times of social and economic upheaval, the disciples have a job. Jesus continued, "And the good news must first be proclaimed to all nations" (Mark 13:10). Jesus predicted that the gospel, or good news, would be taken to "all nations," meaning Gentile nations—Israel alone was a Jewish nation. While Mark does not show Jesus commissioning his disciples with a charge to "go," nevertheless he uses the word "must" about taking the gospel to all the families of the earth.

Matthew and the Gentile Mission

Matthew's Gospel followed Mark's. In fact, Matthew used Mark's Gospel as one of his sources. Sometimes he quotes Mark verbatim. Other times, he edits Mark, often by abbreviating. He mostly follows Mark's order of events in Jesus's life, inserting scenes Mark did not have, but then returning to Mark's order. So Matthew was later than Mark. That means Matthew wrote after the horrific Jewish War that ended with the Roman victory, the destruction of the temple, and tens of thousands of deaths. Many others fled. Most have recognized that Matthew's Gospel has a distinctly Jewish flavor, but what kind of Jewish community of followers of Jesus were they? There are good reasons to believe that Matthew's community comprised war refugees who had escaped the fighting and ended up in Syria. Now this Jewish community, which recognized Jesus as the Messiah, was living among Gentiles, including Gentile "Christians." (It is anachronistic to call these early communities of Jesus-followers "Christians." That title came later, but it is a convenient shorthand.) There, they faced an identity crisis. "Who are we now?" Now that they lived outside of Israel, now that there was no temple, now that there were no priests. Should they remain a strictly Torah-observant expatriate Jewish community, which would mean isolating themselves from Gentile Christians, or should they embrace the Gentile mission while retaining their distinctly Jewish customs, thus integrating with the wider church? Some have argued that Matthew's Gospel was written to address that identity crisis.

They wanted to be faithful followers of Jesus, whom they believed had commanded them to remain faithful to observing Torah. Matthew tells us that Jesus said, "Do not think that I have come to abolish the law (of Moses) or the prophets; I have come not to abolish but to fulfill. For truly I tell you, until heaven and earth pass away, not one letter, not one stroke of a letter, will pass from the law until all is accomplished" (Matt 5:17). Perhaps that mandate was meant only for Jews and was not binding on Gentiles; but as Jews, they were to remain faithful to Torah, the law of Moses. What was Jesus's position on Gentiles? Matthew's Gospel faces the dilemma head-on.

Matthew is the only Gospel to report that, as he was sending his twelve disciples on a mission trip, Jesus gave them these instructions: "Go nowhere among the Gentiles, and enter no town of the Samaritans, but go rather to the lost sheep of the house of Israel" (Matt 10:5–6). In fact, Jesus described his own ministry in those exclusivist categories as well, saying, to the Canaanite woman with the daughter in need, "I was sent only to the lost sheep of the house of Israel" (Matt 15:24). How does Jesus go from those ethnic exclusions to the Great Commission that he gives as the culmination of Matthew's story: "Go therefore and make disciples of all nations" (Matt 28:19)?

Matthew has two ways of getting there. One is a theological interpretation of recent history, the other is a literary strategy. The way Matthew theologically interprets recent history—that is, the Jewish War and the crushing Roman victory—is to understand it as God's punishment of the Jewish authorities, both religious and political (if you could make a meaningful distinction between the two), for their rejection of the gospel of the kingdom that Jesus proclaimed. The leaders led the people to reject the Messiah, culminating in arresting and executing Jesus. Matthew places the blame squarely on the leaders, exonerating Roman Governor Pontius Pilate in the process.

> Now the chief priests and the elders persuaded the crowds to . . . have Jesus killed. . . . So when Pilate saw that he could do nothing, but rather that a riot was beginning, he took some water and washed his hands before the crowd, saying, "I am innocent of this man's blood; see to it yourselves." Then the people as a whole answered, "His blood be on us and on our children!" (Matt 27:20, 24–25)

By the way, those words of the misled crowd have become the basis for anti-Semitism, programs, persecutions, and discrimination against Jews throughout history. Misusing the Bible has a long and dark history in which the church has been complicit. The absurd irony of Christians, whose Christ, when he walked the earth, was a Jewish man, is utterly ignored. Anti-Semitism is ignorance on steroids.

The leaders of the nation, "the chief priests and the elders," persuaded the people to acquiesce to the murder of Jesus by crucifixion. The risen Lord responds to this rejection by commanding his disciples to make disciples of "all nations." This is Matthew's theological interpretation of recent history that justifies the Gentile mission.

How do you then tell the story of Jesus with an eventual acceptance of Gentile inclusion? Matthew has a second strategy, a literary one. Matthew gives glimpses of the eventual climax from the beginning of the Gospel and throughout the story. Scholars refer to the beginning of the Gospels as prologues. A prologue functions like a symphonic overture, in which the orchestra plays the musical themes that the full piece will develop. The prologues of the Gospels announce the themes that will emerge in the story. In Matthew's prologue, the theme of Gentile inclusion is presented in several ways.

Matthew begins with a part everyone likes to skip: the genealogy of Jesus, starting with Abraham (Matt 1:1). In that genealogy of fathers and sons, Matthew inserts four women: Tamar, Ruth, Rahab, and Bathsheba. Why these four? All were considered Gentiles. The Jewish tradition identified Tamar as a Jewish proselyte. Ruth is a Moabite. Rahab is a Canaanite from Jericho. Bathsheba's ethnicity is not specified, but her husband Uriah is identified as a Hittite (2 Sam 11:3). The implicit message is inescapable: Gentiles play a crucial role in the Jesus story, including being part of Jesus's DNA. That is how Matthew starts. Can anyone claim "pure" bloodlines? Jesus cannot.

Matthew then tells us the episode about Joseph, his reaction to Mary's pregnancy, his plan to break off their engagement, and the visit he received from the angel. The angel informed him that her pregnancy was not a result of unfaithfulness but from God. Then the angel quoted from the Hebrew Bible, applying an ancient prophecy to Jesus, still in utero, in an epithet, saying, "Look, the virgin shall conceive and bear a son, and they shall name him Emmanuel, which means, 'God is with us'" (Matt 1:23). The *with-ness* of God is precisely what Jesus will affirm as an ongoing reality for the disciples as they take the gospel to "all nations:" "Go therefore and make disciples of all nations. . . . And remember, I am with you always, to the end of the age." (Matt 28:19–20).

Next, Matthew tells the story of Jesus's birth. Though we tell the Christmas story like a creche scene with shepherds and wise men crowding around the baby Jesus in a stable, lying in the manger, that is a mash-up of Matthew and Luke, whose birth stories are quite distinct. Luke alone has the shepherds and the angels at the manger. Matthew alone has the visit of the wise men (Matt 2:1) to the "child" (Matt 2:2) (not "infant" as in Luke's telling—English versions fail to distinguish the two), Jesus in a "house" (Matt 2:11) (not a stable, as implied in Luke's telling).

Who were the wise men? Some translations call them magi (e.g., NASB), which is an English transliteration of the Greek word. *Magi* originally meant Persian members of the priestly class, but the term was more fluid by the time of Jesus. The distinction between priests, magicians, and astrologists was fuzzy. Whatever they were, they were not Jewish. And yet, they show up at baby Jesus's house, offering him expensive gifts befitting the true "king of the Jews" (Matt 2:2). What do these Gentiles do when they find Jesus? "On entering the house, they saw the child with Mary, his mother; and they knelt down and paid him homage" (Matt 2:11). "Homage" means "do obeisance"—in other words, "worship."[1] Gentiles, from the start, worship Jesus as the "king of the Jews," the same title that Pilate will hang on the cross at Jesus's crucifixion (Matt 27:37). The theme of the rejection of Jesus by his own people, and the worship of Jesus by Gentiles, is a major literary theme of Matthew's Gospel.

Still in the prologue, Matthew tells the story of how the magi frustrate Herod's plan to find the child Jesus. His solution is to slaughter all the male children two years old or less. Joseph and Mary flee for safety to Egypt, where they live until Herod's death. Upon their return, they learn that Herod's successor, the madman Archelaus (Matt 2:22), was reigning in Judea, and so they decide to settle in Nazareth instead of Jesus's birthplace in Bethlehem. This, Matthew tells us, fulfills a prophecy that predicts "he will be called a Nazorean" (Matt 2:23). Nazareth is located in what Matthew will call "Galilee of the Gentiles" (Matt 4:15). In Syria, where Matthew was

1. BDAG, s.v. "προσκυνέω."

written, one of the names for a Christian was *Nazorean*, as it still is in places like Iraq. When ISIS invaded Iraq, they painted the Arabic letter *N* on the gates of suspected Christians. From the beginning, Matthew is anticipating Jesus's ministry as Messiah to the Gentiles. And Matthew is just getting started.

After the execution of John the Baptist at the hands of Herod's son, Antipas, Jesus felt the need to withdraw from Nazareth to Capernaum "in the territory of Zebulun and Naphtali" (Matt 4:12). Matthew draws attention to this area again as "Galilee of the Gentiles" and finds in it another fulfillment of prophecy, saying, "So that what had been spoken through the prophet Isaiah might be fulfilled: 'Land of Zebulun, land of Naphtali . . . Galilee of the Gentiles—the people who sat in darkness [Gentiles] have seen a great light, and for those who sat in the region and shadow of death light has dawned'" (Matt 4:14–16).

Matthew and Luke both record the story of Jesus healing the centurion's servant. When the centurion told Jesus that he believed Jesus could heal his servant at a distance without needing to come to his house, Jesus was "amazed" and said, "Truly I tell you, in no one in Israel have I found such faith" (Matt 8:10, Luke 7:9). Only Matthew records Jesus's reflection on the deeper meaning of this Gentile's faith. "I tell you, many will come from east and west [Gentile areas] and will eat with Abraham and Isaac and Jacob in the kingdom of heaven, while the heirs of the kingdom [descendants of Abraham, Isaac, and Jacob] will be thrown into the outer darkness, where there will be weeping and gnashing of teeth" (Matt 8:11). This summary describes what the Jewish war refugees in Matthew's community in Syria had just witnessed. They had seen Israel's *no* to Jesus and the destruction of Jerusalem, and they had seen many Gentiles turning to Jesus. From the perspective of the people who knew the end of the story of Matthew, including Jesus's Great Commission, the Gentile centurion's amazing faith was the first indication that people "from east and west" would be included in the great banquet of Messiah in the coming age. Those Gentiles would take their places at the table alongside the ancient patriarchs of Israel, Abraham, Isaac, and Jacob.

In Matthew, Jesus describes what the last days will be like (Matt 24:3). He predicts that difficult times will be ahead. There will be "wars and rumors of wars" (Matt 24:6). It will be hard for the followers of Jesus in those days, "they will hand you over to be tortured and will put you to death, and you will be hated by all nations because of my name" (Matt 24:9). So, Jesus says, persevere, because "the one who endures to the end will be saved" (Matt 24:13). But it is not all bad news. Even amid all this distress, the good news of the kingdom will still be advancing. Jesus said, "And this good news of the kingdom will be proclaimed throughout the world, as a testimony to all the nations; and then the end will come" (Matt 24:14). Throughout his Gospel, Matthew has repeatedly tipped his hand that Gentiles will be included in the kingdom. From the beginning, Matthew has prepared his readers for the climax announcement of the Great Commission, when Jesus charges his followers to "go . . . make disciples of all nations" (Matt 28:19).

Luke-Acts and the Gentile Mission

Luke planned and wrote a two-volume work that, now, through the accidents of history, has been divided. Luke-Acts exceeds the maximum length of a single scroll, so probably two were required. Now, in our Bibles, the Gospel of John stands between volume one, the Gospel of Luke, and volume two, the book of Acts. However, Luke's introductions to both books show that he planned his two-volume work from the start. In volume one, the Gospel is dedicated to a person he calls "most excellent Theophilus," probably the sponsor of his work (Luke 1:3). He begins volume two with these words, again to Theophilus, "In the first book, Theophilus, I wrote about all that Jesus did and taught from the beginning until the day when he was taken up to heaven" (Acts 1:1–2). As he said, volume one was about Jesus. Volume two is about the way the gospel goes into the Gentile (or Greek) world, first through Peter, then through Paul's missionary ministry. Luke knew from the beginning of his Gospel that the story would include the Gentile mission. Does he foreshadow that movement from Israel to the rest of the world? Yes, he does; from the very start.

Luke tells us that Jesus's parents took him as an eight-day-old infant to the temple to be circumcised. There they encounter Simeon, whom Luke describes as "righteous and devout, looking forward to the consolation of Israel, and the Holy Spirit rested on him" (Luke 2:25). The Spirit inspired him to take Jesus in his arms and pray, "My eyes have seen your salvation, which you have prepared in the presence of all peoples, a light for revelation to the Gentiles and for glory to your people Israel" (Luke 2:30–32). Already, the destiny of Jesus to be a "light for revelation to the Gentiles" is forecast. After praying over Jesus, Zechariah turns to Mary and says these ominous words, "This child is destined for the falling and the rising of many in Israel" (Luke 2:34). Notice that the falling precedes the rising. First, as shown in the Gospel, Jesus will be rejected by his own people, Israel. Only afterward will some of his people, and many Gentiles, rise to faith.

Another moment that telegraphs the direction that the story will take, from Israel to the Gentile world, is in Luke 4. That story was told in chapter

12 of this book. In his inaugural message at the synagogue in Nazareth, Jesus told his hometown family and friends that God's concern included people outside of Israel, such as the widow of Zarephath in Sidon, and Naaman, the Syrian leper. That anti-nationalistic message so enraged them that they tried to murder him. From the start of his Gospel, Luke anticipated the Gentile mission, which would be the subject of Acts, volume two.

In one of the most striking of his parables, Luke again forecasts the two-step process of the gospel going to the Gentiles. Step one is the rejection of Jesus by the Jewish establishment. Step two is the open door to the Gentiles. The parable known as the "Wicked Tenants" is found in Luke 20. It begins with a vineyard, a symbol for Israel in the Hebrew Bible (e.g., Isa 27:2 et al.). The vineyard owner makes a contract to lease it to tenant farmers in exchange for rent. When he sends a succession of three slaves to collect what was due, however, the tenants turn ugly. They mistreat them and beat them and send them away empty-handed. Finally, the owner sends his own son, saying, "I will send my beloved son; perhaps they will respect him" (Luke 20:13). Instead of respecting him, the tenants killed him. Jesus then asks the Jewish leaders, his audience, "What then will the owner of the vineyard do to them?" He answers his own question: "He will come and destroy those tenants and give the vineyard to others" (Luke 20:15–16). The meaning is clear. The vineyard is Israel. The owner is God. The tenants are the leaders of Israel who reject Jesus, the "beloved son."

To make sure those leaders, who considered themselves the spiritual builders of Israel, fully grasped his meaning, Jesus quoted to them from the Psalms:, "'The stone that the builders rejected has become the cornerstone" (Luke 20:17 = Ps 118:22). According to Luke, Jesus is making a play on words. The "stone" (*eben* in Hebrew) is rejected by the builders, just as the son (*ben* in Hebrew) was rejected by the tenants. Therefore, God, the vineyard's owner, will take it from them and give it to "others." They got the point. It made them so mad that they wanted to kill Jesus right then and there, but could not because the supportive crowds in Jerusalem for the Passover festival protected him. "When the scribes and chief priests realized that he had told this parable against them, they wanted to lay hands on him at that very hour, but they feared the people" (Luke 20:19).

Now we come to Luke's second volume, the book of Acts. Acts begins with Luke's version of the Great Commission. The disciples meet the risen Jesus in Jerusalem, where he tells them, "you will receive power when the Holy Spirit has come upon you; and you will be my witnesses in Jerusalem, in all Judea and Samaria, and to the ends of the earth" (Acts 1:8). The rest of the book of Acts demonstrates how the present eleven disciples, plus Paul, fulfill that commission. The disciples were witnesses of Jesus in Jerusalem, then in all Judea and Samaria, and finally to the ends of the earth, which to them meant the Roman Empire. The story starts in Jerusalem (Acts 2:1–8:1), continues into of Judea and Samaria (Acts 8:1–11:18), and spreads all the way to Rome (Acts 13:1–19:20).

The transition from Jewish space and people to the Hellenized world and its Gentile people is not seamless. It remains difficult for Jewish people like Jesus's disciples to grasp the concept. They have been used to living under the mandate of the Jewish law with its demands of circumcision, Sabbath observance, and kosher food restrictions. Luke tells several stories about how that barrier, that Ephesians later described as "the dividing wall of hostility" (Eph 1:14), could be breached. The first story is the experience of Pentecost, in which the barrier of language is overcome. Another is Peter's experience, which begins with a dream and ends with the conversion of a Gentile centurion. Those stories will be the subjects of the next two chapters.

The Gospel of John and the Gentile Mission

The Gospel of John does not have a scene in which Jesus commissions the disciples to take the good news to the entire world. From the beginning, however, John's Gospel has a worldwide scope. In John's prologue, he speaks of Jesus, saying, "In him was life, and the life was the light of all people" (John 1:4). John quotes Jesus saying, "And I, when I am lifted up from the earth, will draw all people to myself" (John 12:32). "All people" portends the movement of the gospel to the ends of the earth. In one of the Bible's most famous verses, John 3:16, Jesus says, "For God so loved the world that he gave his only Son, so that everyone who believes in him may not perish but may have eternal life." Just before that, Jesus said, "Whoever believes in [me] may have eternal life" (John 3:15). The word "whoever" shows up in John twenty-four times, extending the invitation indefinitely, as in John 8:12 where Jesus says, "I am the light of the world. Whoever follows me will never walk in darkness but will have the light of life."

Perhaps "whoever" is vague enough to mean "whoever among the chosen people." Jesus, however, makes his understanding of the universal reach of the gospel clear. Though the chosen people are God's particular flock whom he shepherds, Jesus said, "I am the good shepherd. I know my own and my own know me, just as the Father knows me and I know the Father. And I lay down my life for the sheep. I have other sheep that do not belong to this fold. I must bring them also, and they will listen to my voice. So there will be one flock, one shepherd" (John 10:14–16). "Other sheep that do not belong to this fold" can only mean one thing: the inclusion of Gentiles. Not that then there will be two folds with separate but equal sheep. Rather, "there will be one flock, one shepherd."

When Jesus's mother came to him at the wedding in Cana, to coax him to do something about the lack of wine, he first demurred, saying to Mary, "My hour has not yet come" (John 2:4). Twice they tried to arrest Jesus, "but no one laid hands on him, because his hour had not yet come" (John 7:30; a similar scene occurs in John 8:20). But in chapter 12 Jesus said, "The hour has come for the Son of Man to be glorified" (12:23). What happened to signal to Jesus that the much anticipated "hour" had finally "come"? John tells the story this way: "Now among those who went up to worship at the festival were some Greeks. They came to Philip, who was from Bethsaida in Galilee, and said to him, 'Sir, we wish to see Jesus.' Philip went and told Andrew; then Andrew and Philip went and told Jesus. Jesus answered them, 'The hour has come for the Son of Man to be glorified'" (John 12:20–23). When the Greeks—that is, Gentiles—come seeking Jesus, he recognizes that his "hour," the culmination of his earthly ministry, has finally arrived. In the same context, after the Greeks came seeking Jesus, he said, "I have come as light into the world, so that everyone who believes in me should not remain in the darkness. . . . I came not to judge the world, but to save the world" (John 12:46–47).

John's Gospel reports that when Jesus was finally arrested, the Roman Governor Pilate had a sign made for Jesus's cross to announce the charge for which he was being crucified. John says, "Pilate also had an inscription written and put on the cross. It read, 'Jesus of Nazareth, the King of the Jews.' . . . It was written in Hebrew, in Latin, and in Greek" (John 19:19–20). Hebrew was the language of the Jews, Latin was the language of the Romans, and Greek was the language of the Hellenized world. Could there be any doubt that the message of Jesus was meant for the world?

We have seen that all four Gospels and the book of Acts show that the mission of Jesus, though it began in Jewish space among the chosen people, was intended for the world. Each author anticipated that move from the start in their own unique ways. Each one showed that Jesus himself authorized the mission to the Gentiles. The Christian vision has never been restricted to one nation or race, not even to the chosen people of Israel alone. The New Testament clarifies that the goal is to have "one flock," not separate, distinct national flocks, because there is "one Shepard." Any claim that people function best when living with their own kind runs counter to the call and ministry of Jesus to take the message to everyone. The blessing promised to Abraham is being fulfilled because it has been extended to all the families of the earth.

15

Pentecost: Babel No More

THE BIBLE HAS BEEN called the most hyperlinked text ever compiled. Texts quote other texts, and stories are told in parallel with other stories. Some stories echo previous stories with keyword connections and allusions. The story of Pentecost in Acts 2 is hyperlinked in that way with the story of the tower of Babel in Gen 11, which deepens and enriches our understanding of Luke's message.

That begs the question, How would Luke, a Gentile, have been so familiar with the Hebrew Bible, even if he had access to the Greek translation, the Septuagint (or LXX)? Luke, in all probability, was part of a group of people that he refers to as "God-fearers," or "worshippers of God" and "lovers of God," who are distinguished from Jews—that is, Gentiles. There are many examples in Luke and Acts. Luke describes Cornelius, the centurion from Caesarea whom we will meet in our next chapter as "a devout man who feared God" (Acts 10:2). In Luke's second volume, the book of Acts, Paul makes the distinction clear saying, "You Israelites, and others who fear God, listen" (Acts 13:16). And again, "My brothers, you descendants of Abraham's family, and others who fear God, to us the message of this salvation has been sent" (Acts 13:26). Luke dedicates both of his volumes, Luke and Acts, to "Theophilus" whose name means "God-lover" (Luke 1:3; Acts 1:1).

These Gentiles were attracted to Judaism. It was a respected and ancient faith that produced people of strong family values and rigorous moral standards. These Gentiles accepted Jewish monotheism, attended synagogue services, and contributed funds. Ancient historian Josephus says that Gentiles as far away as Asia and Europe had been contributing to synagogues for a long time, making them wealthy. Were they considered converts to Judaism? Some were called converts, as we will see. Insofar as being a full convert would include the obligation to become circumcised, not many went that far. They were content to be God-fearing, God-worshipping, or God-loving, without taking that final step.

As a Gentile God-fearer, Luke would have become familiar with the narratives of the Hebrew Bible from years of synagogue participation. At some point he became a Christian. As he writes the book of Acts, his version of the spread of the good news from Jewish space to Gentile space, he deepens the story with allusions to the Hebrew Bible. He tells the story of Pentecost by allusions to the story of the tower of Babel, as we will see.

Pentecost

The story of Pentecost, as we call it, is both straightforward and odd. The risen Christ has instructed the disciples to stay in Jerusalem after he departs until they are baptized with the Holy Spirit (Acts 1:5). The story that follows in Acts 2 describes how that happened. When the disciples were all together, "suddenly from heaven there came a sound like the rush of a violent wind, and it filled the entire house where they were sitting. Divided tongues, as of fire, appeared among them, and a tongue rested on each of them. All of them were filled with the Holy Spirit and began to speak in other languages, as the Spirit gave them ability" (Acts 2:4). Here, being "filled" with the Holy Spirit means the same as being "baptized" in the Holy Spirit. The experience included sound, "like the rush of a mighty wind" and sight, as the "tongues of fire" appeared. Then the effect was experienced by each of them as they were miraculously enabled to speak in "other languages," or literally, "other tongues."

This is where the oddities start. The scene shifts from inside the house, where the disciples had gathered, to outside. Luke sets the stage by informing us that "there were devout Jews from every nation under heaven living in Jerusalem" (Acts 2:5) who somehow heard the voices from inside. As improbable as it seems, the sound of the voices inside was sufficient to draw a crowd. Stranger still, the crowd "was bewildered [literally "confused"] because each one heard them speaking in the native language of each" (Acts 2:6). Now it seems that the miracle was not so much in the mouths of the disciples but in the ears of the diverse crowd. Nor does Luke explain why hearing someone speaking your own language would cause you to be "bewildered" or "confused." The crowd is also somehow aware that the disciples are Galileans, who were not expected to be multilingual.

Luke has told us that all this is happening on the day of Pentecost (Acts 2:1). Pentecost was a big Jewish festival, which helps account for the crowd in Jerusalem. What was the Pentecost festival all about? Here comes another oddity. At that time, several festivals were called Pentecost. "Pentecost" literally means "fiftieth." According to Lev 23:15–16, on the fiftieth day after Passover, a festival was held. It was a harvest festival when the first fruits of the grain were harvested and offered in sacrifice. It was also called the Feast of Weeks (Exod 23:16) because it came after a period of seven weeks of harvesting. In Luke's time, the Jews also considered it the anniversary of the day God gave Moses the law, or Torah, on Mount Sinai. This was one of the three great annual festivals that brought huge crowds to Jerusalem from throughout the Jewish diaspora; the others were the Passover, which came earlier in the year, and Tabernacles four months later.

To complicate matters further, at least some Jews, like those at the Qumran community, celebrated three Pentecost festivals. Each of them was fifty days apart. After the Pentecost—called the Feast of Weeks, the grain harvest festival—came the festival of New Wine, followed by the festival of New Oil. It is possible that Luke, the Gentile, did not appreciate the difference between them. Although the Pentecost harvest festival occurs before the grape harvest, and hence before the production of "new wine," the bewildered crowds explain the cacophony of foreign languages being spoken simultaneously as the speech of people who have had too much "new wine." "Others sneered and said, 'They are filled with new wine'" (Acts 2:13). How speaking in foreign languages could sound like drunken talk is also left to the reader's imagination.

Luke gives us a detailed list of the diverse people comprising that crowd. Fifteen countries or ethnic groups are listed. The list itself is similar to lists of nations found from ancient Babylon to Greece, so some speculate that Luke was working off a list from another source. The list of fifteen may have originally had only twelve, but Luke, in an offhanded way, after the twelve adds that there were "both Jews and proselytes, Cretans and Arabs" (Acts 2:10–11). Jews, Cretans, and Arabs add three more. Proselytes could have been from any non-Jewish nation or people. Proselytes include the God-fearers, Gentiles who were circumcised, and converts to Judaism. Luke has just slipped in the information that this diverse group, whom he is going to address as "fellow Israelites" and "brothers" in his coming sermon, is actually a mixed group of Jews and Gentiles. In this way, he is foreshadowing the Gentile mission that Jesus's commission had authorized and that the book of Acts is going to describe. Gentiles who were "God-fearers," "God-lovers," and sometimes "God-worshippers," like Luke and Theophilus, as well as fully converted proselytes, will soon become Christ-followers.

The Hyperlinks with Babel

According to the Hebrew Bible, God gave his word to Moses at Mount Sinai. On Pentecost, the celebration of the anniversary of that occasion, God's word to the people is being proclaimed in the native languages of everyone in that international crowd. The linguistic disunity that has characterized humanity has now been transcended. It is almost utopian, like a new creation in which the human race's unity is restored. In this way, at least in this one moment, the confusion of languages that started, as the Bible describes, in the story of the tower of Babel has been reversed.

Did Luke intend this allusion to that story? Apart from the reversal of the "confusion" of languages, a word used in both stories (Gen 11:7, 9 and Acts 2:6, where the NRSV translates it "bewildered"), there is another link. According to Jewish tradition, the tower of Babel was destroyed by a violent wind. That was precisely how Luke described the sound that came with the Holy Spirit on the day of Pentecost when "suddenly from heaven there came a sound like the rush of a violent wind" (Acts 2:2). Luke told the story of Pentecost this way to link it to the story of the tower of Babel.

Why did Luke want his readers to make that connection? Let's review the story told in Gen 11. It begins with a description of humanity in the ancient world as completely unified. "Now the whole earth had one language and the same words" (Gen 11:1). The setting is a flat plain somewhere in Mesopotamia. Then, without any reason given, they said to one another, "Come, let us make bricks, and burn them thoroughly" (Gen 11:3). Bricks are mentioned first, before they have agreed to build anything. Then, using a phrase commonly found in many inscriptions on buildings in the ancient Near East, Genesis says, "And they had brick for stone, and bitumen for mortar" (Gen 11:3). Finally, they come to the reason. They plan to build a city and in it build "a tower with its top in the heavens" (Gen 11:4).

All of the details show that the tower they plan is a ziggurat. A ziggurat is a multistage tower-temple, a prominent feature of most ancient Mesopotamian cities. The name comes from an Akkadian word meaning "to build high."[1] In other words, it is a symbolic sacred mountain. Extending from earth to the sky, it was the meeting point of heaven and earth, a place for contact between the gods and humans. The phrase "with its top in the sky or heavens" is a cliché in Mesopotamian building inscriptions, especially ziggurats. Why did the story of the tower building in Genesis begin with bricks first? The author of Genesis would have known the Mesopotamian creation story, which includes the account of building a ziggurat. The story

1. Sarna, *Genesis*, 172.

says that in the first year, they ceremonially made the bricks for that sacred purpose, and in the second year, raised the head of the tower to the sky. The bricks came first, just as Genesis tells the story.

The reason the people gave, in Genesis, for building the sacred tower was to "make a name for ourselves" (Gen 11:4). Ancient kings inscribed their names on monumental architecture to ensure their lasting glory. *Name* and *monument* almost became synonymous. The prophet Isaiah imagined a future time in which foreigners would be "joined to the LORD" and would be given "a monument and a name," making them eligible to participate in temple worship, "in my house and within my walls," alongside Jews (Gen 56:3–5). Having a lasting monumental name is both what the people in Genesis wanted and what foreigners, in Isaiah, are promised.

What good would be a monumental name for the people of Genesis? They supply the further explanation: "Otherwise we shall be scattered abroad upon the face of the whole earth" (Gen 11:4). The sacred tower with its name inscription was meant to help unify them. A common feature of religion is its unifying force; that has long been recognized.

But this quest for a religiously based unity, according to Genesis, displeased Yahweh, who was not to be found at the top of a man-made mountain. In an ironic scene that is almost comical, in spite of their attempt to reach God's abode with the tower, Yahweh has to come down to get close enough to see them at work. "The LORD came down to see the city and the tower, which mortals had built" (Gen 11:5). He disapproves of the project, and so deliberates in an internal dialogue, saying, "Come, let us go down, and confuse their language there, so that they will not understand one another's speech" (Gen 11:7). The crowd's confusion in Acts 2 echoes the confusion of languages here.

Back to the story of Pentecost in Acts 2, after hearing the accusations by the crowd of being drunk with new wine at the premature time of the grain harvest, Peter stands up to explain what has happened. He says that the tongues, or languages, that everyone heard proclaiming the good news are a fulfillment of prophecy from the Hebrew Bible. It was a common belief in the Judaism of the New Testament period that prophecy had long since ceased. They were living in the post-exilic times, when God's word came not by Spirit-inspired prophets but through the study of Torah. There was, nevertheless, the expectation that at some future time Messiah would come and prophecy would again flourish. Peter quoted Joel's prophecy that "in the last days it will be, God declares, that I will pour out my Spirit upon all flesh, and your sons and your daughters shall prophesy" (Acts 2:17). The Spirit-inspired tongues the disciples spoke to the international crowd, Peter said, is the fulfillment of that prophecy. He said to them, "This is what was spoken through the prophet Joel" (Acts 2:16).

What then should the people do? "Repent, and be baptized every one of you in the name of Jesus Christ so that your sins may be forgiven; and you will receive the gift of the Holy Spirit" (Acts 2:38). Why? Because "everyone who calls on the name of the Lord shall be saved" (Acts 2:21). The name they should call upon is not the name inscribed on a ziggurat. It is rather "the name of Jesus Christ [Messiah]" (Acts 2:38). On the celebration of the anniversary of the day Moses received the word of God, Torah, on Mount Sinai, a new prophetic word from God announces the way of salvation, found in the name of Jesus, the Messiah. This monumental name, Isaiah had predicted, would one day be worn by Gentiles. Peter also opens that same door saying, "The promise is for you, for your children, and for all who are far away, everyone whom the Lord our God calls to him" (Acts 2:39). The phrase "those who are far away" includes both "Jews and proselytes," another foreshadowing of the mission to the Gentiles that Peter himself will soon inaugurate. The message was a huge success. Luke tells us that three thousand people accepted his message with joy and agreed to be baptized that day (Acts 2:41).

Worldwide Unity

On the occasion of the harvest festival of Pentecost, the first fruits of the ecumenical harvest are gathered in. The separated nations of the world have been reunified under the name of Jesus, Messiah. This is the basis for a new international unity far beyond that which any sacred tower could produce. This new unity in Jesus's name could overcome the famously hostile division between Jew and Gentile. As Ephesians says, "You who once were far off have been brought near" because "he has made both groups into one" (Eph 2:13–14). The separate languages and ethnicities represented by the fifteen national groups gathered for Pentecost have experienced the reversal of the separation of Babel. The violent wind that knocked down that ancient ziggurat has now blown the breath of God's Spirit into the mouths, ears, and hearts of people willing to repent and be baptized in the name of Messiah, Jesus.

Any quest to undo that gospel unity is a scandal. Every nationalist desire to separate what God has joined together runs counter to the entire biblical vision of a new humanity made one in Christ. The nationalist desire to live among one's own kind to the exclusion of others fights against the purpose of God, which is to overcome exactly those divisions, according to the Bible. From its first hints in the promise of God to Abraham to bless all the families of the earth, the biblical story repeatedly shows that the circle of God's concern encompasses everyone. No one is outside its scope because of national origin or ethnicity. The new wine of the kingdom requires new wineskins large and flexible enough to embrace all the families of the earth.

16

Peter and Cornelius

THE EARLY CHURCH SPREAD quickly in North Africa and Egypt, but Luke does not mention that anywhere. How did it spread? Who were the movement's missionaries? Who led the movement? How did it relate to the apostles in Jerusalem? We know nothing about it. Luke is uninterested. From that fact alone, we can conclude that Luke's purpose was not to write a comprehensive history of the early church. What can we glean about Luke's purpose and goals from what he was interested in? He has several goals. Luke wants to show that the early church was unified, led by the apostles from the headquarters in Jerusalem, and was never a threat to Roman political power. When trouble arose, it was not started by Christ-followers, but by jealous Gentiles or angry Jews. In Luke's telling, Roman civil authorities keep finding the movement not guilty of anything anti-Roman. All of these show the legitimacy of the early church movement.

However, there is a larger, more important reason for Luke's work. It is to show the legitimacy of the Gentile mission. Some have argued that everything else, for Luke, is a prelude or a side show. Because the length of a story and repetitions are signals of its importance, it is worth noticing that the story of the conversion of Cornelius is both the longest one Luke tells, and the one with the most repetitions.

We can see Luke's goals at work as he tells the story of Cornelius, the Roman centurion from Caesarea, the city named for Caesar. Cornelius is the first convert identified as a Gentile. While the conversion of the Ethiopian eunuch has already been told, his status as a Gentile, even if obvious, is not mentioned. His origin, Ethiopia, is the point in that story. After Philip's evangelistic work in Samaria, the Ethiopian eunuch shows that the fulfillment of the Great Commission is underway. The good news has been proclaimed "in Jerusalem, in all Judea and Samaria, and to the ends of the earth" (Acts 1:8), as symbolized by Ethiopia.

Cornelius and His Vision

Here is how the story of the conversion of Cornelius the centurion unfolds. First, we are introduced to Cornelius, a centurion of the Italian cohort, who is described in glowing terms. He is as pious a Gentile as they come. He is a devout God-fearer who gives alms generously and prays constantly (Acts 10:1–2). Readers of Luke-Acts will recognize the parallel with the centurion Jesus encountered (Luke 7). You may recall that in Luke's version of the story, the Jewish leaders come to Jesus on his behalf, describing him as "worthy of having you do this for him, for he loves our people, and it is he who built our synagogue for us" (Luke 7:4–5). The fact that Jesus had positive contact with a Gentile centurion sets up and lends legitimacy to Peter's parallel contact with the centurion Cornelius.

Cornelius has a vision one afternoon at the oddly precise time of three o'clock, in which he is addressed by an angel. Telling unimportant details, like the hour of the day, is how an author slows down the action of a story, making it longer, showing its importance, and keeping the focus on the primary plot. The vision of the angel terrifies Cornelius, but he replies with the humility born of devotion, saying, "What is it, Lord?" (Acts 10:3–4). The angel tells him that his prayers and alms have "ascended as a memorial before God" (Acts 10:4) like the smoke of a sacrifice. These kinds of good works, as meritorious, seem to be at odds with the "by grace through faith apart from works" theology of Ephesians, but this is Luke's story. The angel instructs Cornelius to go to Joppa to find a man named Simon, who is called Peter, who has rooms in the seaside home of a tanner, also named Simon (Acts 10:6). These details are the ancient form of a house address and they are sufficiently precise. The angel does not bother telling Cornelius why he should find Peter, and oddly, Cornelius does not ask. But he is a soldier who knows how to take commands from his superiors. So Cornelius dispatches two of his household slaves and another devout soldier serving under his command, who find the right address.

Peter's Vision

Then the story shifts away from the Cornelius delegation to Peter himself. This part, too, is sprinkled with unimportant details. We find Peter on his roof, praying, but getting hungry. "While [a meal] was being prepared, he fell into a trance" (Acts 10:9). The lunchtime trance is about food, but not the kind of food a kosher-observant Jew ever eats. The Hebrew Bible has many food restrictions. The reasons given are now obscure. For example, we do not understand what difference it makes if an animal has a split hoof and does or does not chew cud like a cow. Cows are good because they have both characteristics, but pigs, which have a split hoof but do not chew cud, are, for that reason, not good (Lev 11:3–7; Deut 14:6–8). And that is just the start. There are prohibitions against eating varieties of fish, birds, and insects, all for reasons we cannot comprehend today. Nevertheless, they are what the law of Moses requires as part of its purity code, so an observant Jew like Peter observes them all.

What we might miss about these dietary restrictions is that they make it difficult—to the point of being virtually impossible—to share a meal at a Gentile's house. How could you be sure that the dish you were offered was kosher? Eating a meal with a Gentile was not explicitly forbidden (although Luke may have thought it was); it did not make you ritually impure, but the meal itself could, so why risk it? Most of the time, they did not. One of the reasons that there was such famous hostility between Jews and Gentiles was that Jews isolated themselves from common meals with Gentiles. Sharing meals has always and everywhere been a primary way humans form and nurture social bonds of friendship and trust. Our word *companion* comes from words that mean to "share bread with."[1] Eating together, or table fellowship, is social glue. But Jews and Gentiles generally did not bond that way.

Back to Peter's hungry trance. People in Peter's day and the ancient world in general believed that the universe had three stories. Most of the Gods were up in the heavens, except those under the earth in the realm of the dead; humans occupied "middle-earth," as Tolkien called it. From God's realm above, Peter sees something like a sheet descending. It is being lowered by its four corners, another trivial detail that keeps our focus fixed. On the sheet are "all kinds of four-footed creatures and reptiles and birds of the air" (Acts 10:12). "All kinds" of four-footed creatures implies those that are clean and those that are unclean. The language may be meant as an echo of the creation story in which God made "living creatures of every kind: cattle and creeping things and wild animals of the earth of every kind" (Gen 1:24), after which "God saw that it was good" (Gen 1:25). If so, it is fortuitous because that is exactly the substance of the heavenly voice's strong command: "Get up, Peter; kill and eat" (Acts 10:13). Kosher-observant Peter

1. Merriam-Webster, "Breaking Bread."

is shocked. He objects strongly, even to this heavenly voice, saying, "By no means, Lord; for I have never eaten anything that is profane or unclean" (Acts 10:14). Then, the way Luke tells it, "The voice said to him again, a second time, [even though this is the first time we are hearing it], 'What God has made clean, you must not call profane.'" This is unexpected. It is not as though Peter had invented the laws on food purity. Those laws came from Moses, and Moses, according to the story, got them directly from God. Visions—even ones from God—like dreams, sometimes play fast and loose with reality.

In any case, Peter is not yet convinced. Luke tells us, "This happened three times, and the thing was suddenly taken up to heaven" (Acts 10:16). The heavenly message seems perfectly clear. But not to Peter, who was quite puzzled about what the vision might mean (Acts 10:17). Why was he puzzled? Because he does not yet know anything about Cornelius's story, and he does not yet know that he is meant to take his vision as a metaphor. It was not about eating animals without distinction between clean and unclean; it was about welcoming people without such distinctions, specifically, Gentiles. He will soon put the pieces together.

Cornelius's Delegation to Peter

As he was puzzling it out, suddenly the delegation sent by Cornelius arrived (Acts 10:17). From the gate (another trivial detail), they asked for Peter. Before he knows he has guests, "the Spirit said to him, 'Look, three men are searching for you. Now get up, go down, and go with them without hesitation; for I have sent them'" (Acts 10:19–20). The words for "without hesitation" can also mean "without discrimination" or "without distinction,"[2] which may be more to the point of the story. The Spirit will soon demonstrate what "without distinction" means.

When they are introduced to Peter they tell him what we already know about Cornelius, that he is "an upright and God-fearing man, who is well spoken of by the whole Jewish nation, [who] was directed by a holy angel to send for you to come to his house and to hear what you have to say" (Acts 10:22). The repetition both slows the story down and lengthens it, lending importance to it. There is one piece of additional information in their report about the angel's message: it is that they are to invite Peter to come to Cornelius's house to hear what he has to say (Acts 10:22). Now Peter learns that he is supposed to go as a missionary preacher. Though Peter is only a lodger

2. BDAG, s.v. "διακρίνω."

in Simon the tanner's home, he invites them in and gives them lodging, providing hospitality, which in that culture is a gesture of solidarity.

It seems odd that Peter interpreted a vision about eating all kinds of animals without distinction as a metaphor for welcoming Cornelius and his family of Gentiles into the faith without distinction. Some have suggested that one of the sources Luke was using had the story of Peter's vision about clean and unclean animals that was originally intended to teach that all foods were clean, and used it here as a metaphor for Gentile inclusion. That is certainly possible. Luke, in Acts, will make the case that the purity laws do not apply to Gentiles but still apply to Jews. Toward the end of Acts, when Paul meets the elders of the Jerusalem church, James tells him that there are "many thousands of believers . . . among the Jews, and they are all zealous for the law" (Acts 21:20). But didn't Jesus declare "all foods clean"? Yes, in Mark's Gospel, he did (Mark 7:19), but Luke did not include that teaching in his version of the story.

It is also worth noting that the heavenly voice Peter heard when he saw his vision of the sheet full of animals left an open door of ambiguity. The voice told Peter, "What God has made clean, you must not call profane" (Acts 10:15). Notice the voice did not say, "Animals that God has made clean. . ." but "What God has made clean, you must not call profane." "What" is open-ended, leaving the door open to interpreting it as meaning "Whatever," which would then include people too. And that is precisely how Peter interpreted it, as he will soon say.

Peter at Cornelius's

Peter travels with Cornelius's delegation to meet him in Caesarea the next day. Cornelius has prepared for them and has invited his relatives and close friends. After some initial greetings with more nonessential details, Peter addresses them, saying, "You yourselves know that it is unlawful for a Jew to associate with or to visit a Gentile; but God has shown me that I should not call anyone profane or unclean" (Acts 10:28). Like rounding off numbers to the nearest ten, Peter compresses the prohibition on eating non-kosher food that had coalesced in his thinking with a complete ban on associating or visiting Gentiles. Then, he shows that the former puzzle in his mind over the divine message had been solved. He reveals his interpretation of the vision and the voice: they were metaphors for people. "God has shown me that I should not call anyone profane or unclean" (Acts 10:28).

Peter then asks Cornelius why he was sent for. Cornelius narrates for Peter, who does not yet know what we know already: he had an angelic vision experience in which he was instructed to send for Peter and was given his address in Joppa. This is another repetition, lengthening the story and adding significance to it. Cornelius concludes they have gathered to hear what God has commanded Peter to say (Acts 10:33).

Peter begins his message by reporting the new view that he has just been converted to, saying, "I truly understand that God shows no partiality, but in every nation anyone who fears him and does what is right is acceptable to him" (Acts 10:34). He goes on to give a schematic overview of the ministry of Jesus, the one "anointed . . . with the Holy Spirit and with power" enabling him to do "good and healing all who were oppressed by the devil" (Acts 10:38). Peter recounts Jesus's death and resurrection appearances, and his commission in which he "commanded us to preach to the people" (Acts 10:42), just as Peter is in the course of doing. The climax of his brief sermon is his announcement that "everyone who believes in him receives forgiveness of sins through his name" (Acts 10:43).

Then, without asking "So who here believes in him?" or any other invitation to express faith, the Spirit suddenly cuts in and demonstrates that God makes no distinction between Jews and Gentiles, just as he has told Peter personally. "While Peter was still speaking, the Holy Spirit fell upon all who heard the word" (Acts 10:44). The circumcised believers, or Jewish followers of Jesus who had come with Peter and witnessed the Spirit's outpouring, "were astounded that the gift of the Holy Spirit had been poured out even on the Gentiles" (Acts 10:45). What was the sign that the Spirit had fallen on Gentiles? It was the same sign that was given when the disciples themselves experienced the outpouring of the Spirit on the day of Pentecost: "For they heard them speaking in tongues and extolling God" (Acts 10:46). Peter noticed the similarity of the two events, saying, "Can anyone withhold the water for baptizing these people who have received the Holy Spirit just as we have?" (Acts 10:47). The phrase "just as we have" makes the connection explicit. This is, then, the Gentile Pentecost. Soon, Paul's ministry among Gentiles will eclipse his, but Peter has opened the door. In confirmation of his new understanding, Peter then accepts Cornelius's offer of hospitality to "stay for several days" (Acts 10:48).

Peter and the Jerusalem Critics

That should have settled the matter of Gentile inclusion once and for all. But this long-standing division between Jews and Gentiles, combined with the boundary between them having been defined as *clean* vs. *profane*, made it hard for kosher-observant Jews to accept. The next scene plays this out.

Peter has returned to Jerusalem, where he meets "the apostles and the believers" who have gotten word that "the Gentiles had also accepted the word of God" (Acts 11:1). Some of them there may have heard about it, but they were not happy about it. Luke tells us that "the circumcised believers criticized him, saying, 'Why did you go to uncircumcised men and eat with them?'" (Acts 11:2–3).

This criticism is unexpected and strange. The Jews with the objections are identified as "the circumcised believers," but their objection has nothing to do with circumcision. They merely object to Peter's table fellowship with Gentiles. The whole issue of circumcision has been entirely avoided in the story of the conversion of Cornelius and his household of uncircumcised Gentiles. They were all baptized without that issue coming up at all. It is not because it was a minor issue—quite the opposite. But Luke is delaying that controversy for a later time. It will come up in the context of Paul's ministry to Gentiles. Acts 15 will recount the story of the council they held in Jerusalem to settle the question: Do Gentiles need to be circumcised to be Christians? But for now, that issue is ignored. The question is about the appropriateness of Peter's table fellowship with Gentiles.

Peter's answer is to recount the story that we have already heard. He details his rooftop vision experience in as much detail as Luke had narrated for his readers. He quotes the divine voice, mentions the threefold repetition, and the simultaneous arrival of Cornelius's delegation. He makes the point in his defense that "the Spirit told me to go with them and not to make a distinction between them and us" (Acts 11:12). If they wanted someone to blame, blame the Spirit, not Peter. He tells about going to Cornelius's house and recounts another part of the story we already know: Cornelius's vision. But in this recounting we learn a detail, omitted previously when Cornelius told the story, that the angel said to him that Peter "will give you a message by which you and your entire household will be saved" (Acts 11:14). Then Peter pulls out his ace card. He tells about the Spirit's outpouring on the Gentiles there. He makes the point that it was exactly like what happened to the disciples in Jerusalem on the day of Pentecost: "And as I began to speak, the Holy Spirit fell upon them just as it had upon us at the beginning" (Acts 11:15). If they wanted a dispute, Peter is saying, they better take it up with God, not him. "If then God gave them the same gift that he gave us when we believed in the Lord Jesus Christ, who was I that I could hinder God?" (Acts 11:17).

Peter's argument is not that he was not guilty of having table fellowship with Gentiles. And he did not pull out any quotations from Jesus or memories of Jesus ministering to Gentiles. He did not cite the prophet Joel about the Spirit being poured out on the last days, as he had done at Pentecost.

He merely recounted that the same Spirit that filled them and enabled them to speak in tongues that day had done the same among Gentiles. He did not even recount to them Cornelius's piety and reputation as a God-fearer, because the point was not that Cornelius himself was deserving, but that God now makes no distinctions between Jews and Gentiles in general. It worked. When they heard this, they were silenced. "And they praised God, saying, 'Then God has given even to the Gentiles the repentance that leads to life'" (Acts 11:18).

The Jerusalem Council's Resolution

The issue of circumcision, however, remained to be settled. Some time later when Paul and Barnabas are reporting on the conversions among Gentiles to the Jerusalem believers, "certain individuals came down from Judea and were teaching the brothers, 'Unless you are circumcised according to the custom of Moses, you cannot be saved'" (Acts 15:1). Things got hot. Paul and Barnabas "had no small dissension and debate with them" (Acts 15:2). They decided to meet to hash out the issue. They held a council in Jerusalem, where the issue of Gentile circumcision was put squarely on the table: "Some believers who belonged to the sect of the Pharisees stood up and said, 'It is necessary for them to be circumcised and ordered to keep the law of Moses'" (Acts 15:5).

To defend both the ministry of Paul and Barnabas and his own experience, Peter stands up and reminds them of his time with Cornelius, though he does not mention him by name. "Peter stood up and said to them, 'My brothers, you know that in the early days God made a choice among you, that I should be the one through whom the Gentiles would hear the message of the good news and become believers. And God . . . testified to them by giving them the Holy Spirit, just as he did to us; . . . he has made no distinction between them and us" (Acts 15:7–8).

Peter knows that Paul's ministry may be suspect because he was not one of the original twelve disciples who were commissioned by Jesus to be his apostles (literally "sent ones"), so he emphasizes that it was he whom God used to open the door to the Gentile mission. In effect, he says, "don't blame Paul, blame me." And again he links Pentecost and the outpouring of the Spirit on Cornelius's household explicitly: "giving them the Holy Spirit, just as he did to us" (Acts 15:8). Again we hear Peter using the phrase "no distinction" that he first heard from the Spirit in Joppa.

After hearing more reporting from Paul and Barnabas, James, who seems to have replaced Peter in leadership of the Jerusalem believers, takes it upon himself to pronounce a final verdict, "I have reached the decision that we should not trouble those Gentiles who are turning to God" (Acts 15:19). Everyone understands that the "trouble" that they should not bother the Gentiles with is circumcision. The matter is finally settled. In a sense, it was already a done deal. Paul and Barnabas had, by then, established many Gentile congregations that had experienced the Spirit. The question was, could those Jewish believers accept that fact and remain united? At this point, they do. Luke, however, will tell us that Paul's later experience back in Jerusalem after a further round of Gentile missionary activity will not go so well (Acts 21). But that is a story for another day.

Luke began his Gospel, volume one, with people in the temple greeting the baby Jesus and foreshadowing Jesus's ministry of being "a light for revelation to the Gentiles" (Luke 2:32). In his first sermon to his hometown crowd in Nazareth, Jesus had anticipated their disapproval of his ministry beyond the limits of Abrahamic bloodline by highlighting the ministries of Elijah and Elisha to non-Israelites (Luke 4). That incident nearly got Jesus killed, so strong was the nationalist feeling there. Luke began volume two, the book of Acts, with Jesus's commission to be his witnesses in the Jewish space of Jerusalem and Judea, to mixed space in Samaria, and finally "to the ends of the earth" (Acts 1:8)—that is, into Gentile space. The ministry of being witnesses, Jesus said, would be enabled because it will happen after "the Holy Spirit has come upon you" (Acts 1:8). The Holy Spirit was the inspiration for that ministry among Gentiles and the confirmation of its fulfillment. The Spirit told Peter that God made "no distinction" and then proved it by coming upon the Gentiles of Cornelius's family "without distinction." Thus, to make distinctions is to oppose the Spirit.

The quest of nationalist movements is to make distinctions. That agenda runs counter to the Spirit's work to dissolve, not reinforce, ethnic or national distinctions. It is an irony of enormous proportions that American "Christian" nationalists are Gentiles. However, some have adopted the notion that they are part of the "city on the hill" with a special "covenant" with God, as John Winthrop had said in his speech to the pilgrims en route to found a Puritan settlement in New England. Though they can quote phrases like that from Matthew's Gospel, and adopt notions of themselves as a new Israel in a new promised land, there is no biblical precedent for co-opting Israel's role in the Hebrew Bible for America, much less using it as the basis for a resurgent Christian nationalism. Doing so would ignore and resist the Spirit's movement, as Luke described, to make ethnic distinctions meaningless. Luke is not alone, nor is he an outlier. From beginning to end, the Bible proclaims a vision of universalism, not a rigid particularism. Yes, there is a tension. Israel was God's chosen people. But the sequence of "to the Jew first and also to the Greeks (i.e., Gentiles, Rom 1:16) is the final biblical model that is inclusive of all the families of the earth.

17

In Christ, There Is No Jew or Greek

Paul had trouble with people. Like a parent who has problem children, Paul had trouble with the Christians in the churches he fathered all over the Mediterranean. He considered himself the spiritual parent to them. He flat out told the new Christians in Corinth, "In Christ Jesus I became your father through the gospel" (1 Cor 4:15). Likewise, he calls the Galatian Christians "my little children" (Gal 4:19) in a maternal metaphor that included experiencing labor pains over them. The Gentile Christians in Galatia were giving him problems because of other people Paul had trouble with: Jewish Christians. Many Jewish Christians did not think their faith in Jesus as Messiah relieved them of their obligation to keep the law of Moses. Laws, like the obligation for males to be circumcised, Sabbath observance, and keeping kosher, were part of Jewish identity. We may think, "But didn't Jesus say. . . ?" but we should ask ourselves: "How much did they know about what Jesus said?" Paul's missionary work occurred in the forties and fifties of the first century. That was before the Gospels or the book of Acts were written. The new Christians heard the gospel through the witness of others, not through reading, which probably most of them could not do anyway. They heard as much or as little about Jesus as their Christian teachers knew and shared. Many, probably most, had never heard the story of Peter and his vision or of Cornelius's conversion, or of the council in Jerusalem.

It is understandable, then, that many Jewish Christians continued to feel obligated to keep the law of Moses. What is more, many believed that if Gentiles wanted to become believers in Jesus as the Jewish "Messiah," which in Greek is translated "Christ," then they also had to keep the law of Moses. After Paul established each congregation, like he did in Galatia, sometimes spending more than a year with them, he would travel to the next place and begin anew. That left the young Christians vulnerable to other traveling teachers and their ideas. Some Jewish Christians had come to Galatia after Paul moved on and taught the Galatians that they needed to keep the law of Moses, including circumcision. Apparently, the teachers were persuasive. Many of the Gentile Galatian "baby" Christians were convinced. Paul heard about it and got mad. His letter to the Galatians gets hot.

In obvious fury, Paul says things like, "You foolish Galatians! Who has bewitched you?" (Gal 3:1), and "I wish those who unsettle you [by advocating circumcision] would castrate themselves!" (Gal 5:12). Even, "If anyone proclaims to you a gospel contrary to what you received, let that one be accursed!" (Gal 1:8). All parents who feel like their children are threatened get hot. What was at risk? For Paul, it was far more than circumcision, food laws, and Sabbath observance. Paul had a vision of a new, reconciled humanity that overcame past divisions between Jews and Gentiles. It went even further. The new humanity left no place for divisions between men and women, and the greatest gulf between people in the first-century Roman world, the division between slaves and free people. Paul taught that now that Messiah (Christ) had come, now that he had been crucified and risen from the dead, a whole new way of relating to God had been opened for everyone equally. From Paul's perspective, embracing Jewish law was a denial of that vision of a new, reconciled humanity; it would ruin everything. The place where this all came to a head was at the table. Eating together was the way you demonstrated that the vision of the new humanity was a reality. Eating at the same table, or having "table fellowship," was crucial to Paul. There could be no new humanity if Jews ate apart from Gentiles. Yes, he got hot about that.

Paul Confronts Peter's Hypocrisy

I said that Paul had trouble with people. Peter was one of them. They had a big conflict when Peter came to Antioch in the Roman province of Syria. Paul says that he opposed him to his face (Gal 2:11). It was about table fellowship. Peter had been eating with Gentiles until "certain people came from James," Jesus's brother, the emerging leader of the Jerusalem church. When they came, they convinced Peter not to. Paul describes the people James sent as "the circumcision faction" (Gal 2:12). Peter's "hypocrisy," as Paul describes it, was that he had previously concluded that it was permissible to eat with Gentiles now that the door had been opened to them—remember his experience with Cornelius—but James's "circumcision faction" persuaded him to back off and eat separately, with fellow Jews.

Let's set the stage for this conflict. It took place in Antioch, a vast, densely populated city—some say as dense as Calcutta is today—the capital of the province of Syria. It had impressive Roman buildings, temples, and statues, but dense Roman cities were not fun to live in. Most people had no sanitation; they used chamber pots and dumped them into the streets. You can imagine the stench and the prevalence of infectious diseases. They lived in cramped, dim apartments, built without building codes, subject to collapse, especially in earthquakes, which they experienced in the first century CE. Many people had short lives, so the city depended on a constant influx of newcomers. They were strangers to each other, which increased the crime rate in a city without a police force. People were desperate to make connections and find support. They found them in the private clubs called *collegia*. Collegia were clubs organized in various ways, by trade associations, religious observances, and even funeral associations that pooled funds for each other's burials. In them the lower classes found community, security, and even fictive kinship, a new family. They also shared communal meals.

In this context, the Jewish synagogues functioned just like collegia. They were a support network organized around a common religion. They were more than religious, however. Synagogues, as Jewish community centers, conducted many charitable activities. There were an estimated twenty to thirty Jewish synagogues in Antioch in Paul's time. These synagogues of Jewish people with their strong families, decent moral lives, and mutual aid attracted many Gentiles. They became known as "God-fearers." Many adopted Jewish customs such as Sabbath observance and kosher food laws. But circumcision was not popular and most did not go that far. At least some of the Jews accepted them to a degree. Some may have even permitted observant Gentiles to eat with them in their communal meals, but an uncircumcised person, no matter how Torah-observant they were otherwise, was still outside the covenant community. God had made a covenant with Abraham and his descendants, and circumcision was required for membership in the covenant community. The law of Moses, or Torah, made that clear. "If an alien [Gentile] who resides with you wants to celebrate the Passover to the LORD, all his males shall be circumcised; then he may draw near to celebrate it; he shall be regarded as a native of the land. But no uncircumcised person shall eat of it" (Exod 12:48). All collegia had to have official sanction from Rome, administered locally. All were obligated to participate in Roman piety—the veneration of Roman gods, including the growing emperor cult—by participating in festivals. All of the collegia were thus obliged—except the Jewish synagogues. Rome made an exception for them. Jews were allowed to gather, to collect tithes, and to pray to their own God as long as they offered prayers for the emperor. They were exempted from military service and from showing piety toward the gods of Rome, a potentially capital offense for everyone else.

Of course, among Jews, there were widely divergent views about the fate of Gentiles. We even find this in the Hebrew Bible. Some believed that in the end, God would judge all the Gentile nations. Micah said God "will execute vengeance on the nations that did not obey" (Mic 5:15; see also Zeph 2:4–15). On the other hand, other texts imagine the future salvation of Gentiles. Isaiah projects a time when "all the nations shall stream to [Mount Zion]. Many peoples shall come and say, 'Come, let us go up to the mountain of the Lord, to the house of the God of Jacob; that he may teach us his ways and that we may walk in his paths'" (Isa 2:3). These opposing expectations of the fate of Gentiles is reflected in the varied views of Gentiles among the Antioch community's Jesus-following Jews. Some, having accepted Jesus as the Jewish Messiah, with no intention of leaving Judaism, had embraced the call to be a missionary movement whose mandate included outreach to Gentiles. If salvation was to come to the Gentiles in the end, then there was an urgency about that Gentile mission, since the early Christ-followers believed Christ's return was imminent. However, how the Gentiles would be saved from "this present evil age" (Gal 1:4) was not clear.

Some Jesus-following Jews believed that to be saved, Gentiles had to become part of the covenant community, and the only way that could happen, for males, was circumcision. That was the position of James and the people he sent to meet Peter at Antioch to persuade him to stop having table fellowship with Gentiles—most likely the God-fearing Gentiles who had joined the synagogues, as their collegia of worship, support, community, and fictive kinship. Circumcision, according to the view at the time, made Gentiles into Jews. Josephus says so explicitly. And that is the problem for Paul. How would God save the Gentiles as Gentiles if they became circumcised, making them, in effect, Jews?

Gentiles Saved as Gentiles

Paul believed that God would save Gentiles as Gentiles and Jews as Jews. He felt so strongly about this that when, after fourteen years of missionary activity among Gentiles, Paul, Barnabas, and their uncircumcised colleague Titus went to Jerusalem to meet Cephas (Peter), James, and John, he stuck to his guns: "But even Titus, who was with me, was not compelled to be circumcised, though he was a Greek [i.e., Gentile]" (Gal 2:3). That private consultation, Paul says, ended in agreement he describes as "the right hand of fellowship" (Gal 2:9). There would be a division of responsibility. Paul reports that "when James and Cephas and John, who were acknowledged pillars, recognized the grace that had been given to me, they gave to Barnabas and me the right hand of fellowship, agreeing that we should go to the Gentiles and they to the circumcised" (Gal 2:9).

All seemed settled—until, that is, Peter came to Antioch and separated himself by eating with Jewish Jesus-followers, at the behest of James's delegation. That is when sparks started flying. Paul says, "When Cephas [Peter] came to Antioch, I opposed him to his face" (Gal 2:11). For house churches, molded after Roman collegia or synagogues, eating together was a core activity. It was an affirmation of their unity in Christ. Eating separately, Jews in Jewish houses and Gentiles in Gentile homes, wrecked that unity. Paul later said as much in Romans: "Because there is one bread, we who are many are one body, for we all partake of the one bread" (Rom 10:17). Peter, eating separate bread, broke that unity.

Strategy 1: Biblical Interpretation

But Paul is still left with a dilemma. How are Gentiles to be included in the covenant community without becoming Jews by circumcision? Salvation, after all, depended on being in the covenant community. Paul uses several strategies; one involves a way of interpreting the Bible, and the other is an argument from chronology. Let's take the Bible first. Paul makes the claim that the Bible itself says that no one is righteous in God's eyes, including those who follow the law of Moses. He makes this point, scholars tell us, by a quote from Ps 143:2 that says, "No one living is righteous before you [God]" (Gal 2:16). Since "no one" includes Jews who keep the law, Paul adds to that quotation "the works of the law," meaning obedience to law like the requirement of circumcision, Sabbath keeping, and keeping kosher. Here is Paul's modified quote: "Because no one will be justified [saved] by the works of the law" (Gal 2:16). No Jewish person would read that verse that way, but Paul did because he had a revelation in which he had heard and seen Jesus Christ (Gal 1:12) authorizing him to take the gospel to the Gentiles, giving him a new way of reading the Bible.

If keeping the law of Moses was not going to make anyone "justified" or saved, then what would? Paul's answer? Faith: "We know that a person is justified not by the works of the law but through faith in Jesus Christ" (Gal 2:16). To prove that it is faith that saves and not by keeping the law of Moses, Paul turns to another text from the Bible. In this one, Paul can do two things at once: prove that it is faith that saves, and, crucially, that faith opens the door to being part of the covenant community. He uses Genesis again, and this time the story of none other than Abraham himself, the father of the Jewish people, to make his point. He says,

> Just as Abraham "believed God, and it was reckoned to him as righteousness" [Gen 15:6], so, you see, those who believe are the descendants of Abraham. And the scripture, foreseeing that God would justify the Gentiles by faith, declared the gospel beforehand to Abraham, saying, "All the Gentiles shall be blessed in you" [Gen 18:18]. For this reason, those who believe are blessed with Abraham who believed. (Gal 3:6–9)

If Abraham was "reckoned" or made righteous (saved) by belief, or trust, or faith, then all who believe, or trust, or have faith are true descendants (literally *sons*) of Abraham. If Abraham is saved by trust/faith, and all the Gentiles will be blessed (saved) through Abraham (Gen 12:2 and 18:18), then they are blessed the same way: trust/faith. To sum it up, those who trust/believe/have faith are blessed (saved, reckoned righteous) along with trusting Abraham.

Someone may object to the notion that just because someone trusts like Abraham, they are necessarily "sons" or "descendants" of Abraham. That sounds like a leap. Paul has more cards in his hand than he has yet played. His ace is Gen 22:18 (using, as Paul does, the Greek translation, or LXX): "And in your seed shall all the nations of the earth be blessed." "Seed" here is a biological metaphor for "descendants." "Descendants" is plural, but "seed" is a collective noun, like water or sand, and is singular. That little grammatical fact allows Paul to make an interpretive move that would drive your English teacher crazy, but was familiar to rabbis. He says, "Now the promises were made to Abraham and to his seed ["offspring" NRSV]; the text does not say, 'And to seeds,' as of many; but, 'And to your seed,' that is, to one person, who is Christ" (Gal 3:16). Paul argues that the promises God made to Abraham, promises of descendants and land, and eventually a blessing to Gentiles (Gen 12:1–3), were made to Abraham and his singular "seed." Who is that one "seed"? Messiah (Christ). The argument is a bit of grammatical sleight of hand, but well played by a skilled rabbi. Thus Christ is the one seed, along with Abraham, to whom the promises were made. Christ is the seed of Abraham; anyone who has faith in Christ is spiritually "in Christ" as well, and hence, belongs to the singular "seed" of Abraham. Remember, Paul has already quoted the Greek version of Gen 22:18, "And in your [Abraham's] seed shall all the nations of the earth be blessed." If

Christ is the "seed," then all the nations (Gentiles) are blessed—that is made righteous, i.e., saved.

By this interpretation, Paul is able to make Gentiles members of the covenant community, not by becoming circumcised Jews, but by being the descendants (seed) of Abraham through faith in Christ. Paul has escaped the dilemma: Gentiles as Gentiles can be saved because by faith they can be included in the covenant community as descendants of Abraham.

Strategy 2: Chronology

Paul has one more problem to solve: what becomes of the law of Moses? For all these many years, Jews have been taught that righteousness before God depends on keeping the laws of Torah, including circumcision. Paul's solution? Chronology. Abraham was given the promises of blessing to him and his seed hundreds of years before Moses came along. He says, "My point is this: the law (of Moses), which came four hundred thirty years later, does not annul a covenant previously ratified by God, so as to nullify the promise" (Gal 3:17). You cannot nullify God's promise of blessing to Abraham and his descendants simply by adding the retirements of the law of Moses, which came "four hundred thirty years later." Those laws were given by Moses to the people of Israel, yes, but they were a temporary fix, like a patch on a garment. He uses the analogy of a child who is promised an inheritance, but before they are of legal age to inherit, they are under the supervision of a babysitter-type person, or, as the NRSV translates it, "disciplinarian." The law was like a supervising babysitter until the child comes of age. The law of Moses supervised Israel until the time was right for Christ (Messiah) to come. But now that Messiah has come, the need for the babysitting law has expired. Paul explains, "But now that faith has come, we are no longer subject to a disciplinarian, for in Christ Jesus you are all children of God through faith" (Gal 3:25).

What is the effect of all of this argumentation? It is to keep Jews as Jews, descendants of Abraham and part of the covenant community, and to embrace Gentiles as Gentiles, descendants of Abraham and part of the covenant community. Now, both Jews and Gentiles have to understand that righteousness before God is based on faith/trust in Christ. A new age has dawned. There is a new, reconciled humanity, "a new creation" (Gal 6:16). This is why, finally, Paul can proclaim the most radical vision of humanity yet uttered: "As many of you as were baptized into Christ have clothed yourselves with Christ. There is no longer Jew or Greek [Gentile], there is no longer slave or free, there is no longer male and female; for all of you are one in Christ Jesus" (Gal 3:27–28). At first this sounds as though all distinctions have been erased. That is not quite the point. Slaves are still slaves, and free people are still free people: Paul was not advocating the eradication of slavery. Men are still men and women are still women.

A Baptismal Creed

In the same way, Jews are still Jews and Gentiles are still Gentiles. Though they are distinct, there is a unity that transcends all these distinctions: class (slave and free), gender (male and female), and race (Jew and Greek/Gentile). The diversity is maintained, but a new oneness is achieved. Scholars have suggested that Paul was not the original author of Gal 3:27–28, but adapted a creed spoken at Christian baptisms. They call it a "baptismal formula." Analysis of that creed and the words that appear to be Paul's adaptations has led to this reconstruction of what the original creed may have been:

> For you are all children [sons] of God in the Spirit.
> There is no Jew or Greek,
> there is no slave or free,
> there is no male and female;
> For you are all one in the Spirit.[1]

The structure is tight. The first and last lines are parallel. The three phrases "there is no. . ." are parallel. The one variation is in the last of the three. Instead of "no male *or* female," it says "no male *and* female." The phrase "male and female" echoes the creation narrative

> So God created humankind in his image,
> in the image of God he created them;
> male and female he created them. (Gen 1:27)

This creed may have described the "new creation" that Christians affirmed at their baptism. It may have been meant to counter one of the oldest clichés of the ancient world. With roots that go back to Socrates, a Jewish rabbi suggested a daily prayer of blessing that went:

> Blessed (art thou), who did not make me a Gentile;
> Blessed (art thou), who did not make me a woman;
> Blessed (art thou), who did not make me a slave.[2]

1. Patterson, *Forgotten Creed*, 25.
2. Babylonian Talmud, Menahot 43b, quoted in Patterson, *Forgotten Creed*, 36.

As a baptismal formula, the vision of a new creation that eliminated those divisions would have been repeated hundreds of times as new converts joined the growing communities of Christ-followers. All the Galatian believers would have known it, and Paul used it to reinforce his message: "In Christ Jesus neither circumcision nor uncircumcision counts for anything; the only thing that counts is faith working through love" (Gal 5:6).

This is why the "circumcision faction" that James's people were a part of, which wanted Peter to stop eating with Gentiles, was so wrong and made Paul so angry. They were called the circumcision faction because they believed Gentiles could only be saved by becoming circumcised, which would make them Jews, not Gentiles anymore. The act of separate eating was just the public manifestation of a view that Jews and Gentiles were on two separate levels before God. One was blessed with salvation, the other not. On the flip side, eating together was a sign that they were one: one bread, one body, one "seed." For Paul, table fellowship was crucial. It demonstrated a profound unity as nothing else could. Paul will go on to say neither "circumcision nor uncircumcision counts for anything" (Gal 5:6), and "real circumcision is a matter of the heart—it is spiritual and not literal" (Rom 2:29). Gentiles, Paul said, had "been cut from what is by nature a wild olive tree and grafted, contrary to nature, into a cultivated olive tree" (Rom 11:24), and "there is no distinction between Jew and Greek; the same Lord is Lord of all and is generous to all who call on him" (Rom 10:12). How could this not affect table fellowship?"

The nationalist vision of a community of similarity that rejects diversity is seeking the very silos that James's circumcision faction sought: to wall off ethnicities from each other. The vision of the Bible is not that we would all look alike, talk alike, think alike, and therefore be able to tolerate each other, but that permanent distinctions, such as race and gender and social class, would not be barriers to fellowship. This is all the more stark when you consider how deep the chasm was in the first century, separating Jews from Gentiles, men from women, and most profoundly, slaves from free people. But those divisions had been overcome. For Paul, the fact that God is one (Gal 3:20) means that God is the God of Jews and Gentiles. Nationalist ideology runs counter to this vision of a unified humanity. In the end, separating Jews and Gentiles, for Paul, would be to deny the oneness of God. That is worth getting angry about, like a parent when her children are threatened. This vision was not just theoretical. From Paul's perspective, it was to manifest in the ultimate Christian virtue: love. He said, "For in Christ Jesus neither circumcision nor uncircumcision counts for anything; the only thing that counts is faith working through love" (Gal 5:6). And, "For the whole law [of Moses] is summed up in a single commandment,

'You shall love your neighbor as yourself'" (Gal 5:15). Love is supposed to be the hallmark of the Christian community. Division is the opposite. Love is meant to be the effect of the promise to Abraham that in his seed, "all the families of the earth would be blessed" (Gen 12:1–3).

18

Paul's Gentile Mission

Paul is a person some people love and some hate. The reasons for those emotional reactions are partly from Paul himself, and partly from the things people wrote in his name, according to many New Testament scholars. I don't think anyone would disagree with the sentiment that Paul was intense. He was an intense pre-Christian persecutor of the faith, or the Way, turned intense evangelist for the faith. Intense people evoke intense reactions.

Something happened to Paul that changed his intense focus from persecution to promotion of the faith. Historically, it is too early to call the faith Christianity because that name implies all that Christianity became, with church councils and creeds. Some use the awkward phrase "Christic movement" to indicate followers of "Christ" or "Messiah." I'll just say, "the faith" and hope you know I'm referring to faith in Jesus as "Christ/Messiah," whom Paul preached as the means of salvation from "this present [and soon to be passing] evil age" (Gal 1:4). Luke tells us that followers of the Way were first called Christians in the city of Antioch (Acts 11:26), and while there is no reason to dispute that claim, that name did not yet imply all that it came to mean over time, as the institutions of Christianity developed. We will stick to calling it "the faith."

What happened to change intense Paul? We have two sources of information about that. One is what Paul says, the other is Luke's story. What Paul says turns out to be very little in any descriptive sense. Luke's story is told in his volume two, Acts. Three times in Acts, Luke narrates the story of Paul's conversion experience (Acts 9:1–19; 22:3–21; 26:9–23). En route to Damascus to persecute the faith, Paul sees a bright light, falls to the ground, hears a voice identifying himself as the risen Christ, and is told he will take the gospel to Gentiles. There is some variation among the three versions, but that is the gist.

Paul never tells that story. There are two things to keep in mind as we explore Paul's sense of himself as the apostle to the Gentiles (Rom 11:13), and Luke's presentation of Paul. First, Paul was a mystic. He describes dramatic spiritual experiences, like being "caught up to the third heaven—whether in the body or out of the body I do not know; God knows" (2 Cor 12:2). He describes receiving revelations, doing miracles among his congregations, and speaking in the "tongues of angels" (Gal 2:2; 3:5; 1 Cor 13:1). Whatever it was that turned Paul from persecutor to evangelist, it was a powerful mystical experience.

The second thing to keep in mind is that Luke was not writing as an academic historian by today's standards. Remember, he said nothing at all about the explosive growth of the church in North Africa. His goal was not to write a comprehensive history but to defend the Gentile mission of the faith and Paul as its primary missionary as it moved from Jewish space in Jerusalem to Gentile space, ending his story in the center of the Roman Empire, the city of Rome itself. These two ideas, Paul's mysticism and Luke's apologetic purpose, will help us appreciate each version.

Paul's Own Story

What would we know if we only had Paul's description of his conversion and call to be an apostle to the Gentiles (1 Cor 9:1; 15:8–10; Gal 1:11–17; Phil 3:2–11)? From his letter to the church he founded in Philippi, we learn that Paul was a Pharisee, the purity police party who practiced and demanded strict adherence to the Torah, the law of Moses. Paul also admits that "as to zeal," he was "a persecutor of the church" (Phil 3:5–6). He recalls both of those attributes in even more explicit terms in Galatians, where he said, "You have heard, no doubt, of my earlier life in Judaism. I was violently persecuting the church of God and was trying to destroy it. I advanced in Judaism beyond many among my people of the same age, for I was far more zealous for the traditions of my ancestors [that is, the law of Moses]" (Gal 1:13–14). In his first letter to the Corinthians, he admits that his history of persecution of the church may cause some to call into question his claim to apostolic authority, saying, "Last of all, as to one untimely born, he [Christ] appeared also to me. For I am the least of the apostles, unfit to be called an apostle, because I persecuted the church of God" (1 Cor 15:8–9). Being "untimely born" gives us no clues as to how Christ "appeared" to Paul. The appearance of the risen Christ, however, does look like a powerful mystical experience. It made the most unlikely candidate for apostleship, a persecutor of the church, into its most successful evangelist.

Whatever that experience was, it made Paul totally reverse his initial estimation of himself as a person who "advanced in Judaism beyond many," telling the Philippians, "Yet whatever gains I had, these I have come to regard as loss because of Christ" (Phil 3:7). What happened to create that great reversal? The closest he comes to a description of the event comes from Galatians. He is insistent that the gospel was given to him as a revelation directly by God, without any human messenger. "For I want you to know, brothers and sisters, that the gospel that was proclaimed by me is not of human origin; for I did not receive it from a human source, nor was I taught it, but I received it through a revelation of Jesus Christ" (Gal 1:11–12). What was the content of that "revelation"? He goes on to say, "But when God, who had set me apart before I was born and called me through his grace, was pleased to reveal his Son to me [literally "in me"], so that I might proclaim him among the Gentiles, I did not confer with any human being" (Gal 1:15–16). The revelation was Christ, "his Son," and that revelation came with a sense of calling "so that I might proclaim him among the Gentiles." He alluded to that vision and calling in 1 Cor 15 where he said Christ "appeared to me" (1 Cor 15:9).

The mystical experience of the risen Christ's appearance that Paul describes was powerful and specific enough to be life-changing. He wrote that he experienced a revelation or vision of Christ who not only appeared to him, but also commissioned him to be an apostle—that is, the one sent (that is what "apostle" means) to the Gentiles.

Luke's Version(s) of Paul's Story

Luke's description of Paul's experience is far more detailed. First, Luke sets the story in a particular place and time and finds Paul engaged in a specific purpose. Paul is on a mission to go to Damascus, find "the disciples of the Lord . . . who belonged to the Way," abduct them, and "bring them bound to Jerusalem" (Acts 9:1–2). This is from the first of his three descriptions of the event. Luke narrates this first version of the story in Acts 9 directly. In the other two versions, Luke describes Paul as recounting the event in his own words to Jews in Jerusalem (Acts 22) and to King Agrippa, the grandson of King Herod (Acts 26). Though each retelling varies according to the audience, the differences do not concern us here. What the three versions all share in common is that, en route to Damascus to persecute the faith, Paul had an experience in which there was a light, a voice, people falling to the ground (Paul, in Acts 9 and 22, or Paul and all the men with him in Acts 26), and an identification of Jesus as the one Paul was persecuting—all of which resulted in a radical change of mission for Paul, who is commissioned to take the gospel to the Gentiles. There were also witnesses in all three, though what they perceive varies.

Paul himself never told this story in his epistles, but he and Luke agree on several main points. Paul had been a persecutor of the faith but had an experience that produced a radical transformation. Paul identified the essence of the experience as a vision of the appearance of the risen Christ (though, oddly, Luke described Paul as blinded, so the "appearance" was not visual, but mystical). Both Paul and Luke note that this experience was Paul's commissioning to take his law-free gospel to the Gentiles. Luke demonstrates the importance of this event by repeating it three times. Paul demonstrates the importance he places on it by making it the basis for his legitimacy as an apostle to the Gentiles, asking, "Am I not an apostle? Have I not seen Jesus our Lord?" (1 Cor 9:1). Both Luke and Paul agree that Paul has received a special divine intervention leading to a commission to take the gospel to a circle wider than the physical descendants of Abraham, but to go to the people included in the original Abrahamic blessing, all the families of the earth (Gen 12:3).

Paul Defends His Mission

An experience, even a powerful mystical vision, is one thing, but it is not, by itself, a theological justification. How did Paul defend his sense of mission to the Gentiles? We know from his letter to the Galatians that there were two times when he made a trip to Jerusalem specifically to meet with the core leaders of the faith. The first time, after three years of ministry in Arabia, he met with Peter (whom he calls Cephas, his Hebrew name) and James, Jesus's brother. Paul does not describe what they talked about (Gal 1:18–24). Then, fourteen years later he went again to Jerusalem "in response to a revelation," this time for a private meeting with James, Cephas, and John (Gal 1–10). Paul describes the purpose of this meeting: "I laid before them (though only in a private meeting with the acknowledged leaders) the gospel that I proclaim among the Gentiles, in order to make sure that I was not running, or had not run, in vain" (Gal 2:2). Paul again does not outline the arguments he made to them. As a literate, educated Torah scholar, trained in Greek rhetoric, there was probably no question about who would prevail in that discussion with likely illiterate Galilean fishermen. Paul describes his victory by saying that, when the meeting ended, "they gave to Barnabas and me the right hand of fellowship, agreeing that we should go to the Gentiles and they to the circumcised" (Gal 2:9).

So far we have not heard Paul's theological arguments, but he had some, showing that he had given the matter a great deal of thought. In our last chapter, we reviewed one of them: that Gentiles, as Gentiles, without being circumcised (which would have made them Jews), could be included in Abraham's family by faith. The promise to Abraham in Genesis was made to him and to his "seed," which Paul, in true rabbinic style, creatively interprets as a reference to Christ. Christ is the "seed" of Abraham, so those who are in Christ, by faith, are included in the seed, or progeny, of Abraham and thus heirs to the covenant. He sums up his argument in Gal 3, saying, "Just as Abraham 'believed God, and it was reckoned to him as righteousness,' so, you see, those who believe are the descendants of Abraham. And the Scripture, foreseeing that God would justify the Gentiles by faith, declared the gospel beforehand to Abraham, saying, 'All the Gentiles shall be blessed in you.' For this reason, those who believe are blessed with Abraham who believed" (Gal 3:6–9). As we noted in the last chapter, God's promise to Abraham was made hundreds of years before Moses and the law, and even before Abraham was circumcised, so Abraham's blessing of salvation had nothing to do with keeping the law of Moses. Therefore, Gentiles saved by faith, like Abraham, do not have to keep the law of Moses either.

Paul understands that removing the requirement of keeping the law of Moses for Gentiles might imply that now there is a two-track system of salvation in place: one for Jews and the other for Gentiles. Paul does not believe that and wants to make sure no one else does either. For him, there are not two people of God, but one. He also has to answer a difficult question that his successful Gentile mission has brought to light: why hasn't Israel, on the whole, accepted Jesus as Messiah (Christ)? It is not as if there were only a few Jewish believers; Luke tells us that James said to Paul, "You see, [Paul], how many thousands of believers there are among the Jews, and they are all zealous for the law" (Acts 21:20). But a movement of thousands is far from overwhelming. Most Jews did not become believers in Jesus. Why not? What happened?

Paul came up with an argument in the form of a metaphor to do two things at once: explain how there is only one people of God, not two; and explain why so many Jews have not accepted Jesus as Messiah. The metaphor imagines the people of God as an olive tree, described in Rom 11.

Before launching into the metaphor, Paul sets the stage by recalling passages from the Hebrew Bible that call Israel out for doing the wrong thing, as if to say rejecting Jesus as Messiah was not Israel's first blunder. Again, Paul pulls out a verse from the Hebrew Bible in true rabbinic style.

This is part of the "Song of Moses" in which he poetically recounts Israel's history, including their past idolatry. Moses says that idolatry, the worship of "no gods," makes God jealous, prompting him to, in turn, make Israel jealous by means of attacks from a "no people" nation. No one knows which nation he is referring to, but the point is that the word *jealous* and the phrase *no nation* are used, allowing Paul to reinterpret them. He is going to make the case that Israel's rejection of Jesus is analogous to their former blunder into idolatry. He will then say that God is using the Gentile's acceptance of Jesus as a means of making Israel jealous—Gentiles, after all, are a "no people" nation in Jewish eyes.

I will quote Moses's words from Deuteronomy here, then follow with Paul's use of the quotation in Romans. First Moses: "They made me [God] jealous with what is no god, provoked me with their idols. So I will make them jealous with what is no people, provoke them with a foolish nation" (Deut 32:21). Now Paul: "Moses says, "I will make you jealous of those who are not a nation; with a foolish nation I will make you angry" (Rom 10:19).

Paul then finds a quotation from Isaiah that does double duty; it is another example of the Hebrew Bible holding Israel guilty for past faithlessness, and it can be interpreted as an oblique prophecy of Gentile faith. Paul says, "Then Isaiah is so bold as to say, 'I have been found by those who did not seek me; I have shown myself to those who did not ask for me [Gentiles].' But of Israel he says, 'All day long I have held out my hands to a disobedient and contrary people'" (Rom 10:20–21, quoting Isa 65:1–2). Jewish rejection of Jesus simply fits a long-established pattern of Israel's blunders, and the open door to the no-people Gentiles, who were not really seeking him, was something the prophets saw coming.

The Olive Tree Metaphor

Now the ground has been prepared for the olive tree metaphorical argument. First, Paul wants to make it clear that Gentile belief in Jesus in no way implies that God rejected Israel. "I ask, then, has God rejected his people? By no means!" (Rom 11:1). He repeats this with another "jealousy" referent: "So I ask, have they [Israel] stumbled so as to fall? By no means! But through their stumbling salvation has come to the Gentiles, so as to make Israel jealous" (Rom 11:11).

If Israel's rejection of Jesus as Messiah is just a stumble, and not a fall, how should Paul's Gentile Roman audience think of unbelieving Jews? They are like branches broken off a cultivated olive tree. And how should Gentile Roman believers understand their relationship to that olive tree? They are like wild olive branches grafted onto it. He reminds them that this is no cause for bragging, it's just God's way. No brag, just fact. "But if some of the branches were broken off, and you, a wild olive shoot, were grafted in their place to share the rich root of the olive tree, do not boast over the branches" (Rom 11:17–18a). Why not boast? Look at a tree; who is supporting whom? Branches or roots? "If you do boast, remember that it is not you that support the root, but the root that supports you" (Rom 11:18b). There is one single tree. Its deep, supportive roots are the long story of Israel, which Gentiles have now been grafted onto. That deeply rooted tree is supporting the newly grafted Gentile branches. Just as God had the power to graft wild olive branches, Gentiles, onto the tree, God can also graft broken-off Israelite branches, if they do not persist in unbelief. He says, "And even those of Israel, if they do not persist in unbelief, will be grafted in, for God has the power to graft them in again" (Rom 11:23).

The metaphorical argument has done its job. God has not rejected Israel, but has opened the door to Gentiles to share in Israel's blessings. They do not need to become Jews by circumcision or by keeping the law of Moses; it is by faith in Christ that they are grafted onto the one single tree. The hope is that Israel will see their inclusion and jealousy will provoke them to faith, after which God will graft back on the previously broken branches. There is one tree and one people of God. Its roots are in Israel's story as God's particular chosen people, but that chosen status has now expanded to universally include all people of faith. Paul sums it up, saying, "For there is no distinction between Jew and Greek; the same Lord is Lord of all and is generous to all who call on him" (Rom 10:12).

Both Paul and Luke spilled a lot of ink making the case that Paul's Gentile mission was initiated by God, empowered by God, and part of God's plan from ages past. The exclusive category of "chosen" people has been blown wide open. The hope is that this will eventually produce the blessing of faith in all of Israel. In the meantime, the single community of believers celebrates God's mercy together in one community, like a tree with natural and grafted branches, supported by a single root system. The biblical vision of a multiethnic community of faith could not be clearer. That is why nationalist aspirations to break up the tree are so misplaced. The nationalist goal of living in mono-ethnic communities is what Paul believed God was working against.

To return to Luke once more, he describes a meeting in Jerusalem where Paul's Gentile mission is the topic. As Luke describes it, the Jewish apostles and elders met together to interview Paul and Barnabas (Acts 15:6). After Peter reminded them that he had conducted the first phase of the Gentile mission (by his ministry to Cornelius's household, which he assumes they knew all about), then Paul and Barnabas got to speak. "The whole assembly kept silence, and listened to Barnabas and Paul as they told of all the signs and wonders that God had done through them among the Gentiles" (Acts 15:12). Then James has the last word. "My brothers, listen to me. Simeon [Peter] has related how God first looked favorably on the Gentiles, to take from among them a people for his name. . . . Therefore, I have reached the decision that we should not trouble those Gentiles who are turning to God [by requiring them to keep the law of Moses]" (Acts 15:13–19). The whole assembly, Jewish apostles and elders, affirmed the Gentile mission. God's will was that these ethnically diverse people should be a single community of faith, which now comprises all the families of the earth.

19

The Royal Nation

We have just explored Paul's vision of the new unity of Jews and Gentiles made possible by Christ. Both Jews and Gentiles are included in the "seed" of Abraham. Both kinds of branches, natural ones (Jews) and grafted ones (Gentiles), are now part of the same olive tree, supported by a single trunk, benefiting from the same roots (the history of Israel). The vision of this kind of unity is astounding, especially given the cultural perspective of the time.

Roman Anti-Semitism

I have noted the fact that the standard animosity between Jews and Gentiles was both mutual and infamous in the Roman world of the first century. We already know how the Jews felt about Gentiles; they were called dogs, unclean, profane, and doomed. How did Roman Gentiles feel about Jews? Now is the time to demonstrate it from the horse's mouth, as it were. Tacitus (ca. 56–120 CE) was a Roman senator and historian. He is considered one of the greatest Roman historians by modern scholars. In book 5 of his *Histories*, he writes what he believes is true about the Jews. He first speculates about their origins, citing a number of possibilities: "Some say that the Jews were fugitives from the island of Crete. . . . Many, again, say that they were a race of Ethiopian origin, who . . . were driven by fear and hatred of their neighbors to seek a new dwelling-place."[1]

Already we can see that Tacitus believes their neighbors fear and hate them. Tacitus offers an alternative origin story that might account for their

1. Tacitus, *Hist.* 5.2.

neighbor's animosity: "Most writers, however, agree in stating that once a disease, which horribly disfigured the body, broke out over Egypt; that king Bocchoris, seeking a remedy, consulted the oracle of Hammon, and was bidden to cleanse his realm, and to convey into some foreign land this race [Jews] detested by the gods."[2] Jews are both a diseased race—expelled from Egypt, left in the desert—and detested by the gods. The anti-Semitic prejudice is thoroughgoing.

How did the Jews survive that expulsion to the desert? Tacitus tells a story about how one of them, named Moses, told them they should follow, as leader, the one who could find a solution for them, especially for their desperate need for water. Moses saw some wild donkeys and followed them to their water source, and led the people to it. This is how he became their leader. After six days of aimless travel, on the seventh day, they came to an inhabited land, expelled its inhabitants, and built a temple. The biblical forty years of wandering in the wilderness is compressed to a week. Besides Moses as leader, the rest of the story is pure fabrication.

Next, Tacitus describes their worship practices, which, he says, are "opposed to all that is practiced by other men."[3] How so? Watch how he mangles Jewish practice with a combination of biblical fact and prejudicial fantasy:

> In their holy place, they have consecrated an image of the animal by whose guidance they found deliverance from their long and thirsty wanderings. . . . They abstain from swine's flesh, in consideration of what they suffered when they were infected by the leprosy to which this animal is liable. By their frequent fasts, they still bear witness to the long hunger of former days, and the Jewish bread, made without leaven, is retained as a memorial of their hurried seizure of corn. We are told that the rest of the seventh day was adopted, because this day brought with it a termination of their toils; after a while, the charm of indolence beguiled them into giving up the seventh year also to inaction.[4]

So far, this sounds like mild derision (Sabbath rest is "indolence"), confusion, and rumor. But it gets much worse. Tacitus speaks of "all their other customs, which are at once perverse and disgusting, owe their strength to their very badness."[5] How bad? Tacitus says,

2. Tacitus, *Hist.* 5.3.
3. Tacitus, *Hist.* 5.4.
4. Tacitus, *Hist.* 5.4.
5. Tacitus, *Hist.* 5.5.

> Among themselves they are inflexibly honest and ever ready to shew compassion, though they regard the rest of mankind with all the hatred of enemies. They sit apart at meals, they sleep apart, and though, as a nation, they are singularly prone to lust, they abstain from intercourse with foreign women; among themselves, nothing is unlawful. Circumcision was adopted by them as a mark of difference from other men. Those who come over to their religion adopt the practice, and have this lesson first instilled into them, to despise all gods, to disown their country, and set at nought parents, children, and brethren.[6]

One may be disgusted by vile sexual practices by a people for whom, "among themselves, nothing is unlawful." But that is a small matter in comparison with their influence on Gentile converts. Those who "come over to their region" are taught to "despise all gods" and, most treasonous of all, "to disown their country."[7] Since the gods protect the emperors and the nation, despising them is traitorous. Accusing Jews of teaching converts to "disown" their country is proof positive of their malevolence and danger to the state.

Overcoming Mutual Antipathy

The authors who gave us our New Testament, however, believed that this deep division between Jews and Gentiles had been overcome in Christ. As impossible and unlikely as it seems, these two groups of people who think of each other as completely incompatible could come to see each other as one, in a new humanity; a single people. This new people would require new loyalties and practices that put them at odds with their neighbors, who will be suspicious of and misunderstand them. Persecution could follow. But such was to be expected of followers of Jesus, who was put to death by Roman authorities. Nevertheless, belief in resurrection enabled them to endure hardship and suffering as they lived with their newfound "living hope" (1 Pet 1:3).

First Peter: A Holy Nation

Here is how some of these New Testament authors expressed this new vision of unity. We will begin with the book of 1 Peter. The authorship is disputed, so we will call him Peter for convenience. First Peter, written to a Gentile

6. Tacitus, *Hist.* 5.5.
7. Tacitus, *Hist.* 5.5.

congregation, is filled with quotations from the Hebrew Bible. From the beginning of the book, the story of the people of Israel is absorbed and becomes part of the story of the people of faith in Christ. It is not as though the church has replaced Israel—not at all! Instead, the Gentiles are addressed as belonging to a new people comprising Jews and Gentiles. Peter says they had been "redeemed from the empty way of life that was your heritage" (1:18; see also 4:3–4). However, they are addressed in the opening salutation as " the exiles of the Dispersion" (1 Pet 1:1). Later, Peter calls them "aliens [or "strangers"] and exiles" (1 Pet 2:11).

Dispersion is the condition in which the Jews found themselves as exiles in Babylon in the sixth century BCE. While it is true that many Jewish people in the first century considered themselves exiles again while they were living under Roman occupation, and even more so after the Jewish War that ended in 70 CE, the story in the background here is not a reference to those events. It is rather the story of Abram. Abraham, as he is eventually called, lived in the city of Ur when, according to Genesis, God called him to leave his homeland and to go to a place God would show him (Gen 12:1). He took his wife Sarah and all his flocks and herds and came to the land of Canaan, the promised land. There, Sarah died. Abraham needed a place to bury her, so he negotiated with the local Hittites to purchase a cave for her tomb. During the negotiations, Abraham confessed to them, "I am a stranger and an alien residing among you" (Gen 23:4). This is the only other place in the Bible, besides 1 Peter, that the words *stranger* and *alien* are found together. The story of Abraham is a perfect metaphor for the Gentile church to whom 1 Peter was written. Abraham was at home in Ur, but became an alien, a stranger, an exile from his homeland. So, too, the Christ-followers of the five areas of Asia Minor to whom 1 Peter is addressed, who were once at home there as Romans, attending public festivals, worshiping Roman gods, and "doing what the Gentiles like to do, living in licentiousness, passions, drunkenness, revels, carousing, and lawless idolatry" (1 Pet 4:3). Becoming people of faith in Christ, however, has involved a change of lifestyle. In many ways, they became "exiled" from their old friends who, Peter says, "are surprised that you no longer join them in the same excesses of dissipation, and so they blaspheme [or ridicule]" (1 Pet 4:4). The believers embraced a new value system at odds with their prevailing culture. Like Abraham among the Hittites of Canaan, they looked at the world differently.

Unlike Abraham, however, the Gentile believers Peter is writing to got pushback for their nonconformity. Early people of faith in Christ were considered atheists by their fellow Romans; after all, they did not believe in or sacrifice to any of the Roman gods. Tertullian, a Roman believer, theologian, and author (ca. 155–220 CE) said in his *Apology*, or defense of the faith, "You say we are atheists, and will not [offer] sacrifice for the life of the emperors. . . . It is upon this account, therefore, that we are convened as guilty of sacrilege and treason."[8] The issue was only partly religious; it was also considered an act of treason to refuse to make sacrifices for the life of the emperors. Besides treason, the gods could be offended; divine disfavor was not a happy prospect; it threatened the empire's safety.

The Romans of Asia Minor did not take treasonous nonparticipation lightly. They reacted negatively toward these Christ-followers who had been their friends but were now acting like "aliens" and "exiles" from some other country. Peter says that the believers "had to suffer various trials" and "suffer for doing what is right" (1 Pet 1:6; 3:14). Were they suffering persecution? Of a mild sort, perhaps. Peter advises them to "keep your conscience clear, so that, when you are maligned, those who abuse you for your good conduct in Christ may be put to shame" (1 Pet 3:16). And he tells them, "If you are reviled for the name of Christ, you are blessed" (1 Pet 4:14). Being "maligned" and "abused" for good conduct and being "reviled" sounds like social ostracism rather than all out persecution that could end in martyrdom. Severe persecution of that sort did happen sporadically, but was often limited to specific locations, not an empire-wide policy in those days. Nevertheless, it felt like suffering for the Gentile people of faith.

Peter's response to their suffering is to encourage them by reminding them, not of what they lost by becoming people of faith in Christ, but what they gained. The most significant advantage was that they had become a new "people" or "nation." They had become one with the chosen people, not replacing them but joining them as heirs to God's promises and blessings to Israel. Instead of merely being "aliens" and "exiles" like Abraham, they were much more than that. Peter uses an avalanche of references from the Hebrew Bible to overwhelm them with their new status before God. Like Israel, Peter says, you are a "chosen race" (Isa 43:20); a "royal priesthood" (Exod 19:6; 23:22); a "holy nation" (Isa 43:21); and a "people for peculiar possession" (1 Pet 2:9–10). Peter says, "Once you were not a people [*laos*, or nation], but now you are God's people" (1 Pet 2:10, from Hos 2:23). In case that deluge of descriptions went by quickly, notice that "chosen race" means that now the Gentiles can consider themselves part of the "chosen people." In fact, that new status is so huge that, compared to it, merely being Roman citizens as they formerly were was like not being a "people" or nation at all. Peter has just made being a member of the world's most powerful nation a nonentity compared with being the "people of God." That may be worth some suffering.

8. Tertullian, *Apol.* 10.

As a new "people," they were now heirs of an "inheritance" (1 Pet 1:4). The primary thing descendants of Abraham inherited was God's promise to bless them (Gen 12:3). Part of that blessing was a share in the promised land. An Israelite's "inheritance" in the promised land was considered inviolate. Even if poverty forced a person to sell their land, they were supposed to get it back every fiftieth year, the year of Jubilee (Lev 25). Who knows if that law was ever observed, but it shows how important that "inheritance" was supposed to be. That concept of birthright inheritance has now been spiritualized. It is no longer land in Palestine, but "an inheritance that is imperishable, undefiled, and unfading, kept in heaven for you" (1 Pet 1:4). Things might be bad now as you suffer social ostracism, but as part of the people of God, you now have "a living hope" (1 Pet 1:3).

Gentiles who put their trust in Christ are now fully integrated into the chosen people, not to replace them, but to join them in every way. All of the characteristics of Israel that made them a unique people to God are now true of Gentile believers as well. We began this chapter highlighting the gross, at times almost comically absurd ways Gentiles viewed Jews. Now we have come to a complete reversal: Gentiles should think of themselves as part of the Jewish community; not that they have become Jews, but together with believing Jews, they are now one people of God.

Paul: Citizenship in Heaven

The book of 1 Peter is not alone in this understanding. We have already noted Paul's take, that in Christ there is no Jew or Gentile—that is, Greek (Gal 3:28). He told the new Gentile believers in the church he started in Philippi, "But our citizenship is in heaven" (Phil 3:20). The word *citizenship* he used did not mean national citizenship but, rather, something more like membership in a community with regulations. In the Roman Empire, immigrants formed colonies in the cities where they settled. These were self-governing, having their own internal leaders and laws. Diaspora Jewish communities were allowed to function in that way. Paul was saying that, like diaspora Jews, the Philippian believers were "citizens" or "members" of a colony of heaven. They were living on earth, but as exiles whose primary loyalty was elsewhere. Paul may be playing with the fact that residents of Philippi had been granted the right of Roman citizenship. That may be great, and even useful, but they should consider their first loyalty to a higher power: they were first and foremost "citizens of heaven," a realm far greater than the Roman Empire. In that realm, there is "no Jew or Greek [Gentile]."

The New Testament has even more to say about Jew and Gentile unity. The book of Ephesians offers an extended reflection on the subject. The authorship of Ephesians has been debated, with scholars on both sides of the question. Whether or not it was from Paul's pen, most agree that it sums up much of Paul's teaching, so I will call the author "Paul." Neither do we know for sure that it was written to the church in Ephesus, since that designation is missing in early manuscripts. Scholars suggest it could have been intended to be a circular letter for several churches. Whoever the intended recipients were, Ephesians is addressed to Gentiles. "So then, remember that at one time you Gentiles by birth, called 'the uncircumcision' by those who are called 'the circumcision'" (Eph 2:11). This shows the centrality of circumcision for Jewish identity; the recipients of this letter were clearly not Jews. It also shows that tensions between the two remained a daily reality.

All that has changed now for believers in Christ. Instead of hostility, Christ has ended the opposition, "For he is our peace" (Eph 2:14). Peace, "shalom" in the Hebrew Bible, is about well-being far more profound than merely the end of conflict. It involves the end of alienation. As such, peace is the expected gift of God to be realized in the end times. Now, Paul says, it has been accomplished. Gentiles who were once "far off" from God have been "brought near" (Eph 2:13). Paul can say that the result of the peace of Christ is that "he has made both groups into one" (Eph 2:14). Just like the one seed of Abraham and the one olive tree, Jew and Gentile believers are to think of each other as a unity. The separation of the two had been a fundamental reality. In 1871, an inscription was discovered on one of the pillars of the balustrade separating the court of the Gentiles from the inner courts and sanctuary of the Jewish temple, which read, "No man of another race is to enter within the fence and enclosure around the Temple. Whoever is caught will have only himself to thank for the death which follows." What has happened to that dividing wall? Christ "has broken down the dividing wall, that is, the hostility between us" (Eph 2:14).

Did Paul intend that reference? It may be doubtful that his Gentile audience in Asia Minor would have caught it, but it does illustrate for us the level of mutual hostility. If not that literal temple wall, what could he have meant? The "dividing wall" is parallel to what follows: "He [Christ] has abolished the law with its commandments and ordinances" (Eph 2:15). The law of Moses that required circumcision, Sabbath observance, and keeping kosher, the three key identity markers separating Jews from Gentiles, has been "abolished." What is the effect? The verse continues, "That he might create in himself one new humanity in place of the two, thus making peace" (Eph 2:15). Believers in Christ have become a "new humanity." This goes far beyond mutual tolerance or respect; Jewish and Gentile believers should not imagine themselves different from one another. Paul continues that Christ's objective was to "reconcile both groups to God in one body through the cross, thus putting to death that hostility through it" (Eph 2:16).

The effect for Gentiles is that "you are no longer strangers and aliens, but you are citizens with the saints and also members of the household of God" (Eph 2:19). First Peter said that Gentile believers were to consider themselves strangers and aliens to the Roman Empire as members of the colony of heaven. But Paul wants to ensure they are not strangers and aliens to the "household of God." Gentiles are now at home with God. Having introduced the metaphor of a house, other architectural metaphors emerge. The household in which they are at home with God becomes a temple: "In him [Christ] the whole structure [house] is joined together and grows into a holy temple in the Lord; in whom you also are built together spiritually into a dwelling place for God" (Eph 2:21–22). Not only do Gentile believers feel at home in God's household, but God feels at home in the spiritual temple that they have become.

The way Paul sees it, this most unlikely outcome, the spiritual unity of Jews and Gentiles, is of cosmic significance. In fact, it is the mystery (or secret plan) God has kept to himself for ages but at last has been revealed. He says this is "my understanding of the mystery of Christ." He explains, "In former generations this mystery was not made known to humankind, as it has now been revealed . . . that is, the Gentiles have become fellow heirs, members of the same body, and sharers in the promise in Christ Jesus through the gospel" (Eph 3:4–6).

The mystery, or secret plan of Gentile inclusion, was tightly kept. The concept of a uniquely chosen people whom God had singled out for special blessing was well established in the Hebrew Bible. It became the basis for an all but complete separation of Jews from Gentiles. There were hints about the mystery's revelation sprinkled throughout the Hebrew Bible; God's blessing to Abraham did have a carve-out for all the families of the earth. Notable Gentiles became part of the story and were included in that otherwise exclusive family, like Rahab and Ruth. Gentile nations, even the Assyrians of Nineveh, could repent and avoid divine displeasure. There was a tension between God's particular choice of Israel and his universal concern for all people. But in the Hebrew Bible, those hints did not rise to the level of solving the mystery. But that has all changed, from the perspective of the New Testament. The mystery has been revealed because of Christ: God's will is that everyone should believe in Christ, who made a new, reconciled humanity a fact.

It is true that people naturally get along better with others who are similar to them than with those who are different. Different nationalities have different customs and cuisines. Language is a difficult barrier. However, those human realities that divide us do not compare in any way with the overwhelming significance of the unity God has accomplished in Christ, according to the New Testament. The nationalist desire to live in comfortable isolation from each other is the exact opposite of God's will for humanity. If the massive dividing wall that separated Jews from Gentiles in the first century can be overcome, then no barrier is strong enough to prevent unity between any groups from knowing each other as one: one body, one household, one commonwealth, even one temple.

20

All Tribes and Peoples and Languages Around the Throne

The theme of the Hebrew Bible, according to some scholars, is the partially fulfilled and partially unfulfilled promise to Abraham in Gen 12. The whole story of Israel is about how that promise of descendants, land, and blessing kept seesawing back and forth between frustration and success. From Egyptian slavery to the triumph of the exodus. From wandering in the wilderness to possession of the promised land. From a loose tribal confederacy to a powerful monarchy. From the debacle of exile to the return to the land. By the time we get to the New Testament, the land of Israel is under Roman occupation. In a sense, the people are in a new kind of exile: in the land but not in possession of it. Whatever the promise to Abraham meant, the part about being a blessing to all the families of the earth is nowhere in sight.

The New Testament introduces a new concept. The promise to Abraham is finally being fulfilled but not as originally imagined. Jesus introduced the concept of the "kingdom of God," which was, he said, "among you" or "within you" or "not far" from you. But that kingdom claimed no territory, had no borders or army or human king. God was king. Jesus bore witness to that invisible kingdom and died at the hands of Rome, which believed he was a revolutionary. Before he died Jesus had innovated his Jewish tradition in significant ways. He had a bold understanding of Sabbath as a day of benefit to people, not a day merely of restrictions. He challenged the notion that sickness and suffering were deserved punishments from God. He crossed social lines to minister to women and children. He welcomed people to common tables of fellowship that were inclusive even of "sinners." And notably, he kept running into Gentiles, or going to their areas, bringing God's mercy and healing to them. He even commissioned his disciples to take the good news of the kingdom of God to the world. They were to be his witnesses in "Judea and Samaria, and to the ends of the earth" (Acts 1:8).

It was left to Paul to put the pieces together. He believed that the promise to Abraham could be fulfilled in Christ. Christ was the seed, or descendant of Abraham, to whom the promise was given. Everyone, including Gentiles, who had faith, like Abraham did, could be legitimate heirs of the promise. Or, switching metaphors, Gentiles, like wild branches, could be grafted onto the Abrahamic tree. Paul and others started small house churches among Gentiles throughout Asia Minor.

Christians in Peril

As years passed, Christians, as they became known, grew in numbers throughout the Roman Empire. They were an anomaly. Like Jews, they worshipped one God alone and so would not sacrifice in honor of the emperor. As long as people thought that Christians were just a sect of Judaism, they had legal protection from prosecution; it was treasonous to refuse to sacrifice in honor of the emperor unless you had special legal protection, which Jews enjoyed. But Jews eventually concluded that people who did not observe the Sabbath, did not keep kosher, and who were not even circumcised were not, therefore, authentic Jews. They understandably kicked the Christians out of the synagogues. Now the Christians had a problem of no small measure. If they became known for not honoring the emperor and thus, in the minds of Romans, endangering the state, they could be considered traitors with all the punishments that entailed. By the time of Emperor Domitian, who ruled Rome from 81 to 96 CE, the climate was getting dangerous. Emperor worship as a necessary civil obligation had been growing for some time; Domitian embraced it wholeheartedly. According to Roman senator and historian Dio Cassius, emperor Domitian took pride in being called "master" and "god," with those titles used in both speech and written documents.[1] Cassius reported that people had been executed for "atheism,"[2] the failure to worship the gods of Rome, including worshiping Domitian himself. Historians tell us that there was no widespread, organized persecution of Christians under Domitian. There was some, but it was sporadic and

1. Cassius Dio, *Rom. Hist.* 67.4.7.
2. Cassius Dio, *Rom. Hist.* 67.14.1–2.

local. But how could Christians feel confident that it would not increase, as later it did?

What were Christians supposed to do under such circumstances? Many were small businesspeople or artisans. Of necessity, they belonged to clubs, or collegia, and funeral associations that we have spoken of in previous chapters. These would involve common meals at which the food provided had been offered in sacrifice to their patron Roman gods. Should Christians eat it? This was one of the issues facing the communities of Christians to whom John wrote Revelation. The book starts with letters to seven churches in Asia Minor, some of which Paul had a hand in starting and others he did not.

But Paul was gone, and John was worried about the direction some of those communities were going in. The challenges they faced were not small. Of the seven cities where the churches he addressed in Revelation were located, at least three had temples to Caesar in John's day (Ephesus, Smyrna, and Pergamum). Sardis had the temple of Artemis, the fourth largest known Ionic temple in the ancient world, as well as temples dedicated to Augustus and possibly Vespasian. Smyrna had a temple to Rome's patron deity, Roma, as well as temples to the deceased emperor Augustus and Asclepius, the god of healing. Besides its temple to Zeus, Pergamum had an entire complex dedicated to Asclepius, as well as temples to Athena, Dionysus, Demeter, and of course, one to Emperor Augustus. You get the idea.

The problem for Christians was that participation in collegia and funeral associations with their obligatory religious practices was the path for upward mobility and economic security in the Roman world. Christians would have been under enormous pressure to accommodate themselves to the Roman world's expectations. As long as they did not witness openly about their belief in the exclusive lordship of Christ and did their best to blend in, they might be able to forestall impending persecutions. If they could keep a low profile as Christians, they could maintain their social, political, and economic security.

It was not as if they would be treating their faith carelessly. After all, there was no real god but God, so idols and offerings to dead or living emperors could be considered fanciful. If the divinity of the emperor is a fiction, why resist it? Offerings to fake gods or eating meat offered to unreal idols could be considered simply participation in a farce with no effect on one's own Christian commitments. Or was something deeper at stake? John believed accommodation to Roman culture, even if the gods of Rome were unreal, was dangerous. He could not tolerate any compromise with activities that proclaimed anyone else as "Lord" or laid claim to a Christian's allegiance. If the promise to Abraham was to come true, if the Gentiles of these churches were the fulfillment of God's blessings to all the families of the earth, then compromise and accommodation were out of the question. John called the Christians to active, albeit nonviolent, resistance. The means of their resistance was to be the same as the Savior they believed in, Jesus, the "faithful witness" (Rev 3:14). John called them to practically pick a fight by witnessing to the lordship of Christ alone. If and when they might encounter resistance or persecution, even martyrdom, rest assured, the final victory was going to be God's. Let us see how John's call to resistant witness plays out.

The Call to Non-Accommodation by Public Witness

John chose to write in a style common at the time, which is now called Jewish apocalyptic. In this genre, a revelation of the future is delivered by an otherworldly messenger, often an angel, to a human recipient. This style involves the use of symbols not intended to be taken literally. In fact, their literal meaning is sometimes contradictory, as when the sky is darkened and the moon, which shouldn't be visible in a completely darkened sky, is turned to blood. Part of the book of Daniel is also written in this style. Beasts are symbolic of kingdoms, for example. Some have compared this style to modern science fiction. John begins his book saying it is "the revelation of Jesus Christ, which God gave him to show his servants what must soon take place; he made it known by sending his angel to his servant John" (Rev 1:1). John gets the message from Jesus through an angel.

What was the summation of the angel's task? The angel "testified to the word of God and to the testimony of Jesus Christ, even to all that he saw" (Rev 1:2). John is introducing one of the key words and ideas from the start. The angel "testified" to the "testimony" of Jesus. The words *testify* and *testimony* come from the word for martyr. A "martyr" is literally a "witness."[3] We could say the angel "witnessed" to the "witness" of Jesus. John calls Jesus "the faithful witness" (Rev 3:4). When did Jesus faithfully "witness" and what was the outcome? It was when he testified before Pilate. John is not as explicit as the author of 1 Timothy, but the thought is the same. Jesus's faithful witness was before Pilate: "Fight the good fight of the faith . . . to which you were called and for which you made the good confession in the presence of many witnesses. In the presence of God . . . and of Christ Jesus, who in his testimony [witness] before Pontius Pilate made the good confession" (1 Tim 6:12–13). The outcome of Jesus's "faithful witness" was his death.

3. BDAG, s.v. "μαρτυρία."

But death was not the end for Jesus. Like John says of God, Jesus "was, he is, and he is to come" (Rev 1:4), and his coming will have a worldwide, universal impact.

> Look! He is coming with the clouds;
> every eye will see him,
> even those who pierced him;
> and on his account all the tribes of the earth will wail. (Rev 1:7)

This is the first but not the last time, John says, that "all the tribes of the earth" will be involved in God's plan for the future. It is almost as if John is intentionally echoing the promise to Abraham and to "all the families [or tribes] of the earth" (Gen 12:3).

John is going to demand that the churches he writes to take the risk of witnessing to the lordship of Christ at great peril to their livelihoods, their social status, and possibly even their lives. From the beginning he gives them the reassurance that the Lord they are called to witness to is none other than the "Son of Man" who holds in his right hand the "seven stars" (Rev 1:13, 16). Emperor Domitian, in the early eighties CE, had coins minted with the image of his dead infant son riding the earth as if it were a horse, surrounded by seven stars. If the stars controlled human destiny, as the Romans believed, then the message was clear. But John reassures his congregations that the Son of Man, not any emperor's descendant, controls the future. Not that it would be easy to be a faithful witness—after all, it wasn't for Jesus—but God is in control. Emperors come and go, but the Son of Man says to John, "Do not be afraid; I am the first and the last, and the living one. I was dead, and see, I am alive forever and ever; and I have the keys of Death and of Hades" (Rev 1:18). Even death has lost its threat potential if God has the keys. He can open death's door for Christians to eternal life.

How does John counsel the seven congregations of Asia Minor, whom he fears are in danger of accommodating themselves to their culture? His first address to the church in Ephesus, and his first words of congratulation are for their nonviolent resistance. They have not accommodated themselves to the social, cultural, and religious expectations that centered around Greco-Roman pagan and imperial worship. He says, "I know your works, your toil and your patient endurance" and notes they have been "enduring patiently" (Rev 2:2, 3). "Patient endurance" includes "bearing up" and not letting yourself grow "weary" for the sake of "my name" (Rev 2:3). The Ephesians have resisted in this nonviolent way specifically by not tolerating "evildoers" who "claim to be apostles but are not," but testing and finding them "false" (Rev 2:2). What were those false apostles teaching? John does not tell us here, but later he will identify others by name (or symbolic name) and make it clear.

John addresses the church of Smyrna next. With its numerous temples, the Roman Senate had conferred on the city the prestigious status of "temple keeper." But the Christians of Smyrna had chosen poverty instead of accommodation. Though they had been prosperous, that was no longer the case: "I know your affliction and your poverty, even though you are rich" (Rev 2:9). Non-accommodation came at a cost, but they had accepted it. In his address to the church at Smyrna, John tips his hand as to why accommodation is so appalling to him. It is not only the case that the gods of Rome were merely fictions; behind them were malevolent forces at work. John speaks cryptically of a "synagogue of Satan" there and about "the devil" who could bring on persecution (Rev 2:9, 10). He encourages them, saying, "Be faithful until death, and I will give you the crown of life" (Rev 2:10).

John next addresses the church at Pergamum. Possibly because the temple of Zeus is there, he locates them as "living where Satan's throne is" (Rev 2:13). He first affirms them: "You are holding fast to my name, and you did not deny your faith in me even in the days of Antipas my witness, my faithful one, who was killed among you, where Satan lives" (Rev 2:13). Antipas was a martyr ("witness") because he was "my witness" who was "faithful." The work of faithful witnessing was what John was calling his congregations to do, sticking their necks out at great risk rather than bowing in accommodation to Rome.

Here in Pergamum, we first discover the nature of the false teaching that has John so concerned: "Some there who hold to the teaching of Balaam, who taught Balak to put a stumbling block before the people of Israel, so that they would eat food sacrificed to idols and practice fornication. So you also have some who hold to the teaching of the Nicolaitans" (Rev 2:14–15).

Apparently, Nicolaitans were teaching the same things. Using the Hebrew Bible story of Balaam as an analogy, the issue is that some of the Christians in Pergamum were led to eat food sacrificed to idols, which, in the language of the prophets, constituted spiritual fornication, even whoredom (Jer 3:9). Eating food sacrificed to idols was what Christian accommodators did to fit in and keep a low profile.

This is the same issue John raises against the people of Thyatira. Although they had been practicing nonviolent resistance by their "patient endurance" (Rev 2:19), nevertheless they were wrong to have tolerated "that woman Jezebel, who calls herself a prophet and is teaching and beguiling my servants to practice fornication and to eat food sacrificed to idols" (Rev 2:20). Using the symbolic name Jezebel, John specifies her teaching: that accommodation is acceptable. Eating sacrificial meat, which, for John, is spiritual fornication, was being justified. That was proof for John that "Jezebel" was a false prophet. He calls her teaching "the deep things of Satan" (Rev 2:24), indicating the spiritual source and grave danger they represented.

The Heavenly Throne Room

After similar addresses to the churches of Sardis, Philadelphia, and Laodicea, John is swept up into a vision of heaven. A trumpet-like voice says to him, "Come up here, and I will show you what must take place after this" (Rev 4:1). Like Isaiah before him, he has a vision of the throne of God: "Coming from the throne are flashes of lightning, and rumblings and peals of thunder" (Rev 4:5). The vision is rich with symbolism, most of which is rooted in the Hebrew Bible. In the course of the vision, the one seated on the throne has a scroll that he gives to the lamb who was "standing as if it had been slaughtered, having seven horns and seven eyes, which are the seven spirits of God" (Rev 5:6). Horns symbolize power. The number seven indicates that his power is complete. Seven eyes, similarly, indicate complete perception. The seven spirits represent the Holy Spirit by whom a Christian has a complete relationship with God. This is the lamb who is worthy to take the scroll from the one seated on the throne. "He went and took the scroll from the right hand of the one who was seated on the throne" (Rev 5:7). The scroll itself contains the plan and purpose of human history so the one charged to open and read it is the one who has been given charge of that history.

When the lamb took the scroll, the others in attendance "fell before the lamb" and "sing a new song" (Rev 5:8, 9). They sing,

> You are worthy to take the scroll
> and to open its seals,
> for you were slaughtered and by your blood you ransomed for God
> saints from every tribe and language and people and nation;
> you have made them to be a kingdom and priests serving our God,
> and they will reign on earth. (Rev 5:9–10)

Peter had called his Gentile congregations a "holy nation" (1 Pet 2:9), which John now affirms, a title originally given to Israel. The people who comprise this priestly kingdom come "from every tribe and language and people and nation." In this climactic heavenly vision, the peoples of the world are no longer separated by tribe, language, and nation. They are one. Together as one new people, they gather to give praise to the one who ransomed them all and gave them a new identity as the people of God. Instead of separate nations, they are now one nation. This is the ultimate victory of God; the lamb is victorious over the dark powers of evil that have enslaved the world for so long. This vision of a final victory is meant to encourage the Christians of Asia Minor to do the courageous thing, to bear witness to the unique lordship of Christ against competing claims of the emperors of Rome. This is the reason they can stand firm and bear witness in the face of impending persecution. This is what can motivate them to refuse to accommodate the overwhelming social, political, and economic pressure of the Roman system. It is the view from the end that will give them the courage to be, like Jesus, faithful witnesses to the kingdom that will outlive Rome, the kingdom of God.

This vision of a worldwide unity in Christ is central to John. He will repeat it several more times in Revelation. In another vision of the heavenly throne, John says,

> After this I looked, and there was a great multitude that no one could count, from every nation, from all tribes and peoples and languages, standing before the throne and before the Lamb, robed in white, with palm branches in their hands. They cried out in a loud voice, saying, "Salvation belongs to our God who is seated on the throne, and to the Lamb!" (Rev 7:9–10)

The innumerable crowd fulfills God's promise to Abraham that his descendants will be as numerous as the sands of the sea and the stars of the sky (Gen 13:16; 15:5; 22:17; 26:4; 28:14; 32:12). These people come from every nation, all tribes and peoples and languages, united together as one people in praise of God. Their white robes indicate that they have been faithful witnesses (Rev 3:2–5, 18; 4:4; 6:11). They have not succumbed to Roman influence, but have risked their lives asserting that Christ alone is Lord.

In John's climactic vision in which he sees "a new heaven and a new earth" and "the new Jerusalem, coming down out of heaven from God," he hears a voice from the throne saying,

> See, the home of God is among mortals.
> He will dwell with them as their God;
> they will be his peoples,
> and God himself will be with them;
> he will wipe every tear from their eyes.
> Death will be no more;
> mourning, crying, and pain will be no more,
> for the first things have passed away." (Rev 21:3–4)

Notice that when God makes his home among mortals to dwell with them, the text says they will be his "peoples," plural. All the peoples of the earth are now together, made one as "his peoples." In this new Jerusalem, John says, "I saw no temple in the city, for its temple is the Lord God the Almighty and the Lamb" (Rev 21:22). Neither is there need of a sun or moon, "for the glory of God is its light, and its lamp is the Lamb. The nations will walk by its light" (Rev 21:23–24). The "nations" again are plural. All the nations become citizens of the new Jerusalem.

The sickness of division, animosity, and exclusion will be overcome. How? The angel that has been narrating John's Revelation shows him "the river of the water of life, bright as crystal, flowing from the throne of God and of the Lamb through the middle of the street of the city. On either side of the river is the tree of life with its twelve kinds of fruit, producing its fruit each month; and the leaves of the tree are for the healing of the nations" (Rev 22:1–2). Finally, the disease of nationalism is healed. The "dividing wall of hostility" has been broken down. The goal that God has had, spelled out in Ephesians, has been realized: "That he might create in himself one new humanity in place of the two [Jew and Gentile], thus making peace, and might reconcile both groups to God in one body through the cross, thus putting to death that hostility through it" (Eph 2:15–16). The assurance of the ultimate victory of God that has enabled people from "every tribe and language and people and nation" to unite in faithful witness to the exclusive lordship of Christ will encourage the Christians of Roman Asia Minor to endure whatever may lie ahead.

This is the climax of the Christian Bible as we now have it. In Christ, the promise to Abraham that extended to all the families of the earth is finally realized. The diseased state of exclusion and separation has been healed. The final vision of the throne room of God is an international, multiethnic, multilingual festival of praise. Rome's unity was based on pacification. Rome bludgeoned its conquered peoples into submission and punished them ruthlessly for attempting freedom from its grip. The Christian vision of unity is liberation from bondage; the redeemed, ransomed people of God are free to join together, not by force, but by transformation. There is now a "new creation" in Christ; a "new humanity" that no longer divides along ethnic or national lines.

Epilogue

When the Europeans arrived in the New World, the land was not empty. People were already living there. The story of the relationship between the newcomers and the indigenous population varied. Sometimes relations were positive, even friendly. Sometimes there was brutal violence. But whatever the relationship was, the Europeans were immigrants. They were not indigenous to the land; they came as aliens.

I am a descendant of those Europeans. My ancestors were immigrants. We were lucky. We Swiss-Germans faced no discrimination when we arrived. Pennsylvania was welcoming to us. The native populations had been pushed out long before my people arrived. We built farms, raised livestock, harvested the food we grew, and survived. We built communities. Churches, schools, town halls, courthouses, jails, and parks. At least, that's the story I've been handed. It did not take us many generations to forget that we were once aliens in our adopted land. Our immigrant history could be forgotten. And it was.

Our family never developed any traditions that tried to keep the memory of our former immigrant status alive. Eventually, as America expanded westward, prairie land opened up in Kansas, so our branch of the Pennsylvania Dutch jumped at the chance. They broke prairie sod into squares to build their first house on the Kansas plains. By my father's generation, we were indistinguishable from any other Kansas family. Nobody even remembers the last German speakers. We ate no German dishes, knew no German songs or dances, celebrated no German holidays; we were just Americans, former immigrants who had forgotten their history. In fact, we had forgotten our history so thoroughly that the Swiss part of being Swiss-German was only uncovered recently by one of us who did the genealogical spade work.

So now, having forgotten how we got here, we do not identify with modern immigrants. We do not remember our family's reasons for making that giant, dangerous, uncertain leap into the New World all those years ago. But they must have had their reasons. They must have concluded that old Europe had no future for them. They must have held out dreams of making a new life in a land with new possibilities in America. Even though they did not speak the language when they arrived, they assumed they would make it, and it would be worth it.

In many ways, my family is like and unlike biblical Israel. According to the biblical account, the Israelites came into a land that they were not native to. They entered the "promised land" as non-indigenous aliens, as immigrants. They had come from Mesopotamia hundreds of years before. They had lived in Egypt as slaves under the Pharaoh for four centuries. They had been wandering nomads in the wilderness of Sinai for a whole generation before finally entering the land. Finally, like the Europeans in the New World, they displaced the native populations. "Displaced" is a euphemism for the wars of Joshua that enabled them to conquer the land. But conquer they did, and eventually it was theirs alone, just like America.

Unlike a genealogy blog, the biblical story is not told to merely recount a distant past for future generations. The story in the Bible is told to form the consciences of future generations into the ethical ideals deemed essential. In other words, the remembered stories are lessons in ethics. By today's standards, however, some of them are ethical nightmares. Holy war? Genocide? All justified because God "gave us the land"? No. Those lessons from the Iron Age need to end in the dustbin of history after further ethical reflection, which they have. No one supports those ideas today, right? (Well, almost no one.) But there are plenty of other ethical ideals that these stories encode that still live and breathe with a vitality that makes them relevant for our times.

What is the ethical guideline given to Israel by God about the treatment of non-Israelites? Here is the law, and the reason for the law:

> When an alien [non-Israelite] resides with you in your land, you shall not oppress the alien. The alien who resides with you shall be to you as the citizen among you; you shall love the alien as yourself, for you were aliens in the land of Egypt: I am the Lord your God. (Lev 19:33–34)

The ethical law has three clauses and a rationale for them:

- No oppression (discrimination, taking advantage of).
- Treat immigrants as citizens (rights, responsibilities, obligations of fair treatment).
- Love the immigrant as you love yourself.

Rationale: You yourselves were aliens in the land of Egypt.

Memory is a basis for empathy.

In other words, God called Israel to do what my ancestors forgot to do. Israel was to be a community of memory. They were to know who they were—former alien immigrants. Remembering who they were was intended to motivate them to have empathy: other people are in the same condition your people were in, so treat them the way your ancestors would have wanted to be treated. A good summary of this ethical admonition might be, "do unto others as you would have others do unto you." The "others" in this case are immigrants.

Losing the memory of who you were has the ethical effect of losing your motivation for empathy. If you cannot imagine people like you being people like them, why should you care about them? But your people were like them. They had reasons for leaving old Europe. They had hopes and dreams that made the risk of immigration tolerable. They wanted a better life, if not for themselves, then at least for their children. They hoped that the New World would welcome them, or at least tolerate them. They did not expect that they would be treated like "citizens," much less that they would be "loved" as the Israelites were commanded to do. They expected only simple human decency and an opportunity to work hard. My people got that opportunity.

As we have seen, the ethical trajectory of the Bible has been toward greater inclusion and compassion. My ancestors experienced an America that had embraced that trajectory. But modern Christian nationalism is moving in the opposite direction. Today, Christian nationalism is gaining adherents and momentum. It had an early start. In 1860, John Winthrop identified the Massachusetts Bay colony as the city on the hill with a special covenant with God, as if they were the new chosen people. That idea had no basis in the Bible. Just the opposite. Indeed, there was once a "chosen people" singled out for God's special blessing. And yet even in that time, non-Israelites became essential parts of the narrative throughout the Hebrew Bible, as we have seen. Gentiles from every tribe, language, and nation who are in Christ by faith are now included in the one new humanity made possible by Christ. This is, at last, the solution to the tension in the Bible we began with. God is both the God of all creation; all people are created in God's image, and God is the national God of one people, Israel. That tension has now been resolved. Paul called it the mystery that had been hidden for ages, now revealed: there is one God for one new humanity.

There is simply no basis for Christians asserting nationalism because breaking down barriers such as ethnicity, language, and culture was implicitly at the heart of Christianity itself. In the New Testament, the blessing to Abraham and his seed that included all the families of the earth culminates in the scene around the throne in heaven when people from every tribe, tongue, and nation gather together as one. That ethical trajectory from particularism to universalism culminates in *shalom*; not just peace, but wholeness, flourishing, and inclusion, the world as it was created to be before things went wrong. The ethical trajectory of the Bible has led to the fulfillment of the Sabbath principle: liberation, and ultimately restoration is for everyone.

Bibliography

Bledstein, Adrien J. "Female Companionships: If the Book of Ruth Were Written by a Woman . . ." In *Ruth*, edited by Athalya Brenner, 116–33. A Feministist Companion to the Bible 3. Sheffield, UK: Sheffield Academic, 1993.

Bush, Frederic W. *Ruth/Esther*. Word Biblical Commentary 9. Dallas: Word, 1996.

Fretheim, Terence E. *Exodus*. Interpretation: A Bible Commentary for Teaching and Preaching. Louisville: Westminster John Knox, 2010.

Linafelt, Tod. "Ruth." In *Ruth and Esther*, by Tod Linafelt and Timothy K. Beal, 1–90. Berit Olam: Studies in Hebrew Narrative & Poetry. Collegeville, MN: Liturgical, 1999.

Merriam-Webster. "Breaking Bread with 'Companion.'" https://www.merriam-webster.com/wordplay/history-of-word-companion.

Nordling, John G. *Religion and Resistance in Early Judaism*. Concordia Greek Reader. St. Louis: Concordia, 2010.

Patterson, Stephen J. *The Forgotten Creed: Christianity's Original Struggle Against Bigotry, Slavery, and Sexism*. Oxford: Oxford University Press, 2018.

Ross, Allen P. *Malachi Then and Now: An Expository Commentary Based on Detailed Exegetical Analysis*. Wooster, OH: Weaver, 2016.

Sanders, James A. "From Isaiah 61 to Luke 4." In *New Testament*, edited by Jacob Neuser, 75–106. Part 1 of *Christianity, Judaism and Other Greco-Roman Cults: Studies for Morton Smith at Sixty*. Studies in Judaism in Late Antiquity 12. Leiden: Brill, 1975.

Sarna, Nahum M. *Genesis*. The JPS Torah Commentary. Philadelphia: Jewish Publication Society, 1989.

Sweeney, Marvin A. *The Twelve Prophets*. Berit Olam: Studies in Hebrew Narrative & Poetry. Collegeville, MN: Liturgical, 2000.

www.ingramcontent.com/pod-product-compliance
Lightning Source LLC
LaVergne TN
LVHW050629100826
845148LV00011B/1801
* 9 7 9 8 3 8 5 2 6 8 9 5 5 *